E. E. CUMMINGS

An Introduction to the Poetry

Columbia Introductions to Twentieth-Century American
Poetry

John Unterecker, General Editor

E. E. Cummings

An Introduction to the Poetry

Rushworth M. Kidder

NEW YORK   COLUMBIA UNIVERSITY PRESS

 Permissions

Permission to quote from the following is gratefully acknowledged: E. E. Cummings, *Tulips and Chimneys, XLI Poems, &, is 5, ViVa*, and *No Thanks*, Liveright Publishing Corporation; "New Poems" from *Collected Poems, 50 Poems, 1 x 1, Xaipe, 95 Poems*, and *73 Poems*, Harcourt Brace Jovanovich, Inc.; all Cummings poems, Granada Publishing Limited. Dylan Thomas, *The Collected Poems of Dylan Thomas*, copyright 1939 by New Directions Publishing Corporation, copyright 1952 by Dylan Thomas, reprinted by permission of New Directions Publishing Corporation; and J. M. Dent & Sons, Limited, and the Trustees for the Copyrights of the late Dylan Thomas.

Quotations from previously unpublished letters and manuscripts of E. E. Cummings are copyright © 1979 by Nancy T. Andrews and are reprinted by permission of Mrs. Andrews, the Houghton Library (Harvard University), and the Humanities Research Center (The University of Texas at Austin).

Library of Congress Cataloging in Publication Data

Kidder, Rushworth M
    E. E. Cummings : an introduction to the poetry.

    (Columbia introductions to twentieth-century American poetry)
    Includes bibliographical references and index.
    1. Cummings, Edward Estlin, 1894–1962—Criticism and interpretation.   I. Title.
II. Series.
PS3505.U334Z72   811'.5'2   79-772
ISBN 0-231-04044-X

Columbia University Press

New York   Guildford, Surrey

Printed in the United States of America

To William York Tindall

COLUMBIA INTRODUCTIONS TO TWENTIETH-CENTURY AMERICAN POETRY

Contents

John Unterecker

Foreword

Obsessed by the big abstractions of love and death, anxious to construct a public image of himself as an "experimental" manipulator of typography yet compulsively drawn to such intricate traditional forms as the ballade and the sonnet, dedicated to the charms of children but more often than not offended by the corruptions of adults, E. E. Cummings is a poet who complicated his own life and his readers' tolerance by an extraordinarily persistent lifetime reworking of a very early established set of fundamentally unchanging perceptions and techniques.

It seems to me that verbs like "change," "develop," "mature," even "differ" are of little use to the reader interested in the total body of Cummings' work. There are changes, all right, and Rushworth Kidder points them out in his excellent introduction to the poetry. But they are all changes in degree rather than changes in manner or matter. Both style and subject are remarkable not for their variety but their constancy. Consider, for example, "fair tall lovers" (poem 6 of 1963's 73 *Poems*). The most astonishing thing about this very good posthumously published poem is how much it resembles the early and deservedly popular "All in green went my love riding" (first published nearly fifty years earlier in March 1916). Or consider the sonnets—hundreds of them—that Cummings produced over his long writing career. Rearranged according to an alphabetical listing of first lines, they make a tonal sequence almost as "natural" as the various small sequences Cummings originally put them in. No one, I am convinced, were he faced with the scrambled sonnets, could by either style or subject tests come up with anything like an accurate chronological sequence.

Some critics, disturbed by this lack of "development," have taken Cummings to task for a failure to mature. But almost certainly the last thing Cummings was interested in was maturity and the second last was probably development. As conservative in art as he came to be conservative in politics, he steadfastly resisted formal change. He experimented—no question of it —but almost always along the lines of his earliest experiments.

In his very first surprising volume, he established the style and tone that would be his trademark for the rest of his life. His patterns set, his project then became the leisurely exploration of a fairly restricted territory. His poetry, consequently, is very much of a piece: usually mannered, frequently metrical, and most often merry. Complaining that Cummings fails to mature is something like complaining that a hummingbird's egg fails to hatch a chicken.

If there is little to be gained by searching for variety in Cummings' technique and subject matter, there is even less to be gained by looking for qualitative "improvements." Though more of Cummings' fine early poems have been anthologized than his equally fine late ones, first-rate poems are scattered in a fairly even diagram over the entire span of his writing career.

It amuses me to play editorial games. Like Yvor Winters, who took his tabulations far more seriously than I do, I entertain myself by making imaginary anthologies: *The Hundred Best Poems of* . . . and fill in whatever seems appropriate—*The Last Hundred Years, San Francisco between 1900 and 1980,* etc.; in this instance—*E. E. Cummings.* What, I ask myself, are the unavoidable poems—the poems so good that everybody should know them?

There's only one way to answer a question of that kind, so, to prepare myself for writing these introductory remarks, I settled down, pencil in hand, to a simultaneous reading of Rush Kidder's manuscript and Cummings' *Complete Poems. Check,* went the pencil, whenever I read a poem that seemed destined for immortality. Though my list isn't identical to that implicit in Kidder's *Introduction,* it's reasonably close.

When I added up my volume-by-volume candidates, I discovered I had ticked off ninety-six poems. What was really interesting about my score sheet, my private list of "Cummings' greatest hits," however, was not its quantity but its distribution. For I found I particularly admired twenty-seven poems published before 1930, twenty-four published during the 1930s, seventeen written and published in the 1940s, and twenty-eight published after 1950. I suspect that this sort of distribution is likely to characterize almost anyone's list. Just as Cummings' poetry doesn't significantly change in technique or subject matter, it also doesn't significantly improve or deteriorate. Time doesn't make it any better; time doesn't make it any worse.

So much, therefore, for critics who fret about development, maturity, improvement, and deterioration. The critical terms simply don't make conventional sense when applied to E. E. Cummings' *Complete Poems: 1913–1962.*

There is, however, one painful fact that any reader seriously interested in Cummings' work must face and face very squarely: whatever else he was as a poet, Cummings was certainly no self-critic. I don't mean that he didn't work carefully at his poetry. Some poems go through dozens on dozens of revisions. But when all of the revisions are finished, Cummings almost inevitably publishes the poem. He seems never to ask himself the hardest question of all: not "Is this poem finished?" but "Is this poem worth finishing?"

The reader going diligently through the *Complete Poems*, whether he checks off those he likes or doesn't, is soon troubled by the fact that mixed in with many excellent poems are a considerable number that range from at best mediocre to at worst dreadful.

Not only was Cummings incapable of pruning out his weakest poetry, he was also grimly determined that no one else —particularly his editors—have a go at it.

Kidder's account of the publication history of Cummings' first three volumes of poetry—the history of an author stubbornly determined to get into either volume two or volume three every single poem that by editorial fiat had been excluded from the first one—can, on the one hand, be read as an example of an author heroically protecting everything that he values or, on the other, as an example of an author congenitally incapable of recognizing work that is slack, pretentious, or simply incompetent. We all, I suppose, prefer the sickly child to the robust one. Cummings' problem seems to have been that he couldn't always tell if a poem was healthy, sick, or plain ordinary dead.

His worst poems make you cringe. It's not just that they're bad, they're out and out terrible. And yet almost always they fail for interesting reasons, usually having to do with a lapse in taste. It's as if something goes wrong not with Cummings ear, which is extraordinarily accurate, but with his whole sensibility.

A splendid example of a poem that starts out with real promise then goes wildly astray is the second of a pair of "Chansons Innocentes" toward the beginning of *XLI Poems*.

Like other considerably more successful Blake imitations (*Songs of Innocence* variety), this one effectively establishes in the first stanza the voice of the naive narrator:

little tree
little silent Christmas tree
you are so little
you are more like a flower

Perhaps this was the point for Cummings to end his poem. It wouldn't have been a major achievement but it would have had precision and a good deal of charm. Instead he went on, not to develop his flower image but to tangle it with a stolen child one:

who found you in the green forest
and were you very sorry to come away?
see   i will comfort you
because you smell so sweetly

This fragrant flower-tree-child comforted by a child narrator leads Cummings into lines that are not just awkward but downright silly:

i will kiss your cool bark
and hug you safe and tight
just as your mother would,
only don't be afraid

(Cummings doesn't bother to figure out how anyone, let alone a child, would be able to fight his way through the evergreen needles without getting considerably torn up, nor does he seem concerned with the picture of a tree's "mother" hugging and kissing it. What, indeed, a tree's "mother" is, is a botanical mystery Cummings presents us with but certainly doesn't solve. Instead, he tells the tree to "put up your little arms" so that the narrator can put a ring on its every finger.)

The fascinating thing about a disaster of this sort is not that Cummings couldn't tell that it wasn't a good poem but that he invested so much energy into making it bad. This poem is not just "worked," it is worked into the ground!

Yet, aside from the badly mixed metaphors, the poem's principal weaknesses—its overt sentimentality and its self-conscious naivité—are the very characteristics most typical of Cummings' strongest poems. It is precisely because in his best work Cummings over and over again approaches, just touches, then backs away from an almost intolerable sentimentality that we can feel such immediate rapport with his poetry. And it is because he makes use of the child in all of us, the innocence we have not so much lost as disguised, that his successful poems restore for us a sense of wonder and unfolding possibility. When he is not wearing his mask of sophisticated, ironical Experience, Cummings really does let us discover, like Shakespeare's Miranda, a brave, new world of extraordinary people.

I know of no one who does not respond with delight to such lovely, risky works as "in Just-/spring," for example, or "you shall above all things be glad and young," or "anyone lived in a pretty how town."

All of these are discussed by Mr. Kidder. I'd like instead to look at a poem just a little less familiar (poem XLVI of 1931's *W* [*ViVa*]) in an attempt to show that controlled naiveté and controlled sentimentality can not only shape a poem and charm its readers but also produce a "signature" uniquely Cummings' own. In order sensibly to discuss this poem, we need it in front of us:

> i met a man under the moon
> on Sunday.
> by way of saying
> nothing he
> smiled(but
> just by the dirty collar of his

jacket were two glued uncarefully ears
in
that face a box of
skin lay eyes like
new tools)

whence i guessed that he also had climbed the pincian
to appreciate rome at nightfall;and because against this
wall his white sincere small
hands with their guessing fingers

did-not-move exquisitely
,like dead children
(if he had been playing a fiddle i had

been dancing:which is
why something about me reminded him of ourselves)

as Nobody came slowly over the town

The "signature" I spoke of is, of course, built into the language of the poem. Dominated by *moon, dead children, dance*
and *smile,* "i met a man under the moon" relies on imagery
familiar to even the most casual of Cummings' readers. Not
quite symbols and considerably more than metaphors, these
and perhaps a dozen other obsessive words and phrases show
up in poem after poem. As we experience them in different
contexts they gradually create—like a dressmaker's reflecting
mirrors—a complicated echoing ambiance of overlapping images and ideas. They trigger responses just a little larger than
those they otherwise might, and we "read into" them material
left over from other contexts. Consequently, "moon" prepares
us for a night of discovery rather than of terror, and "dead children" are not just cadavers but fragile messengers from the
world of night. "Dancing" is here imagined dance, dance as po-

tential, dance that does not have to take place but, instead, like imagined music, moves us through harmonies of ideal space. And a "smile," freighted with possibilities, fills us with communions richer than those carried by other words.

Terminology of this sort binds lyric to lyric in an interwoven tissue of felt but never explicitly stated meaning. When it is as delicately handled as in this poem, it achieves a shimmering precision/imprecision that is immensely satisfying.

If the imagery of "i met a man" provides one kind of a "signature," the controlled naiveté creates another. Readers of Cummings poetry are likely to recognize this man with small hands and guessing fingers and dirty collar. They recognize him by his shy but sincere smile and the bright eyes that communicate "by way of saying/nothing," and by the fiddle that he doesn't have to play. He is cousin, of course, to Cummings' most memorable hero-failures: the little lame balloonman, the frail man dreaming dreams, Uncle Sol who was a born failure, and perhaps even Olaf glad and big. He is the eternal innocent and, as in this poem, he shares not just secrets with the narrator ("something about me reminded him of ourselves") but habits of behavior as well. (One of them has guessing fingers and the other guesses why his double has "climbed the pincian.") And both of them are ambiguously linked to the white innocence of dead children in the ominous white world of a moonlit landscape.

For the entire poem is governed by the death-pale radiance of the moon. The smiling man with "white sincere small/ hands" and the narrator freeze into position to watch the white moon, the only moving form in a motionless world, slowly drift its terrible, compelling innocence across the sky: "Nobody came slowly over the town." Personification, that got Cummings in trouble in "little tree," here seems superbly appropriate as the man-under-the-moon and the man-in-the-moon echo each other and share their moon world with a moonstruck narrator.

I spoke of this as a poem of both controlled naiveté and controlled sentimentality. It is, of course, easy to see how close it comes to pulling out all the sentimental stops: dead children and a dirty-collared, sincere, smiling, bright-eyed, innocent fiddler are tossed into the same hopper with moonlit Rome and a would-be-dancing narrator. It risks ruin from top to bottom. And yet it never falters—partly, I think, because the sentimental temptations are undercut by verbal wit.

When Cummings fails, he fails, more often than not, because he becomes so caught up by the "message" of the poem that he neglects to distance it from himself. Wit is his most effective distancing device, and in this poem it is brilliantly used. Here, for example, Cummings manages to get the sun into a moon-flooded sky by having the moon appear on *Sun*day. That may not seem a major literary achievement, but it instantly defuses the potential sentimentality of the opening lines. A "Sunday" moon plays with language, its pseudo-opposition wittily starting the poem not with naked feeling (as in "little tree") but with feeling transmuted by mind into poetry.

Similar pseudo-opposition occurs when "climb" and "fall" meet in the middle of the poem. But the climber doesn't fall. Instead, night does. Almost all of the "opposites" of the poem work this way. They're oblique opposites. Even "nothing" and "something" are, in context, as obliquely opposed as the first line's "man" and the last line's "Nobody." The latter pair, indeed, both oppose and complement each other (partly because in the same lines there is an under/over apposition). Put first and last lines together and they beautifully "enclose" the action of the lyric, even to binding it with the partial rhymes of *moon* and *town:*

> i met a man under the moon
> as Nobody came slowly over the town

Wit, rhyme, and echoing patterns of sound, at least as they are used here, control sentimentality by shifting attention away from the statement of the poem toward its technical mastry. I mentioned the wit of balancing moon against *Sun*day, but should certainly also have pointed out the verbal dexterity that goes with it, for if we listen carefully we can hear the opening lines hum. Five of the syllables end in *n*, four of them preceded by unlike vowels and the fifth rhyming. That alone is flashy. But then tack on three more syllables of neighboring full rhyme and the poem becomes a buzzing amalgam of sound. All we have to do is pull the crucial syllables out of context to hear them at their work:

man/ *un*/ moon/ *on*/ *Sun*// *day*/ *way*/ *say*

Once we are tuned in to this ingenious sound system, we can delight in Cummings' use of shoulder rhymes (rhymed or assonant words that are next to one another) in the first and last lines of the second stanza (*two glue*[d] and *new too*[ls]) as well as a wide variety of internal rhymes and partial rhymes (*fall* / *wall* / *small* in the third stanza, for example, or *did* / *dead* / *had* in the fourth).

Yet all of this analysis really does not solve the poem's mystery or account for its success. Like the other ninety-five poems that I'd preserve forever, it evades pigeonholes. It breathes a life of its own, different from my life, different (I assume) from yours, and (I'm willing to bet) different from Cummings'.

In spite of which we go on trying to "solve" poem after poem. Because Cummings is not merely a poem maker but a puzzle maker as well, we're lucky to have so cogent, so eloquent, and so perceptive a reader as Rushworth Kidder to show us not only how precise the structure of these poems is but how brilliantly one poem can light up—can help "solve"—the richly satisfying obscurity of others.

Preface

This book is designed as a reader's guide to individual poems. The rationale for this approach is based largely on my experience as a teacher: it is evident that many of Cummings' poems are not comprehensible to the reader unfamiliar with his idiosyncrasies. My students and I have often spent a good deal of time groping in a fog of syntactical and semantic confusion before locating a clearly paraphrasable meaning upon which to construct our sense of the poem. In our labors, we have found Cummings' commentators to be invaluable aids. Most of them, however, deal with his poems thematically rather than individually; and while they nicely address the broader questions about his thought and style, they often stop tantalizingly short of providing full readings of particular poems. This book, while it also may stop too short too often, is intended to supply several needs. I have tried, in the first chapter, to untangle some of the prevalent notions about Cummings' poetry and life. Thereafter, I have tried to provide careful readings of a broad number of poems. And I have tried to indicate the importance of the arrangement of poems within each volume.

The order of chapters here corresponds to the chronology of Cummings' various volumes of poetry, and the discussion generally proceeds through the volume from beginning to end. In the interest of conserving space and covering as many poems as possible, I have not quoted extensively from other critics, but have added an Appendix which directs the reader to those pages in the critical literature where he can find useful explications of individual poems. I have also refrained from extended quotation of the poems themselves, trusting the reader to consult his own copy of the text.

A note on texts is called for here. I have followed the order of the poems as they were first published in each of the twelve separate volumes. The contents of these volumes is preserved intact in *Poems 1923–1954* (New York: Harcourt Brace, 1954), which reprints all the volumes through *Xaipe*, and in the now-standard *Complete Poems 1913–1962* (New York: Harcourt Brace Jovanovich, 1972), which adds to the 1954 edition the contents of his two last volumes, *95 Poems* and *73 Poems*. Readers will find it most convenient to use *Complete Poems 1913–1962*. They may, alternatively, use the earlier *Poems 1923–1954*, supplemented with the two later volumes (available in paper). Or they may use the individual volumes, either in their original editions or, as they become available, in the typescript editions currently published by Liveright. In addition, either of the two English editions will serve. Readers are warned, however, against trying to use the well-known *Collected Poems* (New York: Harcourt Brace, 1938), which is both misnamed and disordered. It is not a full collection, but rather a strictly pruned selection from earlier volumes; and the poems it includes are completely rearranged. Like the later *100 Selected Poems* (New York: Grove Press, 1959), it provides reliable texts of the poems it includes but ignores the original order and relation among poems. Because of the variety of acceptable texts available, I have referred to poems by number rather than by page. In citing poems from the first four volumes, where poems are grouped into short sections, I have had to include volume, section heading, and poem number; thereafter, volume and poem number suffice.

I have incurred many debts in writing. Richard Kennedy, who is currently writing an exceptionally thoughtful biography of Cummings, has provided invaluable pieces of information and much encouragement. Edwin E. Williams has been a model of kindness in providing access to the Harvard libraries during my sabbatical year and in helping me locate and reproduce material in the Cummings Collection at the Houghton Library. Marty Shaw and the staff at the Houghton have been courteous, prompt, and inventive. George Firmage has gone out of his way to provide facts and insights and has been most generous in securing the necessary copyright permission. Several of Cummings' acquaintances, including William O'Brien and Horace Gregory, have shared their recollections with me. My own colleagues at Wichita State University have provided me with funds for research, a library staff eager to help, and a schedule that allowed me to write. They have also provided me, in the fall of 1976, with a wonderful class of four graduate students— Michael Calvello, Michael Moos, Carl Stach, and Tom Sullivan—in whose presence so many of these ideas began to unfold. Finally, my wife and family have patiently excused me from chores large and small; to them I owe a debt of affection which Cummings, of all people, would have understood.

Wichita, Kansas
May 1978

Chronology

1894   Edward Estlin Cummings born October 14 to Edward
Cummings, a teacher of sociology and political
science at Harvard since 1891, and Rebecca Haswell
Cummings.

1899   Cummings' parents buy Joy Farm, their summer
home near Silver Lake, New Hampshire.

1900   Cummings' father ordained minister of South Congregational Church of Boston.

1911   Cummings enters Harvard, lives at home. First poem
published in *The Harvard Monthly*.

1913   Elected to board of editors of *The Harvard Monthly*.

1915   Graduates *magna cum laude;* delivers commencement
address, "The New Art."

1916   Receives M.A. from Harvard. Mentions "Miss Orr,"
fiancée of Scofield Thayer and later Cummings'
wife, in letter. Moves to New York, applies for and
is refused position with *Vanity Fair*. Takes job with
P. F. Collier & Son.

1917   Joins Norton-Harjes Ambulance Corps, sails for
France in April. Imprisoned by French authorities
(September 21–December 19) on suspicion of treason. *Eight Harvard Poets*, including eight poems by
Cummings, published.

1918   Returns to New York, paints and writes. Drafted into army, sent to Fort Devens, Massachusetts, in July.

1919   Exhibits paintings at The Penguin Gallery in New York and at the annual exhibition of the Society of Independent Artists in New York (with which he exhibits fairly regularly into the early thirties). Daughter (Nancy) born to Elaine Orr Thayer.

1920   Publishes first poems and drawings in *The Dial*. Finishes writing *The Enormous Room*.

1921   Exhibits at Wanamaker's in New York. Moves to Paris, remaining abroad until December 1923.

1922   *The Enormous Room* published. Exhibits with Modern Artists of America.

1923   *Tulips and Chimneys* published.

1924   Marries Elaine Orr Thayer on March 19; lives with her in New York until summer, when they separate. Publishes the first of many essays in *Vanity Fair*. Moves to Patchin Place in Greenwich Village, his New York address for the rest of his life.

1925   Divorces Elaine, February 7. Publishes *&* (February 14) and *XLI Poems* (April 11). Meets Anne Barton. Wins *Dial* Award.

1926   *is* 5 published. Edward Cummings dies in automobile accident, November 2.

1927   Lives with Anne Barton. *Him* published. Last publications in *The Dial*, which ceases publication in 1929. Publishes nothing more until summer of 1930.

1928   *Him* produced (April 18–May 13) in New York by Provincetown Players.

1929   Marries Anne Barton, May 1.

1930   Publishes [No Title].

1931   Exhibits with Society of Painters, Sculptors, and Gravers in New York. Travels to Russia, May

10–June 14. Publishes *CIOPW* (containing ninety-nine reproductions of his art work in charcoal, ink, oil, pencil, and watercolor) and *ViVa*. Separates from Anne.

1932 Meets Marion Morehouse, well-known fashion model, with whom he remains for the rest of his life. Exhibits watercolors at Painters and Sculptors Gallery, New York.

1933 In Paris and Tunisia with Marion on Guggenheim Fellowship. Publishes *Eimi*, a journal of his 1931 Russian trip.

1934 Exhibits at International Art Gallery, New York. Divorced from Anne.

1935 Travels to Mexico City and California. Publishes *Tom*, a ballet, and *No Thanks*.

1936 1/20 [One over twenty], a selection of twenty poems, published in England.

1938 Publishes *Collected Poems*, a selection from his earlier volumes with twenty-two new poems.

1940 Publishes *50 Poems*.

1944 Publishes *1 x 1*. Exhibits fifty-nine paintings at the American British Art Center in New York.

1945 Exhibits at Rochester Memorial Gallery.

1946 *Santa Claus* published. *Harvard Wake* devotes special number to Cummings.

1947 Mother dies in January.

1949 Exhibits fifty-one paintings at the American British Art Center, New York.

1950 Academy of American Poets fellowship awarded. *Xaipe* published. Exhibits at Rochester Memorial Gallery.

1951 Guggenheim Fellowship.

1952 Charles Eliot Norton Professor at Harvard (through spring 1953). Delivers first of the nonlectures.

1953   *i:Six Nonlectures* published.
1954   *Poems 1923–1954* published.
1955   National Book Award citation for *Poems 1923–1954*.
        Exhibits at 1020 Art Center, Chicago.
1957   Reads at Boston Arts Festival. Receives Bollingen
        Prize in Poetry. Exhibits at University of Rochester
        Fine Arts Gallery.
1958   Publication of 95 *Poems* and *E. E. Cummings: A Miscellany*.
1960   Travels to Italy, Greece,. and France.
1962   *Adventures in Value* (photographs by Marion Morehouse, text by Cummings) published. Dies September 2 in New Hampshire.
1963   *73 Poems* published.

E. E. CUMMINGS

An Introduction to the Poetry

Chapter 1

Introduction

The Man

Poets are image-makers, and they make, among other things, images of themselves to tell us who they are. But poets are not always the people they tell us they are, and Edward Estlin Cummings was no exception. His literary career, stretching from the time of World War I to his death in 1962, was a prolific one: it produced, as he noted in his first "nonlecture" at Harvard in 1953, "a pair of miscalled novels; a brace of plays, one in prose, the other in blank verse; . . . an indeterminate number of essays; an untitled volume of satires; and a ballet scenario"— as well as twelve volumes of poetry containing over seven hundred poems.[1] Readers and critics have drawn from these writings an image of Cummings which, while it contains much truth and has gained great currency, is in some respects more caricature than portrait. The image is that of a man of feeling. And so he was—in part. In his personal life, as well as in his poetry, his expressions of feeling ran from the virulent and abrasive to the magnanimous and gentle. He had, as his friend John Dos Passos recalled, a mind that was "essentially extemporaneous," one that was apt to "go off like a stack of Roman candles" in unpremeditated volubility.[2] Spontaneous, effusive, he once, on the spur of the moment, felt sorry for his long-time friend Bill O'Brien, who was suddenly jobless, and offered him the contents of an unused bank account. The account, containing Cummings' honorarium from his year in residence at Harvard, had ten thousand dollars in it; O'Brien, deeply touched, refused. With the moment's other spur, however, he could rail mercilessly against the state of the arts, politics, and society, and fire pistol shots to frighten trespassers away from his New Hampshire farm.[3]

The voice that speaks in his poems—often wrongly confused with the voice of Cummings himself—is also a voice of feeling, given to such pronouncements as "let's live suddenly without thinking" (&, "Sonnets—Actualities," IX) and to well-wrought arguments assuring his lover that "feeling is first" (*is 5*, "Four," VII). This persona reserves his bitterest vitriolics for the individual who "does not have to feel because he thinks" (*No thanks*, 23). Reason is for others; and those who live by it alone—in which class reside scientists, politicians, and, at one time or another, nearly everyone else—are doomed to "the trivial torments of ordinary, hum-drum, common or garden life."[4] Cummings' poetry is probably best known for this antirational view: rebellion against the insensitivities of modern technocracy energizes such lines as:

> I'd rather learn from one bird how to sing
> than teach ten thousand stars how not to dance
> > (*New Poems*, 22)

and

> (While you and i have lips and voices which
> are for kissing and to sing with
> who cares if some oneeyed son of a bitch
> invents an instrument to measure spring with?
> > (*is 5*, "One," XXXIII)

The public image of Cummings also takes note of his interest in the visual configuration of his poems. Here the portraiture suffers not because it is caricature but because it is merely silhouette. In noting this concern, Cummings' readers have barely touched upon an aspect of his thought that is at once deeply significant and greatly neglected. For Cummings was—to judge by the devotion of time, energy, and thought—as much a painter and draughtsman as a poet. Some two thousand paintings are still in existence; the Cummings collection at Harvard alone has catalogued over eighty sketchbooks and more than ten thousand sheets of drawings. Wholly serious in his art, he regularly, if modestly, exhibited his work throughout his life. This aspect of his career is beginning to receive the attention it deserves, and discussions of it may be found elsewhere.[5] It is important to recognize here, however, that the spatial arrangements of his poems are the work neither of a whimsical fancy nor a lust for novelty. Poetry and visual art grew, in Cummings' mind, from one root; and while their outermost branches are distinct enough, there are many places closer to the trunk where it is hard to know which impulse accounts for a piece of work. Throughout his life he labored to articulate, in his essays and especially in his unpublished notes and journals, the relationship between literature and the visual arts. A number of his poems, too, deal verbally with visual ideas—not only with transcriptions of visual patterns (a common enough phenomenon in poetry) but with attempts to articulate visual thinking and bring into poetry the aesthetic principles of the painters.

The portrait that gives us the man in the round, then, must include proper emphasis on Cummings as a man of feeling and as a man of visual responsiveness. But it must do more. Primarily and essentially it must also portray him as a man of thought. For underneath the antirational guise, which delights or disgusts readers according as they see in it the purely childlike or the merely immature, lies a core of knowledge and a capacity for abstract and analytic thought strongly buttressed by something that can only be called scholarship. His five years as an undergraduate and graduate student of language at Harvard provided him with a scholarly habit of mind which never left him. He spoke and wrote French fluently, and he translated Greek with some regularity. He had a habit of making vocabulary lists: odd words used by Shakespeare, useful words he came across in miscellaneous reading, and, when he was traveling, necessary or interesting words in German, Spanish, Italian, Russian. He read, if not voraciously, at least thoughtfully. Throughout his career he apparently did his best thinking with pen in hand. His worksheets—typically on plain typing paper, with notes organized in logical progression down the page— address themselves to such subjects as the relation of color to sound, the effect of visual processes on reading, the nature of optical sensation, or the symbolic significance of up and down. Occasionally a flash of pithy insight interrupts, and he writes it out. "RED IS THE PRESCENCE OF THE ABSCENCE OF GREEN," he writes in the sheet illustrated here (see figure 1); elsewhere he is moved to jot down such things as "loudness is circular," "Melody is Silhouette," and "NOUNS are STUFFED BIRDS, their lice are adjectives."[6] For the most part, however, the worksheets, although written in elliptical fashion with ditto marks, arrows, and parentheses charting the path, are carefully worked out in step-by-step sequence. Even in later years, when he was reading widely less for research than for love of learning, he took copious notes: his papers include hundreds of pages of single-spaced typed digests of books, reviews, encyclopedia articles, and magazine essays, in which he emphasizes important ideas by shifting his typewriter to the red ribbon. And when he decided that his portrait painting could benefit from the study of anatomy, he went into it with characteristic diligence: his an-

I have just realised something:metaphors are everywhere, the silences and
the solidities which we call things are not things,but metaphors;and if
things were, metaphors are the hoppings of one thing to another which we
mistakenly call ideas:they copulate in laughter,in your smallest gesture
are born myriads which die in the next and incredibly are reborn;they
are eaten and drunken,we swallow them and we breathe them,under different
names;we do not stroke edges and feel music,but only metaphors;they are
the brightness and savour of all things--there are a billion on an in-
stant,on a coatsleeve--they are what we call sounds and flavours,the difference between this face and another

       everything is dangerous or fatal to everything else

    there are no entities,no isolations,no abstractions,but there are
    comparisons,contagions:consciousness is a heap of jackstraws,
    but this heap is not static,inert;it is a poise
    stresses quotion,of innumerable perfectly interrelated
    a product and a
    strains:thinking is an subtraction of one item,of a single unit,
    without the least budging of the whole.

the silences and solidities which we call things are not things,but

--thirstier than flies at a cow's eyes,thicker than memories in a blind
man.

the silences and solidites which we call things are not things,but
poises,self-organising collections; there are no entities,
no isolations,no abstractions,but there are differences,contagions:
I have seen consciousness as a heap of jackstraws,but this heap is
not static,inert;it is in a poise fatally or accidentally composed
by mutually dependent stresses,a product and quotient of innumerable
perfectly interrelated strains:

the least intensity of red is the greatest abscence of green

RED IS THE PRESCENCE OF THE ABSCENCE OF GREEN.

                it is thepresecence of abscences which
                constructs a whole

a given surface
    i take a flat surface,let us say a piece of canvass:and i put a
    colour anywhere,here: what has happened? The
    canvass, has lost its homogeneity:it is now,
    The homogeneity of the canvass is destroyed
    two things--an amount of colour, and an amount of canvass surround-
    ing this amount of pigment. The position of the pigment as regards
    the limits of the canvass,the size of

Figure 1. A typical Cummings' worksheet
cr. By permission of the Houghton Library, Harvard University

atomical drawings, some of them done in colored pencil with typewritten labels, indicate that he was copying at various times from at least nine different books on anatomy which he found at the New York Public Library. The result was over five hundred pages illustrating bodily structure and a much more competent hand at portraiture.[7]

In many respects, then, Cummings was hardly a man willing to "live suddenly without thinking." Nor did he conform to the pattern of the social rebel. Commonly seen as a Greenwich Village bohemian, he in fact remained a right-of-center Yankee in a left-leaning age. In *Eimi* (1931), the prose journal of his trip to Russia, his excoriations of the loudly touted Soviet system set him starkly apart from most of his contemporaries in American literature, for whom Communism seemed the hope of the ages. He was later to take an unpopular view of Franklin Delano Roosevelt, referring to him as "the great pink supermediocrity" (*Xaipe*, 37), and assuring his New Hampshire friends that he planned, as usual, to vote Republican.[8] His acquaintances thought him anything but radical. His first wife, telling the critic Edmund Wilson that "Cummings was the most conventional man in the world," warned, " 'Don't ever be fooled by this idea of Cummings the rebel.' "[9] And Dos Passos, noting some "Emersonian streak in his early training," quickly identified him as "the last of the great New Englanders."[10]

The necessity for our having a correct portrait of this "great New Englander" may be seen in the problems raised by misinterpretation. In 1931 the American critic R. P. Blackmur, looking back over Cummings' first decade of published work, leveled a lengthy and articulate blast which has sent wisps of gunsmoke through much of the criticism since.[11] Placing Cummings in the "anti-culture group," Blackmur attributed to him "a sentimental denial of the intelligence" and accused him of making "the deliberate assertion that the unintelligible is the only object of significant experience."[12] He objected to the "distortion" in the verse as "a kind of baby-talk."[13] Citing many examples—for he was by no means a slipshod scholar—Blackmur did his best to relegate the poet to the ranks of romantic egoists. He also laid out his own critical biases plainly. "Poetry," he wrote, "if we understand it, is not in immediacy at all. It is not given to the senses or to the free intuition. Thus, when poetry is written as if its substance were immediate and given, we have as a result a distorted sensibility and a violent inner confusion. We have, if the poet follows his principles, something abstract, vague, impermanent, and essentially private."[14]

Those who would defend Cummings from these charges had two courses open to them. They could, on the one hand, object to Blackmur's critical stance and justify Cummings precisely because he *was* a poet of immediacy. They could, in other words, take the view that Cummings was wholly a man of feeling, to whose poetry such rational criticism was inapplicable. On the other hand, they could agree with Blackmur's premises and labor to demonstrate that underneath the exterior distortions and the apparent solipsism lay a deeper and much more intellectual strain. His supporters most often chose the former path. They had, it must be said, the apparent support of the poet himself, who continued to write poems capable of being interpreted as banners of the "anti-culture group," and who publicly adhered to Rilke's pronouncement that "Works of art are of an infinite loneliness and with nothing to be so little reached as with criticism."[15] The result has been the perpetration of the idea that Cummings was an antirational poet—and that his antirationalism is perfectly acceptable.[16]

This view of Cummings rightly emphasizes the strong place he gives to feeling: to intuition, to the sensibilities, to the human capacity for responding to metaphysical reality in ways that are beyond the rational. But the view has largely ignored

Cummings' lively sense of the dangers inherent in the antirational. These are the sort of dangers that surface when what Eliot called "the general mess of imprecision of feeling" and the "Undisciplined squads of emotion"[17] find expression in forms that are commonplace and sentimentalizing. The fact is that Cummings uses logic, thought, and a great deal of calculated skill in writing poems which assert that feeling is first. Surely there is a paradox worth investigating here. And surely the investigation must consist of a close and thorough reading of individual poems—word by word, syllable by syllable, and in many cases letter by letter. Such a reading recognizes that there is much that cannot be grasped by limiting our study to syntax and semantics alone.[18] But it also recognizes that we can only touch the substance of the poet's feeling by beginning with the structure of his thought as it appears in the arrangement of his words. That arrangement is all a poem gives us to look at; we cannot reach through to feeling by ignoring structure.

Cummings himself was unremitting in his scorn for the critic who refuses to analyze. In a 1927 *Vanity Fair* essay, he puts the most abhorrent critical principles he can think of into the mouth of a fictitious lady reviewer. In her essay on a sculptor he names "Ivan Narb," Cummings has her write:

> Now, in closing, the present writer begs to apologize for the incompleteness of this little essay. Her only hope is that she has at least avoided the pitfalls of analysis into which many would-be critics of this new, unrecognizable sculpture have humiliatingly tumbled. As previously stated, the very essence of Ivan Narb's art is its perfect unanalysability. Once analysis is applied, all is lost. Either you instinctively feel the beauty inherent in these occult forms, wrought by the mysterious hand of genius from lowly materials, from humble substances which have never before been called upon to bear the lofty message of aesthetic emotion, or—to put it bluntly—you do not. . . .
>
> For example: To the privileged man or woman or child who per-

ceives the secret locked in Ivan Narb's sculpture, a certain vaguely ellipsoidal form of which I am now clearly thinking, is a source of irrevocable bliss, of ceaseless revelation, of unending joy. To someone whose eyes are sealed by materialistic considerations, this same form is merely a potato.
Here, as elsewhere, it is our duty and our privilege to choose.[19]

The choice lies between a trite and sentimentalized enthusiasm for the mysterious—which poises on the edge of plausibility while spinning out cliché after cliché—and a clear perception of the ordinary. Cummings urges us toward the latter, toward calling a potato a potato.

To make such a choice is not to affirm, however, that Cummings is to be seen only as an intellectual. His importance lies in the skillful combination of feeling and intelligence in his work. Always laboring to be as articulate as possible, he nevertheless refused to allow the thrust toward articulation to sweep aside the delicate moments of feeling. It is the recognition of the balance between these forces that makes, for example, a comment on his wife, typed into some of his reading notes in 1955, so significant. "How amazingly important language is!" he writes. "Marion—who's one of the few women I've ever known who can appreciate Nature—exclaims 'well look at the sunrise. Isn't that lovely. My goodness.' If I didn't know her, I'd think her Soul was like those unwords."[20] Recognizing the value of her capacity for feeling, Cummings simultaneously recognized that the *articulation* of feeling was something separate from the feeling itself, and "amazingly important." That he could forgive the inability or unwillingness to articulate, without for a moment surrendering his conviction in the importance of language, is characteristic of his particular blending of these two strains of feeling and intellect.

One other detail needs to be added to the portrait here. Cummings wrote—it will not do to mince words—some bad poetry. Moreover, he occasionally published it. The same is true in his painting. He seemed unwilling to consider the wastebasket his ally. Perhaps he was not a sound critic of his own work—which may mean no more than that he could not take the proper distance on it. As Edmund Wilson observed, "he never seems to know when he is writing badly and when he is writing well. He has apparently no faculty for self-criticism."[21] More probably, Cummings simply partook of good old New England husbandry: his parents, too, in saving religiously his letters, papers, scrapbooks, and even childhood sketches, amassed a mighty collection of indifferent things. The task for the reader, then, is one of sorting. If he is willing to trust his own discriminations, and if he is willing to read carefully, he need not be put off by the occasional inferior piece as he locates and appreciates the many excellent ones, nor need he labor to defend the indefensible. To do this, however, demands a certain skill in reading Cummings' idiosyncratic language, a skill that can best be fostered by an overview of Cummings' poetic style.

The Poetry

It is Theseus who, in *A Midsummer Night's Dream*, exactly summarizes the difficulty Quince has in reciting a few lines of verse without proper punctuation. "His speech," says the Duke, "was like a tangled chain—nothing impaired, but all disordered" (v, i, 125). The assessment is an apt one for some of Cummings' poems. The reader who would fathom his syntax and penetrate to the heart of his meaning must keep in mind Theseus' analysis: for although it is often "disordered," it is "nothing impaired" and still holds together its "chain" of meaning. The process of disentangling is easier if the reader observes some general rules for paraphrasing.

1. *Treat each stanza as a separate syntactical unit.*
Usually (although not always) Cummings brings his ideas to a conclusion at the end of a stanza, whether or not punctuation announces a point of completion. When syntax is puzzling, the assumption of syntactically independent stanzas is usually safe. Often, too, it is safe to assume that the syntax *within* a single stanza will ride across the line divisions and bind them together into a unit.

2. *Supply punctuation and capitalization as necessary.*
Cummings often deletes periods, commas, colons, and quotation marks, which need to be reinserted by the reader. The first two stanzas of "this mind made war" (*No Thanks,* 56) illustrate the difficulty:

> this mind made war
> being generous
> this heart could dare)
> unhearts can less
>
> unminds must fear
> because and why
> what filth is here
> unlives do cry

Assuming a full stop between stanzas and adding punctuation and capitalization helps resolve the syntax:

> This mind made war.
> (Being generous,
> this heart could dare).
> Unhearts can less.

> Unminds must fear
> "because" and "why."
> "What filth is here!"
> unlives do cry.

The fourth line, however, is still in confusion. It illustrates the need for another rule, which is to

3. *Sometimes add words to complete the sense.*
Cummings is a remarkably elliptical poet. In the line "unhearts can less," for example, the understood words, paralleled from the previous lines, are "only dare to do," so that the restored sense of the line is "unhearts can only dare to do less."

4. *Rearrange words within lines as needed.*
Cummings does not usually use both ellipsis and distorted word order in a single line. When a line needs rearranging, it is best to assume that he has supplied all the necessary words, and that nothing need be added to restore the sense. For example, the lines

> swim so now million many worlds in each
> least less than particle of perfect dark—
> > *(Xaipe,* 5)

become, on rearranging,

> so many million worlds now swim in each
> least particle of less than perfect dark—

a comment, as it turns out, on the stars.

5. *Connect fragments from line to line.*
Letters often need to be recombined into words:

a gr

eyhaire
d(m
utteri
ng)bab
yfa

ced

dr(lun
g)u
(ing)
nk . . .
(95 *Poems*, 33)

becomes "a greyhaired muttering babyfaced lunging drunk."
And pieces of words such as

rub,
!berq;
:uestions
(*ViVa*, xi)

become "rubber questions."

6. *Treat parentheses carefully.*
There is no infallible rule for reading around or through parentheses. They are usually to be treated in standard fashion, as marks that isolate inserted material, whether they come between or within words. In "yes but even" (95 *Poems*, 36), for example, the lines that describe

4 or(&
h
ow)dinary

businessmen are describing *four ordinary (and how!)* business-men. On some occasions, however, we must ignore the paren-theses: the last lines of "n(o)w" (*ViVa*, XXXVIII), which appear as

>)all are aLl(cry alL See)o(ver All)Th(e grEEn
> ?eartH)N,ew

end with the words *over all the green earth new.*

7. *Pay attention to context.*

With Cummings, as with so many poets, meaning develops from relationships among poems, and the reader will do well to examine neighboring poems in deciding among possible in-terpretations. In making sense of "who were so dark of heart they might not speak" (*Xaipe*, 51), a poem open to a Christian interpretation in its idea of "innocence" as a redeeming quality, the reader needs to take account of the previous poem, "no time ago" (50), about the narrator "walking in the dark" and meeting "christ / jesus." And in deciding how to construe the line "away the they" ("nonsun blob a," *1 x 1*, 1), the reader will do well to insert a colon after "away" and put "they" in quota-tion marks. In this way, "the 'they' " is given its proper empha-sis as "the others," the undifferentiated mass. Support for this interpretation comes from the following two poems in *1 x 1,* both of which make similar use of the word "they."

These rules, it must be emphasized, are useful largely for paraphrase. And paraphrase, because it reduces to prose all the glories of the poetic art, is a great destroyer of rhythm, asso-nance, consonance, and a host of other devices. Cummings' lines, through inversion, fragmentation, ellipsis, and punctua-tion, open up to a wealth of interrelationships and overtones not present in most prose; and any reading of a poem that contents itself with paraphrase and fails to account for these effects has not finished. It is equally true, however, that any reading that fails to make paraphrasable sense of a poem by means of the simple rules given above has not even begun. Cummings' poetry is meant to be understood—not, as Dylan Thomas once quipped about Surrealist verse, "by sucking it in through [one's] pores,"[22] but by making conscious and logical sense of its progressions of ideas. If this book helps the reader into a clearer grasp of such meanings—and then helps him out again into a fuller sense of the significance of the artistry in the language—it will have fulfilled its purpose as an introduction to the poetry.

Chapter 2

Tulips and Chimneys

Tulips and Chimneys (1923), Cummings' first collection, gathered together only some of his many early poems. He had already published some two dozen poems in *The Harvard Advocate* and *The Harvard Monthly* during his student days, and had appeared in print in an anthology titled *Eight Harvard Poets* (1917).[1] His career began in earnest, however, with publication in *The Dial*, a respected periodical newly refurbished by his friends Sibley Watson and Scofield Thayer and managed by former *Harvard Monthly* editor Stewart Mitchell. Cummings made his debut in the first number (January 1920) with seven poems and four line drawings; in following years he continued contributing in both media. By the time *Tulips and Chimneys* was published, readers of *The Dial* had seen twenty-seven of his poems. They had also seen eighteen drawings, and they must have wondered whether to call Cummings a poet or an artist.

Cummings, at that period, thought of himself as the latter. From Paris he had written his father that he was producing "the usual five million drawings a month and now and then a sentence or three, sometimes suitable for 'poetic' consumption that most hideous of diseases."[2] Even after the publication of *Tulips and Chimneys* he felt himself to be "primarily a painter."[3] Perhaps it was unavoidable that his lower-case *i* and unconventional typography should, in the early twenties, seize the public attention more than his line drawings. The drawings, skillfully conceived and deftly executed, adhered to the conventions of the day; but his audience had never seen anything quite like the jaunty freedom of his poem on Buffalo Bill, which had appeared in that first issue of *The Dial*. In any case, *Tulips and Chimneys* was widely reviewed, and Cummings the would-be artist found himself a much-discussed poet.

The book which the reviewers discussed in 1923 was not the version Cummings had originally wanted to give them. The manuscript Dos Passos brought over from Paris late in 1922 and presented to various American publishers had contained 152 poems. Considerations of bulk, of quality, and of censorship—even *The Dial* had shied away from some of his more earthy works[4]—seem to have militated against its publication: the book Thomas Seltzer finally brought out contained only sixty-six poems, with the remainder left to find places in Cummings' next two books.

With his usual penchant for verbal play, Cummings referred to *Tulips and Chimneys* by such pseudonyms as "Daisies and Fireescapes" and "Geraniums and Elevators."[5] A typed page among his notes, on which he worked out well over a hundred other candidates for the title—among them "fishhooks and pajamas," "lilacs and monkeywrenches," "starfish and phonographs," "squirrels and efficiency," and "doughnuts and tranquility"—indicates that the selection was a matter of no little significance.[6] His final choice suggests a number of oppositions: the country to the city, the organic to the lifeless, the natural to the manmade, and the beautiful to the ugly, as well as (in shape) the female to the male and (in the pun on *tulips* and the waste-disposing function of chimneys) the oral to the anal. It may well suggest, too, the essential division in the book: the section headed "Chimneys" comprises only sonnets, while "Tulips" includes a good deal of free verse.[7]

Beyond this major division, *Tulips and Chimneys* is further segmented into fourteen sequences, each containing from one to ten poems. Cummings' interest in conjoining short individual poems into larger sequences persists throughout his career; his practice of identifying these sequences by separate titles, however, continues only through *is* 5 (1926). Except for the division of *1 x 1* (1944) into three parts, the volumes after 1926 simply number the poems from beginning to end; and even *Collected Poems* (1938), although it draws heavily on his early volumes, abandons the earlier subdivisions. His interest in these patterns is nevertheless instructive. Always fascinated by the happy accidents of individual words—the puns, the multiple meanings, the words-within-words—he was also fascinated by the ways in which whole poems, since they always appeared to a reader within a context, inevitably and somewhat accidentally interacted with that context. In his collections of poems, sequence determined context and provided a means for making larger statements. A thoughtful examination of his sequences reveals that Cummings had much more to say than could be said in individual short poems.

It is equally clear, too, that Cummings' talent did not run to long poems. *Tulips and Chimneys* begins with "Epithalamion," an extended poem as traditional in its structure as it is classical in its reference. Here Cummings, not unlike a figure skater who must demonstrate precision in conventional school-figures before undertaking more inventive work, proves his mastery of the poet's traditional domain of rhyme, rhythm, metaphor, assonance, consonance, and a host of other literary devices listed in most handbooks of prosody. Here, too, he tactfully opens his assault on the conventions of poetry with an uncontroversial overture, saving the shock and dazzle for later. These twenty-one eight-line stanzas display a dutiful adherence to their common rhyme-scheme, although the rhyming words are sometimes (*emboss / diadumenos; alchemist / amethyst*) intriguing. Rhythmically, the poem rarely departs from ten-syllable pentameter lines. And, true to its traditional ancestry, it begins with an apostrophe ("Thou aged unreluctant earth") and ends with an envoy ("bless / thy suppliant singer and his wandering word.") Here the poet demonstrates his proper acquaintance with the classical pantheon and even assumes similar knowledge in his readers, who need to know, among other things, that the "crippled thunder-forging groom" is Vulcan, the "scared shepherd" is Paris, and the "prince of artists," sculptor of the "diadumenos" (a statue of an athlete crowning himself) is Polykleitos. Here, too, he echoes more recent poets: Hopkins' "dapple-dawn-drawn Falcon," riding the morning air, seems close behind the lines "On dappled dawn forth rides the pungent sun, / with hooded day preening upon his hand," and Keats's "still unravish'd bride," the "foster-child of silence and slow time," probably underlies Cummings' "O shining girl / of time untarnished."

For all its propriety, the poem is nevertheless a kind of cold-frame for Cummings' later style. The overt subject (praise of sensual delight) and the metaphor (spring) will grow up to become Cummings' favorites; even the suggestion in the final lines that this is a poem about poetry has parallels in numerous later pieces. Some phrases—the "grave / frailty of daisies" and the "small intimate / gently primeval hands"—seem to belong to later periods in their linking of paradoxical adjectives to conventionally "poetic" nouns; and at least one phrase—"silence immaculate / of God's evasive audible great rose!"—looks forward to his moments of knotty ambiguity. Reaching this far, he at times overreaches, with Swinburnian excess, into effects merely precious or patently labored—as he does, for example, in his image of dusk, in which "surpassing nets are sedulously spun / to snare the brutal dew." But the very surfeit in diction betrays a central theme in Cummings' (as in Hopkins') poetry: an ambivalence toward sensuality that, while it will produce images of great tenderness and beauty, will also produce, in some of his salacious sonnets, images of violence, distortion, and gross ugliness.

"Of Nicolette," the second poem in the volume, appeared originally in *The Harvard Advocate* (March 1913) during Cummings' sophomore year. There, the thirty-two-line one-sentence poem began with a capital letter; here, the capital disappears, but the final period remains. Perfectly rhymed, ethereal in its emphasis on whiteness and light, the poem, like "Epithalamion," is a spring song celebrating May. But where the earlier poem employed classical imagery, "Of Nicolette," with its castles and troubadours, is distinctly medieval. The next poem, "(thee will i praise between those rivers whose," is the first of a six-poem sequence entitled "Songs"; it celebrates May in much the same willowy diction as "Of Nicolette." It, too, is a single sentence. Here, however, Cummings has gone a step further in introducing his reader to the peculiarities of his style: neither initial capitalization nor terminal punctuation braces this poem, which begins and ends with parentheses and includes a lower-case *i*. The imagery, too, advances from the classical and medieval modes of the previous poems to a kind of Renaissance pastoralism, where references to "shadowy sheep" and the "tall mysterious shepherd" seem a nod in Spenser's direction, and where such lines as "let not thy lust one threaded moment lose: / haste" recalls the *carpe diem* argument of Sidney and the Petrarchans. More than a mere echo from older poets, that argument also looks forward to scores of similar poems of persuasion in Cummings' later work. The later tone is also anticipated in occasional phrases which use favorite words in oxymoron ("a rain fraily raging") and in the distinctive precursors of his conceptual vocabulary ("almostness," "the far-spaced possible nearaway").

"Always before your voice my soul" ("Songs," II) demonstrates Cummings' archetectonic skill. The first sentence is carefully threaded through four stanzas: paraphrased roughly, it reports that the speaker is awkward when the lover speaks (stanza 1), weak when she is silent (stanza 2), and lowly or insignificant ("mean") when she is thinking (stanza 3). When her words come again (stanza 4) these three conditions smite his heart in "trembling thirds" (fractions, or musical intervals), just as the twilight "shakes" with fright at the flight of "thirty birds" (a multiple of three). Syntax, not yet as gnomic as in later poems, requires only rearrangement to make clear sense. At times it is self-consciously poetic: "it is the autumn of a year" takes a full line to express what he will later learn to say in one word. But the effects are sometimes powerful:

> . . . through the thin air stooped with fear,
> across the harvest whitely peer
> empty of surprise
> death's faultless eyes.

Although death reaps his days, the transcendental mode so evident in his later poems is already apparent here as the speaker looks beyond mere physicality to "an earthless hour." His attention to assonance, fused with an imagery which, in a "rare / Slowness of gloried air," is orchestrated on flute, bassoon, and "a wild and thin / despair of violin," has about it an aura akin to that of the plays of Maeterlinck or even the illustrations of Maxfield Parrish. Nevertheless, the poem is artfully crafted: even the capital letter which begins one line in each stanza is not dropped in at random, but changes place stanza by stanza according to definite plan.

References to music, rather than innate musicality, qualified the first two entries for inclusion in the "Songs" sequence. The third, "Thy fingers make early flowers of," is justified by a graceful lyricism built from the literary counterparts of musical devices. Theme and variation ("sings,saying" and "says;singing"), refrain ("though love be a day"), and a careful attention to rhyme mark the piece as more song than statement. Employing a free-verse cadence within a rather tight structure, Cummings draws his effects both from accentual verse, as in the repeated spondees in the third line of each stanza, and from syllabic verse, as the common measure of the second, fourth, and fifth lines in each stanza demonstrates. In substance, the *carpe diem* argument to his lady depends on a simple repetition of motifs: praise of "Thy fingers" and "thy hair" in stanza one parallels praise of "thy whitest feet" and "thy moist eyes" in stanza two. The last stanza focuses on "thy lips," noting that Death, even if it misses everything else, is rich if it catches them. The lyric ends with just enough ambiguity to give it a nutty solidity: the lines "(though love be a day / and life be nothing,it shall not stop kissing)" leave unresolved the antecedent for "it," which may be love, life, or Death. In any case, nothing elevates the lover's intentions here: body is all, kissing is the goal, and promiscuity ("for which girl art thou flowers bringing?" she asks) is the order of the day. In tone, the poem, as Friedman notes, is in Cummings' "most serious formal style";[8] in subject, however, it belongs to his sensual rather than to his transcendental mode.

"All in green went my love riding" ("Songs," IV) first appeared in *The Harvard Monthly* (March 1916). Like Pound's "The Return," it seems deliberately vague in its referents; something is being described, but there is no certainty about the identity of the subject or its significance. Recalling Pound's "silver hounds" which are "swift to harry," Cummings' "lean hounds" and "swift deer" run in a "silver dawn." Like a scene from a medieval tapestry, the poem seems to demand an allegorical interpretation. Whether the repetitive "four" and the "great horse of gold" owe anything to he four horsemen of the apocalypse, and whether the final "heart" which "my love" has slain is also to be heard as *hart* (a male red deer), is open to interpretation. In its superbly balanced incremental repetition, however, it is one of Cummings' most musical poems, rivaling Wallace Stevens' "Sea Surface Full of Clouds," which appeared in book form the same year. In the light of Cummings' predilection for the sonnet—he published, during his career, one hundred and ninety-one of them—this poem is an interesting variation of that form: its fourteen stanzas, like the fourteen lines in a Shakespearean sonnet, fall neatly into three "quatrains" and a final pair. And, like the sonnets of Wyatt, Surrey, and Spenser, it depends on the courtly metaphor of deer-hunting.

The last of the songs ("when god lets my body be"), a parting shot at the cruel lady behind this sequence, is not unlike Shakespeare's sonnet 71 ("No longer mourn for me when I am dead") in its effort to evoke his lover's pity. In this sonnet variant, the poet envisions a time when his body will be (rather grotesquely) atomized and infused throughout nature. The poem may be, as Doris Dundas notes, a parody on Joyce Kilmer's "Trees," upended to prove that the poet can indeed make trees as well as poems.[9] Parody or not, the final line—"With the bulge and nuzzle of the sea"—is an accurately observed and wonderfully assonant description of the action of the ocean around, say, the pilings of a wharf.

Following "Songs" in a section by itself is "Puella Mea," a 290-line poem favorably comparing "my lady" with all the dead lovelies of mythology and history. It is a work which proves only that Cummings is best in shorter poems. Learned, repetitive,

the poem depends on adjectives and adverbs to flesh out its tetrameter lines. Writing to his father after the poem appeared in
The Dial (January 1921), Cummings noted that it was written
"in a tent a year ago last August, if I remember rightly," which
may explain its genesis as a literary wish-fulfilment.[10] Nevertheless, it does at moments prefigure his later style: he praises his
lady's legs by noting that "each is a verb," and he comments on
"the minute / spontaneous meadow of her mind"—where "minute" may be less a deprecation of her mentality than a praise of
her "spontaneous" freedom from stifling intellection.

The three poems in "Chansons Innocentes" are united in
their concern for the innocent and "wonderful" world of childhood, and also in their suggestions of an underlying presence
inimical to that very innocence. The first, "in Just-," is, as
Cummings told his father, "a hint of youth and Norton's
Woods," an evocation of his own boyhood neighborhood in
Cambridge, Massachusetts.[11] Like Dylan Thomas' "The Hunch-
back in the Park" or Lawrence Ferlinghetti's "The pennycan-
dystore beyond the el," it draws on the poet's own childhood
and finds there both joy and foreboding. The "balloonman" is,
in one dimension, simply a sign of returning spring and a focus
for childhood's delights in fragile and evanescent toys. In another
dimension, however, he is a distorted version of adulthood,
lame, strange, and, like Pan or any satyr, "goatfooted." Goats
conventionally emblemize lust—clearly not a childlike quality—
and the capital in the final "balloonMan" emphasizes the adult's
presence in the child's world. Like the Pied Piper, he draws
children out of their separate boyish ("marbles and / piracies")
and girlish ("hop-scotch and jump-rope") concerns and toward
each other, toward a world of complex adult interrelationships
which, while still "far / and / wee," is ominously waiting. Nevertheless, in "Just- / spring"—in the earliest spring, or in the
spring which brings its own inevitable justice, or perhaps in the

only season ("just in spring") in which such things could possibly happen—there remains a "mud- / lucious" and "puddlewonderful" sense of relish for things which adults are supposed to dislike.

The last of the "Chansons," "Tumbling-hair," comments on the end of innocence, and was in fact titled "Epitaph" when it appeared as the last of Cummings' poems in *Eight Harvard Poets*. With an economy which will later become his hallmark, Cummings identifies the character and sets the scene in the first two lines: a child, carelessly spontaneous in her appearance, is absorbed in the "wonderful" task of picking wild flowers. The flowers she picks, each of which has a specific name and identity, increase in size from tiny "buttercups" to "big bullying daisies," paralleling her own growth. The first four lines apostrophize this picker; the last four describe "Another" who comes with eyes that are "a little sorry" and picks "flowers" indiscriminately, without distinguishing types. While meaning is clear here, significance is not. Is this sorry-eyed person meant to be Death, or (as Cummings described it in "Puella Mea") the "Eater of all things lovely—Time"? Is this poem addressed to a former lover who has been superseded by another? Is "Another" the poet himself, who loses his sense of the fine distinctions among beautiful things in the rush of adult life? Or is "Another" the same "Tumbling-hair" child grown older? Whatever the case, the "field wonderful" of youth is, like the "farm forever fled from the childless land" in Dylan Thomas' "Fern Hill," doomed to disappear.

The six poems of "Orientale" are all of a piece. Eastern in their imagery, symbolic and ceremonial in their eroticism, they speak of such things as incense and porphyry and satraps. The second, "lean candles hunger in," apparently describes a worshipper of temple prostitutes involved in strange rites, while the third, "my love," seems to parody the language of the Song of Solomon. The last, "the emperor," is a fairly straight-forward description of activities in a harem, and is notable only for its inclusion of the word "stiffenS," whose internal capital is an advance beyond the earlier "ballonMan" in Cummings' use of that now-famous device. Strange and foreign, these poems demonstrate rather forcefully that experience, for Cummings, was a better muse than fantasy.

"Amores," containing eight poems, treats of love, parting, and reconciliation. The last two, "O Distinct" and "your little voice," are poems of praise that are, respectively, among the best and worst in the volume. "O Distinct / Lady of my unkempt adoration," begins the singer ("Amores," VII); addressing his love, he bids her forgive the "unkempt" appearance of his verse as it appears in "a certain fragile song"—this very poem, perhaps. Unlike the trite songs of "the others," his is stamped with his own individuality: where he has been true to "Nothing and [that] which lives," they have wallowed in conventional description ("the handsome / moon," "the / pretty stars"), and have been faithful to "the serene the complicated / and the obvious." The word "complicated," meaning "consisting of many parts not easily separable," comments on their lack of single-mindedness: "they have been faithful," the poet sneers, "to many things." Here even Cummings' adjectival excess can be excused: the guilty line ("placid obscure palpable"), after all, parallels the earlier "serene," "complicated," and "obvious." The poem is, finally, another *carpe diem* piece, without the logic of persuasive argument but with all the imagery of an "eligible day," an "unaccountable sun" (not subject to any responsible reckoning of consequences), and the "noise of worms." It is also, not surprisingly, a poem more about poetry than love.

The section entitled "La Guerre" presents a brace of poems concerning the effects of war and the subsequent and inevitable renewal of the earth. In each, human skill—whether it manufactures "the bigness of cannon" or produces the impertinences of philosophy, science, and religion—submits to larger forces: to death, or to spring. The free verse of "O sweet spontaneous" ("La Guerre," II) is constructed in four-line stanzas, which, unlike the abstract categorizations practiced by the researchers it describes, ultimately breaks down into a scattering of "spontaneous" final lines.

The five poems in "Impressions" all refer to night. Primarily about the city rather than the country, they are, to a greater or lesser degree, verbal transcriptions of visual effects seen in the sky. Cummings was a lover of sunsets, not only in his paintings and poems, but in nature as well. Bill O'Brien, a frequent visitor at Cummings' summer home in New Hampshire, reports that house-guests, wherever else they might roam during the day, were to be back on the west porch to watch the sun set behind Mount Chocorua each evening.[12] Cummings took the same delight in city sunsets: in "the sky a silver" ("Impressions," I), the city twilight is "resolved" like a dissonant chord into a harmony of "jewels" (stars). The stars are "trite" both because they, like "correct" harmonies in music, are commonplace images in poetry, and because they, unlike sunsets, are invariably the same. By contrast, the mothlike moon, low on the horizon, "flutters and flops" among trees, grass, and houses until it disappears into the river. The second poem, "writhe and," describes the city as a painting of the sort Cummings himself was doing in these years. The buildings, "putting off dimension," seem to lose depth in the approaching darkness, just as, for the modern abstract painter, represented reality reduced itself to the flatness and two-dimensionality of the picture plane. Adding commas (lines 3, 5, 8, and 9) and a dash (line 10) clarifies the syntax. The alarm clock in the third poem is followed, quite properly, by "the hours rise up putting off stars and it is / dawn" ("Impressions," IV), where poems are made at twilight and unpoetic reality intrudes during the day. The final poem, "stinging," was titled "Sunset" on its appearance in *Broom* (July 1922); it describes spires and a townscape as dusk changes them from gold to silver and at last to rose. If punctuated— semicolons after "spires" and "litanies," dashes after "rose" and "fat bells"—the syntax makes sense, although the cryptic metaphor of sunset as religious ceremony (with a "tall / wind" as *pneuma,* spirit) suggests more than it says.

The ten "Portraits" in the next sequence are essentially city poems. The first seven describe, respectively, a twenty-dollar prostitute lying drunk in the street, a youth with "hurt girl eyes," burlesque strippers (a favorite subject in Cummings' art as well as in his writing), a "dirty" child out walking with her parents, a conversation with Death at Dick Mid's brothel (for more on Dick Mid, see "Sonnets—Realities" IV in *Tulips and Chimneys* and "Sonnets—Realities" XX in *&*), a cemetery, and, perhaps, a mourner in the cemetery. The progression leads neatly into Cummings' famous comment on death, the cryptic "Buffalo Bill 's."

Apparently reading the obituary of William F. Cody in the New York *Sun* on January 11, 1917,[13] Cummings began "Buffalo Bill 's" ("Portraits," VIII; note the space before the *'s*) as a kind of elegy for a figure in whom he recognized a significant blend of hero and charlatan, a figure whose image reflected something he felt was at the very pith of the American character in the twentieth century. Buffalo Bill, more like a concept than a man, is not simply dead but "defunct." With him has gone not only a link with the myth of the frontier but another sign of the human penchant for reducing heroic deeds to circus stunts and for applauding the glib and the fraudulent: this performer, after all, merely broke clay pigeons instead of Indians. Central to this two-stanza poem (the second begins in line 8) is the word "Jesus." Obviously an expletive, it is also a substantive: for just as the enjambment in lines four and five produces "a water-smooth-silver / stallion," so lines five and six produce "pigeons-justlikethat / Jesus." In the reduction of his heroic deeds into polite religious convention, Jesus, "just like" Bill, has been made by modern Americans into nothing more than an intriguing breaker of insignificant objects—or, if pigeon, for Cummings as for Joyce, meant Holy Ghost, into a kind of spiritual sharpshooter. Bill was "handsome"; so, too, "Jesus / he was a handsome man." But "handsome" is a word Cummings denigrated in the poem "O Distinct" as belonging to the cliché-ridden language of singers of "the obvious"; these two poems, in fact, appeared together in the January 1920 issue of *The Dial*. So what good is it (asks the narrator) to be "blueeyed," "handsome," and as clever as Buffalo Bill? "Mister Death" takes all such clichéd things, for only the truly alive (a favorite word of approbation for Cummings) can escape ultimate destruction. As Cummings' later poetry makes clear, the transcendent and metaphysical were not in themselves objects of his scorn; the counterfeits of these things, however—the merely superficial manifestations, whether political, intellectual, or religious—were not to be spared. And Cumimings may have written this poem with one eye on his own family: he was, as Gertrude Stein would later note in *Everybody's Autobiography*, a minister's son, and, while he remained on the best of terms with his parents, he lost few opportunities in the 1920s to assert his independence from their religious standards. The poem, then, is much more a comment on varieties of worship, secular and religious, than it is often taken to be; and Sibley Watson's mother, a "High Church Episcopal" who, Cummings reported, "raised such a cry over the 'Jesus' in *Buffalo Bill*" when it appeared in her son's periodical, may have spoken better than she knew.[14]

"Portraits" ends with two poems which focus on the power of

spring. In "spring omnipotent goddess thou dost" (IX), the poet
concocts the delightful mixture of archaic grammar and contemporary diction (evident in such phrases as "thou stuffest")
which will characterize later satires. Coming like an irresistible
slut, spring makes the poet "so very / glad that the soul inside
me Hollers." Here, as in many of his poems of praise, Cummings is not far from Biblical language: the lines of a central
passage ("When you sing in your whiskey-voice / the grass /
rises on the head of the earth / and all the trees are put on
edge") appear to blend the phrase "and all the trees of the field
shall clap their hands" (Isaiah 55:12) with the words "the children's teeth are set on edge" (Jeremiah 31:29). Otherwise the
poem is straightforward, except for some ambiguity in the concluding lines ("feet incorrigible / ragging the world"), where
"ragging" may mean *tearing to rags* or *covering with rags*, as
well as *dancing a rag-time rhythm.* The first lines of the last
poem in the section ("somebody knew Lincoln somebody Xerxes," X) may be paraphrased "Somebody knew Lincoln, somebody knew Xerxes, and somebody knows this man." The man
here appears to be a famous elderly gentleman, perhaps one of
Cummings' neighbors, whose activity is reduced to a daily walk
in the park. Spring, troubling his sense of "lean and definite"
order, comes and secretly enlivens the city houses, which "con-
verse" in a "nervous" and "furious" language reminiscent of
Gertrude Stein's prose. But they cease their animation and become merely objects with no human responses ("irresponsible")
when he appears. Pigeons, dogs, and children, however, "Are":
they assert themselves, and so live, and even the old man's conservative sense of propriety cannot suppress the "beautiful nonsense of twilight." The poem's placement is significant: "Portraits," ostensibly about people and society, ends with a
reassertion of the power of life, spring, and poetic language over
social convention and conformity to factual analysis.

"Post Impressions," the final sequence of "Tulips," contains six poems. Of these, the third ("into the strenuous briefness") is the most vigorous. Normalized, the first lines read: "into the strenuous briefness (Life: handorgans and April, darkness and friends) I charge laughing." As in the later "i will wade out / till my thighs are steeped in burning flowers" (*XLI Poems,* "Songs," XI), the narrator describes his passion for the evanescent. Characteristically, the progression of four-line stanzas is concluded by a variant stanza—here, the single line "(of solongs and,ashes)"—which brings a finality to both the subject (saying *so long* to the earlier "roses & hello") and the form. Whether Cummings had these roses and ashes in mind when he settled on *Tulips and Chimneys* as a book title is uncertain. Writing to his father on the poem's appearance in *The Dial* (May 1920), he did say, however, that it was "later in composition than the other 4 [in the same issue], and to my mind more perfectly organized. I am confident that its technique approaches uniqueness. After all . . . it is a supreme pleasure to have done something FIRST—and 'roses & Hello' also the comma after 'and' ('and,ashes') are Firsts."[15] A similar device appears in the prose poem which ends the "Post Impressions" sequence ("at the head of this street a gasping organ is waving moth-," VI): describing an organ-grinder's monkey, he uses punctuation to denote gesture in the lines "(if you toss him a coin he will pick it cleverly from, the air and stuff it seriously in, his minute pocket) Sometimes [. . .] the monkey will sit, up, and look at, you with his solemn blinky eyeswhichneversmile."

"Tulips" gathered together a rather broad cross-section of Cummings' early work. While its individual sequences usually had discernible themes, the section as a whole was more aggregation than organization. "Chimneys," however, is a tightly composed work. The seventeen sonnets, most having something to do with love, are divided into three groups: "Sonnets—Realities," "Sonnets—Unrealities," and "Sonnets—Actualities." The first sequence deals mainly with prostitution and the harsher "realities" of sexual relationships. Commenting on the second sonnet ("goodby Betty,don't remember me") Horace Gregory and Marya Zaturenska noted that it "says very nearly everything that many American novelists of the period had to say, and it has the advantage of saying it with greater art and in fewer words."[16] The other poems portray a dancer (III) whose conception of death can take her no farther than a simile of emptiness in a social context—"like Coney Island in winter"—a visit to Dick Mid's brothel (IV), and a teen-aged prostitute (V). The last is a rather skilled and highly ironic poem ("when thou hast taken thy last applause,and when"), titled "A Chorus Girl" in *Eight Harvard Poets,* which feigns sentimentality as it describes the narrator's lust.

The best of the sequence, however, is the first, "the Cambridge ladies who live in furnished souls." "Cambridge," here, is a word charged with significance. Having grown up under the shadow of Harvard, Cummings knew well the kind of old New England intellectual strain represented by these arbiters of social life. Apparently espousing the liberal humanitarian causes, they remain rigidly conservative. Not unlike "Buffalo Bill 's," the poem is essentially about the failure to make distinctions between the significant and the trivial. These ladies live in "furnished souls": the surprising appropriateness of the phrase (we expect "live in furnished rooms") contrasts the real intellectual and social life of Cambridge, going on perhaps in the furnished rooms of transient students, with the states of feeling and sentiment which these permanent residents have taken over readymade from their environment. Having the accouterments of soul without its vital capacities, they also have "comfortable minds"—full of safe clichés, the product of second-hand association with a heady university atmosphere without any first-hand experience of studious endeavor. They also have daughters, but only "with the church's protestant blessings": their successors have been born strictly within the bonds of marriage, but the church protests a little at the sexual implications behind child-bearing. In any case, the daughters themselves are devoid of female charm: "unscented shapeless," they are too "spirited" and wraithlike to possess much physical attractiveness.

These ladies "believe in Christ and Longfellow, both dead": just as, in "Buffalo Bill 's," the modern age confuses Jesus and a showman, so here the ladies make no distinction between the founder of Christianity (in whose honor Harvard, as a school for the ministry, began) and a safely orthodox if sometimes insipid poet, himself a denizen of Cambridge. Capturing their own tones of voice in the next lines (tones meant to suggest the prose of a society page, perhaps), Cummings tells us that they are "invariably interested in so many things"—constantly interested, but also without any variation in routine. Their "delighted fingers" are "knitting for the is it Poles? / perhaps"— even the ladies themselves cannot distinguish the purpose behind their efforts. Carefully groomed in their permanents, bandying "scandal of Mrs. N and Professor D" (note the *n* and *d* sounds here), they finally betray their real interest: gossip. The point is that they "do not care" to differentiate between beauty and comfort, to distinguish the religion of Jesus from the philosophy of Longfellow, to contrast international crises and local gossip, or even at last to discern such universal portents as the moon rattling "like a fragment of angry candy" in the sky above Cambridge, from their own petty lives. Failing to distinguish, they tend to reduce all things to their own terms: even the moon, although she behaves like a goddess angered at the indifference of mortals, is seen through the simile of parlor sweets as a useless "fragment" in a fancy round "lavender" box. Surreal and ominous though it is, the image cannot jar the ladies from their complacency: like the dozens of socialites, politicians, and scientists Cummings will excoriate in later poems, they are unconcerned with the things which, to the poet, matter most. The next sequence, "Sonnets—Unrealities," comments on the idealized and sentimentalized aspects of love. It moves toward the metaphysics of its concluding poem ("a connotation of infinity," vi), which anticipates Cummings' later transcendent bent so well that it seems oddly out of place in this early work. The first poem ("it may not always be so;and i say") is an unabashed piece of sentiment in the tradition of Elizabeth Barrett Browning; the second, in startling contrast, begins "god gloats upon Her stunning flesh," but reveals itself to be explicitly about the sea and only metaphorically about women. The third meditates on unrequited love, and the fourth, again taking sea as metaphor, addresses its waves as "counted petals" which signify "the exquisite froms / and whithers of existence," and sees the moon as "the white ship of thy heart." The fifth, "a wind has blown the rain away and blown," seems less logic than incantation, less a poem to be read silently than aloud. A fine piece, it recalls Cummings' earlier landscape paintings of dark trees and crescent moons.

"Sonnets—Actualities" is a sequence which, ostensibly praising love and the lover, is really rather acidulous. To speak of a kiss in so anatomical a phrase as "the little pushings of the flesh" (i), and to speak of love as "building a building" (ii) where, in a kind of dungeon, the lover's "surrounded smile / hangs / breathless," is surely to treat the lover with more mockery than affection. The narrator of the third poem spins out extravagant metaphors ("yours is the music for no instrument / yours the preposterous colour unbeheld") to woo his lover, only to end with an aside ("or so thought the lady") betraying his insincerity. The last two poems apparently draw their metaphors from allied arts: from a painting of a madonna and child (IV) and from something akin to the love-and-graveyards ambience of Jacobean drama (V). Hardly as "tender" and "whimsical" as they have been called,[17] these poems end the volume on a note consonant with Ortega y Gasset's insight that readers in the mid-twenties could hardly interest themselves in "a poem, a painting, or a piece of music that is not flavored with a dash of irony."[18]

Chapter 3

XLI Poems
and &

Early in 1925 the remainder of the poems from the original
Tulips and Chimneys manuscript were published in two volumes, & [*And*] and *XLI Poems*. Although & happened to appear
two months before *XLI Poems*, it should be considered the later
volume.[1] Along with some new poems, & contains the leftovers
refused by the publishers of *Tulips and Chimneys* and *XLI
Poems*. Writing home in May of 1924, Cummings told his
parents that "Mr. Lincoln MacVeagh has accepted a group of
poems(41) (by simple process of rejecting the rest of the T & C
ms.)for publication via 'The Dial Press.' "[2] The poems left behind, as Cummings later explained, were simply too hot for
publication. "I have one book [&] on the press & one [*XLI
Poems*] should be by the end of this week," he writes on January 5, 1925. "The 1st will not be suppressed(for obscenity)only
because labelled 'privately printed' . . . . The 2nd is harmless."[3] Shortly after & appeared, he wrote home that "this con-
catenation of poems, if found in a Cambridge bookstore, or on a
table in the Cummings,Sr.,home,would cause liberal arrests
lawsuits mayhems and probable massacres."[4]

XLI Poems is, indeed, "harmless"—a charming, if slightly effete, collection. While it indulges in some experimental word
disruptions and typographical oddities, it presents none of the
extraordinary curiosities of &; and while it contains protests of

love for city streets "(by god i want above fourteenth / fifth's deep purring biceps, the mystic screech / of Broadway" ("Sonnets," XVI), they are mild and polite in contrast to other poems from the original *Tulips and Chimneys* manuscript. Cummings' feelings for the volume can be gauged by noting that he salvaged few poems from it for later volumes. *Collected Poems* (1938) eliminates sixteen of the forty-one, and *100 Selected Poems* (1959) represents the 1925 volume by only two entries.

XLI Poems, like *Tulips and Chimneys*, has "Songs," "Chansons Innocentes," "Portraits," "La Guerre," and "Sonnets." The poems in "Songs" tend to be rather slight. Many of them take twilight, dawn, or night as context for meditations on love or on "the mystery / of my flesh" (XI). Three of them ("the / sky / was," "between green / mountains," and "the hills") are verbal sketches of scenes which Cummings frequently delineated in oils and watercolors during this period: the pyrotechnics of sunset, the "magnificent clamor of / day / tortured / in gold" (X) by the "flinger / of / fire" (VII). He seems to have had painters in mind. In an early draft, the first six words of "the / sky / was" are divided into monosyllables; scrawled beneath is the phrase "cf. pointists," probably referring to the pointillists of the late nineteenth century, who represented luminous surfaces by using variously colored dots or short strokes all of a similar size.

Of particular interest to the sequence and to Cummings' early work in the visual arts is the second poem, "of my." The poet describes a particular "street" in his "soul" as being full of the "prettinesses" of Picabia, the "stark . . . throttling trees" of Picasso, "Matisse rhythms," and "Kandinsky gold-fish." Cataloguing some of his own artistic influences, the street also provides a refuge where "my soul / repairs herself" to get away from "the gripping gigantic / muscles of Cézanne's / logic"— where the poet-painter can escape the unrelenting demands of the master's example by fleeing into the significant ("prisms of sharp mind") but nevertheless secondary atmosphere of more modern art. That Cummings ranked the French postimpressionist first is evident from his published and unpublished comments: speaking of Cézanne's "incredulous and otherwise energetic intelligence," Cummings praised him for succeeding "not by superficially contemplating and admiring the art of primitive peoples, but by carefully misbelieving and violently disunderstanding a secondhand world."[5] He had no such loyalties to the other moderns. Toward Picasso, for example, his attitude was much less approving: while he once called him "the world's greatest living painter,"[6] he had also written of him, in unpublished notes, as "a far inferior master" and as "a cynical Spaniard" who was "spiritually defunct."[7] In this poem, Picasso and the other painters inhabit "a street . . . / where strange birds purr." Cummings' own canvases at this period, as "strange" as these hybrids of flying and feline ("purr") creatures, are in keeping with those of his contemporaries; but they are not, as he must have recognized, up to Cézanne's "logic."

Several of the "Portraits" from *XLI Poems* continue this painterly theme. The poem beginning "Picasso / you give us Things / which / bulge" ("Portraits," III) appeared in the same issue of *The Dial* (January 1924) as Henry McBride's review of Picasso's recent work. McBride observed that Picasso was "first and foremost a stylist, as concerned with simplifications and purities of expression as ever . . . . Intellectually all the other painters of the day pale beside him."[8] Cummings takes up similar points, emphasizing the ideas and the solid tangibilities of this "Lumberman of The Distinct." The metaphor throughout is of woodworking, tools for which are suggested in the "brain's / axe" with which the artist can "hew form truly," the "squeak of planes" (both flat Cubist surfaces and carpenters' tools), and the "circular shrieking tightness" of a power saw. Unlike Picabia's "prettinesses" in the earlier poem, Picasso's bodies are "lopped

/ of every / prettiness," for his instinct "only chops hugest inherent / Trees of Ego"—only the most meaningful and significant aspects of being, shorn of all ornament. It is characteristic of Cummings that he should see Picasso as a painter of sounds. The poem is full of "squeals" and "solid screams," just as Cummings' own paintings of this time—in several numbered series whose works bear such titles as *Noise Number 13* and *Sound Number 5*—attempted to present the visual equivalent of audible sensations. It is also characteristic that Cummings' poetic self-portrait in this volume ("my mind is," "Portraits," vII) employs a vocabulary and imagery remarkably similar to that of "Picasso." Cummings' comments on other artists and writers regularly reflect upon his own practices, and it is not accidental that he saw himself here through metaphors he used for Picasso, and that in praising the painter's powerful economy of form he delineated his own poetic and artistic ideals.

"Chansons Innocentes," the second sequence in the volume, contains two poems which, attempting childlike simplicity, remain merely immature. The nine poems of "Portraits" move closer to the low-life subjects of *&*. Three of them ("conversation with my friend is particularly," "as usual i did not find him in cafes,the more dissolute," and "at the ferocious phenomenon of 5 o'clock i find myself") are prose poems. The first of these (I) probably describes Scofield Thayer, whose "electric Distinct face . . . clinched in a swoon of synopsis" Cummings has caught well in various drawings.[9] The next ("Portraits," v), which comes midway through the sequence, was originally entitled "Arthur Wilson" after Cummings' roommate in New York in 1917. It describes, in the first part, the poet's search for his friend through crepuscular city streets. The latter part describes their room, complete with the Harvard-colored "comforter" (mentioned in letters from this period) and littered with Cummings' canvases ("the carouse of geometrical putrescence"), which the forthright criticism of his roommate has, figuratively if not literally, "wheeled out on the sunny dump of oblivion." The last of the prose-poems, ending the "Portraits" sequence, is a self-portrait narrating the poet's trip to the top of the Woolworth Building during New York's rush hour. Dealing with three individuals Cummings knew well, these prose-poems compose a sequence of their own, a framework within which the rest of the portraits are hung.

These remaining portraits (excluding "Picasso" and "my mind is") depict urban low-life. The second, "one April dusk the," describes a café. Its Greek name is nothing less than The Parthenon, and its central figure, a tramp, is grandly known as Achilles. Here the poet smokes "Haremina" cigars with feet up against the sloping attic (note the pun) ceiling. Poet and reader, here, observe ironies which are lost on Nicho' the waiter, for whom Achilles, and all that name suggests, seem no more significant than the shishkabob he offers the poet. Occasional flashes of language stand out in this sequence: the tramp is described as "peeling / off huge slabs of a fuzzy / language with the aid of an exclamatory / toothpick," and the poet in the Turkish café (VI) notes that the proprietor's "peaked head smoulders / like a new turd in April." The latter phrase exemplifies a strain in Cummings' style evident in later poems: he fastens to conventional indicators of spring, love, or beauty ("April") some generally overlooked unpleasant characteristic associated with the image ("a new turd") which is both disgusting and, because surprisingly apt, amusing.

The two poems in "La Guerre" are specifically iconoclastic. In the first, "earth like a tipsy / biddy with an old mop" brings to light, in her cleaning, "hidden obscenities" and "dusty heroisms." In her awkwardness she upsets and smashes a crucifix, which is "thrown on the ash-heap" along with the "discobolus" of "Myron." The discobolus, ascribed to the Greek sculptor Myron, is a statue of an athlete about to throw a discus; although copies exist, the original has been lost. This "ashheap," then, is the depository for icons which are no longer useful—nor even original. Once on the ash-heap, it hardly matters whether the image was pagan or Christian. Cummings, who throughout his poetry shows more respect for spirituality than for religion, equates the crucifix with the latter, and expresses no concern at its loss. But the poem need not be read as a statement of the poet's faith: "earth," not the poet, is the iconoclast, and (given its place in "La Guerre") the poem may be saying that the natural processes of earth, like the unnatural ones of war, smash all traditions and reduce all distinctions between the worship of classical muscularity and Christian love to barely distinguishable refuse.

"Humanity i love you," the other poem in the sequence, nicely illustrates the intertwining of affection and disgust so prevalent in Cummings' work. Each of the six reasons adduced for loving Humanity are in fact cause for loathing it, and by the time the reader has sniffed out the mockery in the praise, he has come upon the terminal phrase, "Humanity / i hate you." No interpretive difficulties arise until the final reason ("because you are / forever making poems in the lap of / death"). Given the sequence title ("La Guerre"), these lines may be meant to suggest that Humanity's ultimate flaw is its propensity for glorifying war, death, and morbidity instead of making poems of praise. Cumings clearly loathed war as much as he did the warlike who applaud clichés. His distaste, like Wilfred Owen's in his bitter World War I poem "Dulce et Decorum Est," is that of the front-line soldier for the stay-at-home politician, except that here, as usual, he leavens his acerbity with humor.

The sixteen poems in the "Sonnets" sequence ending *XLI Poems* are largely drawn from the "Sonnets—Unrealities" sequence in the original *Tulips and Chimneys* manuscript. The

result, especially in the first twelve poems, is a heavy effluvium
of fin de siècle decadence, a tone evident in such lines as "wish-
ing by willows,bending upon streams" (VII). These are largely
early poems: five of them (I, III, IV, VIII, and IX) appear in an
unpublished notebook marked "France, 1917," one (XII) is in a
similar notebook dating from Cummings' army stint at Fort
Devens, Massachusetts, in 1918, and two (IV and V) appeared in
Eight Harvard Poets. These latter two ("this is the garden:col-
ours come and go" and "Thou in whose swordgreat story shine
the deeds"), alike in praising conventional subjects, testify to
that inclusiveness, that proclivity for saving anything and everything, which sometimes interfered with Cummings' capacity for
self-assessment. Like so many in this sequence, they are rich in
imagery but devoid of significant comment.

Several others ("if learned darkness from our searched world"
and "come nothing to my comparable soul" are examples) betray a problem with which the effusive and spontaneous Cummings was perhaps inevitably confronted. Beginning with a flash
of inspiration and wit, some of his poems, particularly those cast
in more formal modes, lose their effervescence as they progress.
The demands of the sonnet form—the requirement for twelve
or thirteen more lines to develop the brief but intriguing insight
of the first line or two—all too often sink his sonnets into mere
verse. As a result, many of his eminently quotable lines come
from disappointingly flat poems, poems which fail to realize the
potential of their better passages. The line "come nothing to my
comparable soul" (VIII), for example, immediately involves the
reader in a syntactical puzzle, which may be resolved by brack-
eting "nothing" in commas as an apostrophized entity. It also
provides an interesting problem of interpretation in the word
"comparable." The remainder of the poem, however, turns into
little more than a conventional embodiment of the fashionable
nihilism of the day. Nevertheless, these poems are not to be

disregarded. Individual words and phrases reward the reader: "peerless," used to describe a frosted window ("Sonnets," III), nicely balances its double meanings (*incomparable* and *incapable of being peered through*), and the lines

> and sweet uncaring earth by thoughtful war
> heaped wholly with high wilt of human rind

illustrate his characteristic distinction between things of the mind ("thoughtful") and of the feelings ("uncaring") while it simultaneously spins out a rich play of sounds.

The last four poems in the sequence, perhaps by virtue of having identifiable places for their narrated actions, are more fully realized. Sonnet XIII ("when i am in Boston,i do not speak") belongs with the earlier "Portraits" set in cafés. This café, on Kneeland Street near Boston's South Station, was no doubt a find for a poet interested in city low-life. The view includes an advertising sign ("the electric When / In Doubt Buy Of(but a roof hugs / whom") whose final words are obscured by the roofscape. The next sonnet ("will suddenly trees leap from winter and will," XIV), while a meditation, is of a different sort from the earlier ones. Alone in his apartment in winter, the narrator wonders whether his lover will "do the exact human comely thing" by coming to visit him, by being comely in her appearance when she arrives, and, perhaps, by coming in a sexual way. The last two sonnets describe city street-life as the painters of the Ash Can School would want it to be, particularly realized by specific detail (the el, Second Avenue, Grand Central Station, Fourteenth Street, Washington Square) and replete with quick sketches of unidentified humanity ("Mrs. Somethingwich," and an "opaque / big girl" who "jiggles thickly hips to the kanoon" in a Greek dive run by "Hassan"). Like the rest of the sonnets here, they do not bear up under much questioning;

they have no profound answers for the reader who asks, "So what?" But they are rendered in an imaginative diction; and, in their eclectic interweaving of snippets of language and hints of images, they move Cummings farther along toward some of his significant experiments.

The other 1925 volume, &, spells its title in the names of its three sections: "A," "N," and "D." Of the seventy-nine poems, forty-three are drawn from the original *Tulips and Chimneys* manuscript; the remainder are new. "A" takes many of its poems from the "Tulips" section of that original manuscript; "N" contains seven new poems; and "D," comprising sonnets, corresponds to the earlier "Chimneys." The title, as Norman Friedman has noted, "means two related things," for the book "contains poems left over from the 1922 manuscript, and new poems added for the present purpose."[10]

Interestingly, there are no "Sonnets—Unrealities" here. Poems from that sequence, generally dealing with a somewhat idealized and unsensual world, readily found favor in the hands of the publishers of *Tulips and Chimneys* and *XLI Poems*, who chose them while leaving behind poems they considered inferior or feared obscene. So while it is not entirely accurate to classify the poems in & as either new, prurient, or poor, it is apparent that the sensual poems are among the liveliest here. If the overall tone of *XLI Poems* tended to pale into polite comment, the tone of & errs on the side of ribaldry: neither had the other for balance.

Essential to the interpretation of many of these poems, especially those in "Sonnets—Actualities," is a recognition of the importance of Cummings' dedication of the volume "To E. O." Elaine Orr had married Scofield Thayer, Cummings' friend and editor, in 1916; and she had been the subject of Cummings' ardor since 1918. The extent of their relationship in the early twenties is unclear—it is documented mainly in letters to his parents, from whom he quite understandably withheld the more intimate details—but after 1922, when Elaine divorced Scofield, she and her daughter were regular companions of Cummings in Paris and New York. To an onlooker like John Dos Passos, Elaine was "the Blessed Damozel, the fair, the lovable, the lily maid of Astolat. To romantic youth she seemed the poet's dream. Those of us who weren't in love with Cummings were in love with Elaine."[11] Her relationship with Cummings, however, was less than harmonious; and in what appears to have been a last-ditch effort to salvage affections, Cummings married her on March 19, 1924. Almost immediately his letters home drop the varnish of comforting assurances and begin to relate, in a seethe of anguished introspection, Elaine's disaffection, her interest in another man, and their separation. In less than a year, on February 7, 1925, their divorce was decreed. One week later ひ appeared.

Cummings' decision to dedicate ひ to Elaine was, as he quipped to his mother, "possibly my affair," a private matter of his own conscience.[12] But in justifying his willingness to help Elaine obtain the divorce as she wished it, he revealed that conscience. Writing in July of 1924 he noted that "she has given me too many proofs of how much she does not love me,& of how much she likes me,for me to interfere any longer in her happiness. In admitting that I am beaten,you will please understand that I consider myself beaten by an unbeatable person whom I love & admire very much & whom I would like to have admire me since she cannot love me. All this is words:gestures,movements,are another thing far too convincing to translate."[13] On July 26 he adds that "whatever suffering you may justly lay claim to—you cannot possibly approximate mine. For this reason,if for no other,I have the right to act as seems to me necessary."[14] And on August 12 he writes:[15]

Only now, incredible as it may seem, do I realise that I had never attempted to understand the person for whom I thought I cared most in life, & who understands me better than anyone alive. Once to understand this person is, for me, at last to understand myself: I owe her everything fine in my life—I have hurt her more than anyone but myself, perhaps, can ever know. There remains only 1 course: one way: to show her how deeply I comprehend my own selfishness & how perfectly I recognize her own fineness—To help her, so far as I can help her, in the divorce. . . .
anyone so magnificent as she should be allowed to entirely live. (Compared with her life, my own does not so much as matter to the wearer)

The dedication of ♭, then, is a final gesture of generosity and affection for Elaine; and some of its poems yield most when interpreted in the light of his experiences with her.

The first fourteen poems, comprising the "Post-Impressions" sequence, have no convenient common denominator. Some are clearly impressions of scenes; some seem more like portraits; and some are love poems or meditations. They are difficult poems from the outset: the challenges to the unraveler of Cummings' language are not introduced gradually here, as they were in *Tulips and Chimneys*. The first poem, "windows go orange in the slowly" ("Post-Impressions," i) is as opaque as the first poem of *Tulips and Chimneys* was lucid. To paraphrase: "Windows slowly go orange in the town at twilight. Then night lightly and quickly sifts darkness on us all. Memories, like stories once told, having returned, gather together 'the / Again,' the repetition and reliving of the past. This retelling dances, churning with wit, and twitters across the 'Our'—that quality which makes individuals into *us*." The final enigmatic lines, a parenthetical gesture of derision by the moon, appear to reverse the ending of "the Cambridge ladies," where the moon, with lots to say, found only inanity among its earthly listeners. Here, the poem ends with the crescent moon pictured as a parenthesis.

The style of the third poem, "the wind is a Lady with," registers an alternative to such knotty compactness. The onward flow, fitting for a poem on the wind, is maintained here by Cummings' constant enjambment: only rarely (as in line 5) does he end a line where the sense of the phrase would normally dictate a pause. Ending instead with articles, prepositions, and pronouns, with verbs separated from their subjects and adjectives from their substantives, he refuses to let the eye come to rest until the poem is finished. Yet the length of the lines, the controlling punctuation, and the need to rearrange the sometimes unexpected syntax all operate to countervail the onrush. The result is a nicely swinging movement, neither halting nor headlong. An early example of his transcendental interest, the poem makes a simple point: although the material world manifests only poorly the ideas of nature, the world's beautiful ideas are part of the "i am" of the wind, or spirit.

Two poems from the January 1923 issue of *The Dial* take Paris as their subject. "Take for example this:" ("Post-Impressions," iv) describes city twilight as the impulse for the creative endeavor which produces both poetry ("a millionth poem") or painting ("one of the thousand selves who are your smile"). And "Paris;this April sunset completely utters" ("Post-Impressions," v), a smoothly wrought verbal statement of a painterly scene, bears a marked resemblance to one of Cummings' sunset paintings.[16] That Cummings had paintings in mind as he composed the latter poem is evident from a nearly complete draft which, penciled on an envelope from his mother postmarked 29 May 1922, is decorated with Cubist sketches of intersecting planes, some annotated with the names of colors.[17]

Many of the remaining poems in the "Post-Impressions"

sequence deal with urban low-life. Two are prose-poems describing details of New York: "i was sitting in mcsorley's" (VIII) and "my eyes are fond of the east side" (XI). These ventures into Joycean language attempt to capture sights, sounds, smells, and conversations. Cummings, who had read part of *Ulysses* as it appeared in the March 1918 *Little Review*, [18] entered a draft of the former poem in a notebook he kept with him at Fort Devens that same year. Like Joyce, he found significance in traditions; and McSorley's, established in 1854, popularized by John Sloan's paintings of its interior and Joseph Mitchell's *New Yorker* stories about its habitués, had plenty of tradition. [19] Like Joyce, too, he experimented here with stream-of-consciousness prose, a technique he carried further when he came to write *The Enormous Room* and *Eimi*. Reading the poem requires an open-minded willingness to abandon grammatical restrictions, a good deal of patience, and a liberal sprinkling of parentheses to help isolate phrases like "I ploc spittle . . . in . . . hopping sawdust" from its matrix.

The twelve poems in "Portraits" suggest what later volumes will make clearer: Cummings rarely wrote about sexual relationships in a wholly approving manner. While most of these poems are explicitly sensual, none is in any way a love poem or a poem of praise. He seems to have glimpsed rather vividly the death's-head at the feast of the flesh: even those poems ostensibly celebrating sensual endeavors frequently employ an imagery and diction that undercuts the praise. The opening portrait, "being," describes a twelve-year-old prostitute; unraveled, it reads: "Old eyed child, who, being merely twelve, hast gonorrhea, what shall death add to the ambitious weeness of tiny boots?" In other words, the poet implies, you already have everything that death could add: you are, in fact, an embodiment of death. By itself, the poem is simply a portrait; the poet makes no assessment of the situation, casts no blame on the girl or her society, and betrays neither lust nor sympathy for her. In the context of the following poems, however, she symbolizes the cheapening of love effected by lust and the corruption of real feelings produced by sensual indulgence. She also stands in sharp contrast to the sort of children Cummings portrayed in his "Chansons Innocentes"—a sequence significantly absent from &.

The grimness and isolation of the prostitute's life, and the discrepancy between professional lust and normal conversational interchange, are the themes of "raise the shade" ("Portraits," v). The voice here is that of the prostitute, and the poem, significantly, is a monologue: although the woman asks three questions, her customer does not even honor her individuality to the extent of replying. While the voice maintains an outward cheerfulness, the sense of desperation creeps through in the poet's skillful deployment of images of the shade (standing between her loneliness and the expansiveness of an outer world) and the rain (here, an image of dreariness), and in her too-much-protested assertion that "we don't care do / we dearie we should / worry about the rain / huh / dearie?" Even as she feigns pity for "awl the / poor girls" who have legitimate jobs and must get up "god / knows when every / day of their / lives," her words are undercut by the poet's emphatic spotlighting of the word "lives" in a line all its own. Those girls at least have life. Here, as the last lines suggest—"not so / hard dear / you're killing me"—is nothing but death, figurative and literal.

Cummings explores the other side of the professional relation in "when the spent day begins to frail" ("Portraits," viii). The speaker is "this blueeyed Finn," who, like "blueeyed" Buffalo Bill, stands for the public conception of handsome masculinity. The poem narrates his confession of the sin which he is about to commit. In the early evening, when stars are just appearing, he instructs "you" (presumably his wife) to believe everything he

will tell when he returns home at one o'clock. What he will tell
her then is that, at the stroke of midnight, he went to a "love-
house" and became (like a werewolf) someone else, only to
emerge, at twenty to one, restored to himself. What he became
when the midnight bell struck (with its patently sexual imagery)
is hardly an object of admiration: "twin / imminent lisping bags
of flesh." Cummings' comment appears in the poem's final lines:
for all its carnal satisfaction, this experience (so curt and mea-
surable that it can be calculated down to the minute) ultimately
produces only a figure of loneliness in a bitter landscape, the
Finn who "buttons his coat against the wind."

Even the most forthright and robust celebration of sensuality
in the sequence ("her / flesh / Came," "Portraits," xi) takes as
metaphor for the sexual act an image which, witty though it be,
is entirely divorced from tenderness or vitality. Her flesh, says
the speaker in run-on words that need separating, "came at me
as sand caving into a chute," and "i had cement for her." The
moment itself is glorified: "merrily / we became each / other
humped to tumbling garble." But the result, as unpleasant as
the wind at the end of "when the spent day begins to frail," is
nothing less than "concrete." Isolated from the rest of the
poem, that final word summarizes the fixed, the heavy, the
merely manmade: active though the sexual endeavor may be, it
results only in something which hardens into lifelessness.

In respite from the prevailing sensuality, two of the best
poems in the sequence take up quite different topics. The portrait of the barroom pianist ("ta," iii) is in subject simply a quick
imagist impression. Once the fractured words are reassembled,
it reads: "tapping toe—hippopotamus Back—genteelly lugubrious eyes LOOP-THE-LOOP as fat hands bang rag." But the
poem no more appears through such paraphrase than a Cubist
portrait can be approximated by a photograph of the sitter: the

effect is less in subject than in execution. A poem about rag, it captures the dislocations of jazz in its first stanza:

> ta
> ppin
> g
> toe.

Just as jazz syncopates rhythms by carrying phrases across the normal divisions of measures and beats, so here the accent on "ppin" comes a little ahead of its expected place in the syllable "ping," and the phrase carries over into the next measure before it ends. The following stanza emphasizes appearance: breaking the word "hippopotamus" so that *hip* and *pot* are revealed, and capitalizing the word "Back," Cummings swiftly defines the image of a corpulent pianist seen from the rear. From toe through hip the poet moves up to the eyes, which are at once genteel (refined, cultured, polite) and lugubrious (full of exaggerated gloominess). And here Cummings tips his hand ever so slightly, showing the reader, as he did more plainly in "Buffalo Bill 's," the degree to which the apparent spontaneity of this player's performance is in fact a calculated display for his audience. The audience expects that a ragtime pianist will pour out his whole soul into music, and that every fiber of his body will quiver with its making. But the expressiveness conveyed so convincingly in his toe and back is at last betrayed in his eyes. Where the sincere blues singer or jazzman would abandon himself to a compelling mournfulness, the pianist here can only muster a polite and hyperbolic gloom. True to the stereotypes of jazz pianists, his eyes roll; but the phrase used to describe them—"LOOP-THE-LOOP"—has more than a tinge of the carnival-ride atmosphere about it. Like the many musicians in

Cummings' paintings and drawings of Harlem dance-halls and burlesque theaters, this one is depicted in a tone that registers something less than complete approbation.

Neither does he approve of Effie ("here is little Effie's head," "Portraits," x), whose brains, he tells us, "are made of ginger-bread." Not a random choice, that word suggests not only the crumbling and commonplace food but also, in Webster's words, "something showy but unsubstantial or tasteless." The story of God on "judgment day" searching for Effie and finding only "six subjunctive crumbs" tells the cause of her undoing. Her problem—which has rendered her so thoroughly unalive that even after death there is nothing for God to find—is her inability to act in any but the conditional mode: the crumbs she leaves behind are named "may," "might," "should," "would," "could," and "must." Her acts, never flowering into fulfillment, remain forever in the realm of the suppositional, the provisional, the wishful. Never to have acted and only to have planned is, for Cummings, the rankest sort of inanition. It is a habit of mind he regularly excoriates in his satires, and one against which the poet pleads in his *carpe diem* arguments to his lover.

The seven poems in the "N" sequence are all new, having appeared neither in the original *Tulips and Chimneys* manuscript nor in periodicals. The first ("i will be / M o ving in the Street of her") experiments in fractured and recombined words. Like the unambiguously sexual ringing of the bells in "when the spent day begins to frail," the poet's movements through the streets of the city suggests intercourse. The city is a woman; the poem distinguishes, however, between the woman of "her / body" and the "you" of "mYveRylitTle / street / where / you will come." The latter is the poet's lover coming to visit him, as she does in so many of these poems, at his apartment somewhere among the narrow, short streets of lower Manhattan; the former, the "body," is the city itself, whose ambience peaks the poet's anticipation. The images entangle, however, and one becomes metaphor for the other. Technically the poem records, by spacing, capitalization, and punctuation, the rhythms of the speaker's experience in a manner foreshadowing (in such descriptions as that of pigeons "SpRiN,k,LiNg an in-stant with sunLight") many of his later experiments.

The third poem, "Spring is like a perhaps hand," is a quiet and limpid statement of a simile: spring is like a hand decorating a shop window. A theme with variations, not unlike "All in green went my love riding," its two parts make, like variant drafts of a single poem, the same point in slightly different ways. The poem itself does in words what it describes the hand as doing in the window and spring as doing in the world: while the reader watches ("people stare"), the poet is "changing everything carefully," revising and rewriting the first stanza into the second right before our eyes. It is finally a poem about poetry, about the juxtaposition of "there a strange / thing and a known thing here," of "New and / Old things," of the familiar with the surprising which is so much the function of metaphor. The poet, the poem implies, must have a sense for even the smallest detail of spacing and arrangement: he must be capable of "placing / an inch of air there" and doing it artlessly, naturally, "without breaking anything."

"Who / threw the silver dollar up into the tree? / I didn't" ("N," IV) is a lode for symbol-digging, a series of clear statements whose relationships to one another are highly ambiguous. The various questions, reduced to their fundamental sense, seem to be asking how the moon got to be where it is; and the answer seems to be that neither Fate (the "little lady who sews and grows every day / paler-paler"), Luck (the crap-shooting elevator operator), nor animal instinct (the dog) can account for it. The failure of human rationality to justify its presence is of no consequence to the moon, however, which continues to smile as it always has. In much the same way, the barber pole in "(one!)" ("N," vi) continues to turn. Aside from the first word (which, like a title, suggests the striking of a clock late in the night), the poem complements the motion of a barber pole and spirals up out of itself: the last line ("A:whispering drunkard passes") can be joined to the first extended line ("the wisti-twisti barber / -pole") to start the process again.[20] True to its first word, the poem is about oneness, about the unity that relates three apparently disparate images of street life. These images, particularly the "sawdust Voices" in "tenements," portray a city not unlike that found in the early poetry of Eliot and in the "Ash Can" paintings of John Sloan and George B. Luks. The subject, in fact, would be little more than conventional were it not that the treatment provokes new insights—insights which Cummings probably arrived at by analyzing, in both words and diagrams, the motion of a barber pole on a piece of graph-paper now at Harvard.[21] As is often the case, it is to Cummings' technique, rather than to any paraphrasable ideas in his poetry, that his success must be charged.

The prose poem "gee i like to think of dead" ("N," v) captures a voice quite apart from the poet's own. Cummings, a superb mimic with an excellent ear for the peculiarities of speech, records unerringly the voice, and thereby the sensibilities, of the vacuous frowzy speaking here. By its very presence, the poem serves warning on the reader not to confuse the speaker in these poems with Cummings himself—a warning which sometimes goes unheeded when his poems are read out of context. Specifically, this poem should shape our attitudes toward the final poem in the sequence ("who know if the moon's," vii), which has too often been taken as a serious statement of Cummings' own transcendental views. But its language suggests that the speaking voice here is far from Cummings' own: the intentional flatness of description ("keen city," "pretty people"), the random connections of disorganized ideas implicit in the repetition of "and," and the simplicity of the conception are very much in the manner of "gee i like to think of dead." The final image, in particular, quietly subverts the explicit argument in the preceding lines: surely the idea that "flowers pick themselves" suggests an activity a little too mechanical, a little too separated from human involvement, to be interpreted as an unequivocal statement of Cummings' ideals.

The individual sonnets in the "D" section of & generally require little explication. The larger statements they make, however, deserve analysis. The two sequences in the section, "Sonnets—Realities" and "Sonnets—Actualities," are, superficially, of opposing tones and attitudes. The cast of the first is appropriately introduced by the initial poem, which begins "O It's Nice To Get Up In,the slipshod mucous kiss / of her riant belly's fooling bore" ("Sonnets—Realities," I). Syntax suggests that the poet is praising; but diction ("mucous kiss," "bullet," "worms," "the skilful mystery of Hell") tells otherwise. "Sonnets—Realities" are, for the most part, poems of plain venery, withholding no detail of the sexual act; and they are so intentionally gross as to repulse the reader by their very surfeit of sensuality. They are poems of "grim ecstasy" (VIII) which describe "the poetic carcass of a girl" (X) in terms such as "the gnashing petals of sex" (IV) and "her small manure-shaped head" (V). These are "propaganda of annihilation" (XXI), and their subject is the "friendless dingy female frenzy" (XXII). One of the best of them (because the most controlled and ironic) is "my girl's tall with hard long eyes" (XVIII). Akin to Shakespeare's "My mistress' eyes," this poem inverts the standard conventions of praise and rejoices in such things as her "long hard body filled with surprise / like a white shocking wire" and her "thin legs just like a vine." There is nothing beyond mere physicality here. Neither is there anything tender. Cummings links the

words "long" and "hard" four times in describing her; the effect—since the words connote male qualities—is to remove
from consideration whatever might suggest her femininity.
Even the love-making that ends the poem is done "grimly."
Horace Gregory and Marya Zaturenska may have had this poem
in mind in noting that "The girls and young women [in this
volume] are drawn from the same models who sat for Hemingway's *The Sun Also Rises* and John Dos Passos' *1919*."[22]

"Sonnets—Actualities" is no less explicit about sexual relations. But the blatant repugnance toward the act is lessened.
These are more meditative sonnets, poems about "i" and about
"my love" which are less patently ironic in their praise. The imagery, nevertheless, casts a peculiar pall over the subject of
love. Buried in the most apparently complimentary catalogues
of the lover's attributes are images surprising for their animality
or—like the "concrete" of the earlier poem "her / flesh /
Came"—notable for their unfeeling hardness. The first three
poems are perhaps meant to provide a transition from "Sonnets—Realities"; they note that "all her beauty is a vise / whose
stilling lips murder suddenly me" (I), they describe the "ner-
vously obscene / need" of his love's "lustfulhunched deeply-
toplay /lips" (II), and they tell of biting "into you as teeth,in the
stone / of a musical fruit" (III). Lips, not only for kissing, are for
eating and devouring.

Sonnet XI ("my naked lady framed") makes this masticatory
metaphor explicit: contrasting the consuming qualities of life
with the permanent qualities of art, it nods in favor of the former. Cummings has approached the theme before (see, for example, the oddly out-of-place poem in "Sonnets—Realities"
which begins "even a pencil has fear to / do the posed body
luckily made"), and he will approach it again in such poems as
"if i have made,my lady,intricate" (*is* 5, "Five," v). Here, the
lady's "niceness betters easily the intent / of genius," so that

"painting wholly feels ashamed / before this music, and poetry cannot / go near." Enchanted by his lady's allure, he raises and dismisses the possibility of catching her in a poem or a painting, electing instead to catch her "in my arms" and to "taste" the "rhythm" of her fleshly presence. Choosing life over art, eating over contemplating, he pays "the price": consuming his potential subject, the artist forgoes the opportunity to create "an imaginable gesture," a gesture of the imagination which constitutes a work of art. But the reward is worth the price; for where art is an approximation, she is "exact," where it is lifeless, she is "warm," and where it sanctifies and distances its objects for worship by the cultured, she remains secular, available, "unholy." Reworking the old cliché, the poem explains that you cannot have life's cake and eat its pleasures. But its very presence on the page contradicts its explanations: here is a poem made out of a subject which the poet says he refuses to make into a poem. This incongruity between the express meaning of the poem and the fact of its experience—an incongruity he exploits in many poems of praise which assert that he is incapable of praise—underlies some of Cummings' most successful poetry.

That an understanding of context is essential to explication is the message behind sonnet XVIII ("—G O N splashes-sink"), a poem Cummings must have known would befuddle the unwary. It comes in a series of poems which have to do with lights, with windows (the last word in the preceding poem), and with the view from Cummings' downtown apartment. The first line ("—G O N splashes-sink"), since it is metrically incomplete by three beats, calls attention to the missing first three letters (whatever they may be) of a word ending in -*gon*. The word— like the words "When / In Doubt Buy Of" in the poem "when i am in Boston,i do not speak"—is meant to be read as a message on a large illuminated signboard, partly obscured by roofs and

"supercilious chimneys." Only the end of the word is visible as
the sign flashes on ("splashes") and off ("sink") while the poet,
waiting for "you," looks toward "west eighth" street in Greenwich Village from his window.

That all his waiting was not in vain is the message of the final
poem in the volume, "i like my body when it is with your /
body" (xxiv). Usually taken simply as a poem in praise of sensuality, it is built on parallel assertions beginning with the
words "i like." Here is the consummation of the poet's relationship with his lady in a poem describing the fulfillment of all
his *carpe diem* persuasions and all the hours of waiting and
meeting described in the sequence. Yet even here, as though
Cummings' own attitudes toward personal morality and ex-
tramarital intercourse were somewhat at odds, the imagery is
not altogether felicitous. It is not, to be sure, the "electric trite /
thighs;the hair stupidly priceless" of the antepenultimate poem
in the volume ("you asked me to come: it was raining a little,"
xxii); but the lines "the,shocking fuzz / of your electric fur,"
especially in the light of the earlier image of hair and electricity,
seem something less than unequivocal in their praise. Missing
here is any sense that the physical sensations provoked by the
lover have any mental or spiritual counterpart. The lover, it
seems, has nothing worth praising beyond carnal charms. Later
love poems, while not ignoring the body, will find much more
to celebrate. It seems not unlikely that the poet's ambivalent attitude toward his relationship with the lover was conditioned by
Cummings' relationship with Elaine.

The fact that the vast bulk of his sensual poetry in these years
blended the sexual with the repulsive suggests that his attitudes
were far more complex than they are usually taken to be. A
careful assessment of the imagery in these early poems rein-
forces the conviction that, while they are obscene, ironic, and
often very witty, they are hardly to be written off as the graffiti

of a goatish mind. To misread them and view Cummings as a youth unashamedly mesmerized by eroticism is to convict him of a tastelessness and an immaturity which neither his age—he was thirty when *&* was published—nor the genuinely affectionate tone of his letters at this time can support. It is also to erect formidable barriers to an understanding of his later development toward a transcendence that moved him leagues beyond the worship of unrelieved physicality—because such a misreading posits a personality that changed rather suddenly from prurience to refinement. In an odd and inverted way, these poems are pleas for purity and balance, stifled cries for a higher vision of human love coming out of a wilderness of sensual indulgence. Much as his diatribes against conformity reinforce his celebrations of individuality, these assertions that flesh is at worst gross and at best slightly unsatisfactory prepare the way of his later metaphysic: to show the repulsiveness of carnality is to prove the need for its opposite. For even in his most sensual early work, the seeds of his mature ethic were planted—sometimes too deep, and sometimes upside down, but planted nonetheless.

Chapter 4

is 5

"Am now confronted," wrote Cummings to his mother in February of 1926, "by the task of making my Voice Weedable for the Gwate Amewican Publick—that is, am supposed to edit my new collection of poems, write a preface, explaining same, and submit to publishers. No sinsh. Particularly as this (coming)volume is entitled: IS FIVE(short for: Twice Two Is Five, hasten to add)."[1] The forword addresses itself to "my theory of technique." Comparing his art to that of burlesque, he observes that he is "abnormally fond of that precision which creates movement," and notes that the poet is "somebody to whom things made matter very little—somebody who is obsessed by Making." Here, too, he confesses his "Ineluctable preoccupation with The Verb." Behind these statements lies his concern for the active and living over the fixed and inert, a concern he elaborated in his 1920 essay in *The Dial* on the sculpture of Gaston Lachaise. There, speaking of children's art, he wrote that "houses, trees, smoke, people, etc., are depicted not as nouns but as verbs. . . . Consequently to appreciate child art we are compelled to undress one by one the soggy nouns whose agglomeration constitutes the mechanism of Normality, and finally to liberate the actual crisp organic squirm—the IS."[2]

The ramifications of his "theory of technique" show up in *is 5* somewhat more clearly than in his earlier volumes. Here, as

Norman Friedman says, "there is an organic relation between the poet's technique and his purposes." Noting that the satirical vein is mined to a new depth in *is 5*, Friedman also observes that "in general Cummings uses metrical stanzas for his more 'serious' poems, and reserves his experiments by and large for his free verse embodiments of satire, comedy, and description. Parody, pun, slang, and typographical distortion are called into being by the urgencies of the satirical mode, which requires the dramatic rendition of scorn, wit, and ridicule. Violence in the meaning: violence in the style."[3] The poetry may, as Friedman points out, have taken some flavor from Cummings' concurrent prose writings: he had published a number of satires in *Vanity Fair* during the eighteen months preceding the publication of this volume. The requirements of writing for that monthly, noted for its debunking manner, had quite naturally sharpened the satirical edge of Cummings' style.

That satirical style had always been there, as such poems as "the Cambridge ladies" attest. But a number of factors may have come together by 1926 to give it greater impulse. He had put behind him a seminal period of his career with his divorce from Elaine Orr in February of 1925, and may have felt less restrained in expressing his bitterness. That experience, to judge from his letters home, drove him toward a new maturity and sense of responsibility, and may have contributed to a shift in focus in his writing away from private vulgarity and toward more public concerns. Then, too, he had nearly severed his six-year-old ties with *The Dial*. He had won the Dial Award in 1925; yet after the appearance of *is 5* on June 14, 1926, he published only once again with that journal. Scofield Thayer had by that time resigned his editorship, and Cummings, looking elsewhere for markets, may have felt liberated from the constraints of having to please Thayer's taste. Somewhere during this period, too, his style in painting began to change. As with so many of his contemporaries in art, Cummings found his abstraction giving way to a more representational style toward the end of the twenties. The age of radical experimentation was over, and the movement toward a more conservative manner was everywhere evident.[4] So it is not surprising that Cummings, for various reasons, found these years a period of change in his own work, and discovered in *is* 5 a voice distinctly his own. The freshness of that discovery informs these poems. "Among all the books of poetry that Cummings published," Malcolm Cowley would conclude years later, "*is* 5 is still the liveliest."[5]

Satire enters forcefully in "One," the first of the five sequences in the volume. Earlier poems, taking their tone from Eliot and the Ash Can painters, had been content to present physical degradation with neither praise nor blame; these poems do not hesitate to condemn, in unmistakable terms, physical and moral corruption. They are generally more complex and thoughtful poems than the earlier ones: the same verve and élan characterize the language, but the thought behind them now extends into various dimensions. Here, more regularly than before, we are reminded that the poet is at work trying to sort out and articulate the tremendous diversity of responses facing him.

The first group of sonnets, "Five Americans," is much more reflective than his earlier sonnets of the demimonde. Rather than picturing the lustful voyeur titillated by his environment, they show the sensitive and questioning poet trying to come to terms with it. "Gert" ("One," I, iii) shows us the poet in the act of composition, deciding among words—"joggle," "jounce," and "toddle" are some of his choices—in his attempt to define his responses to a prostitute. His proper and poetic language fails, forcing his admission that "there 's no sharpest neat / word for the thing." He is left only with her own language as the most fitting description of her being, and he records its dialect as directly as he can. Her choice—a "swell fite" at "Rektuz" (Rector's) on "Toysday nite" (Thursday night)—is ultimately his. In place of the analytical abstractions of a sharp and neat language, she (and he) chooses experience itself, where drunks throw lobster salad and emotion erupts into violence. The irony remains, however, that the denial of the efficacy of language is embodied in this piece of language.

As though to reaffirm that "there 's no sharpest neat / word" except the informal language of the speakers of his age, Cummings writes many of the following poems in voices that are far from his own. Sometimes he stands aside for a moment and comments, in the proper voice of a poet, on overheard language, as he does in "even if all desires things moments be" ("One," VIII). Sometimes the poet's voice enters only in a few lines to cap a description, as in "on the Madam's best april the" ("One," XXII), a poem wrapping up snippets of speech from a conversation between an "Irish,cook" and her beau in a park.

And sometimes, as in the well-known "nobody loses all the time" ("One," X), he withdraws completely and lets the speaking voice carry the entire poem. Illustrating the opening proposition with an anecdote, the speaker, who is more narrator than philosopher, lets the evidence of his Uncle Sol's life make his case. Unsophisticated in his language, he tumbles ahead at a breathless pace, catching up a diction at once formal ("to wit," "the auspicious occasion of his decease") and colloquial ("highfalootin," "splendidferous"). His very ineptness provides much of the humor and not a little of the complexity of the poem: when he says that "my Uncle Sol could / sing . . . like Hell Itself," he uses the simile both as an intensifier (he was a "hell" of a singer) and, conversely, as a condemnation (his singing was simply hellish). That he sees "farming" as an "inexcusable" luxury tells us something of his city-bred background: only a society comfortably far from its frontier days, and perhaps longing to return to

its pastoral images, could take such a view. Sol, romantic that
he was, indulged in that luxury: a "born failure," he became, in
death, a success with his "worm farm." Behind the speaker's
zany tale lie some of the familiar Cummings devices. The notion
of social stigma attached to bad odor ("skunks"), the presence of
the trade name ("Victor / Victrola"), and the use of a song title
("McCann He Was A Diver"—itself an ironic prefiguring of the
downward-tending Sol) echo such pieces as "POEM, OR
BEAUTY HURTS MR. VINAL." And the mechanization of the
funeral customs suggested in "somebody pressed a button" fore-
shadows Cummings' virulent philippics against the encroach-
ments of technology.

At times Cummings steps into roles so complex that the
reader can neither laugh at the character (for fear that character
and poet share too many traits) nor take at face value all that is
being said. Such is the case in two poems which, standing back
to back, seem to support each other. The first ("mr youse
needn't be so spry," "One," XVIII), adopting the language of the
tough who favors the "he-man's solid bliss" over "arty" questions and mere "ideas," ends with a statement which in one
breath both affirms Cummings' commitment to the "actual crisp
organic squirm" of life and brands the speaker as a cultural lout:
"a pretty girl," naked, is "worth a million statues." The second
("she being Brand," "One," XIX) takes up two of America's favorite fetishes—automobiles and sex—as metaphors for each
other. That the same language perfectly describes intercourse
and driving is the source of humor here, as double entendre
rises to a pitch recalling Shakespeare's low-life scenes. The occasional use of place-names lends a dimension of subtlety to the
poem: "Divinity / avenue" locates the ecstatic climax, and "the
Public / Garden" suggests the lover's return to a consciousness
of a world beyond. Here, as in "nobody loses all the time," the
wit is rapidly paced by Cummings' propensity for ending lines

on articles, conjunctions, or other words whose syntax demands the immediate completion provided in the next line.

Similar in its interweaving of two diverse ideas is "curtains part" (One," III), which contrasts a "peacock-appareled" stripper named "dolores" with Professor Josiah Royce of Harvard. She, though "small in the head," is "keen chassied like a Rolls / Royce." Reversing the automotive trade name, Royce "rolls" along Cambridge's Kirkland Street; ungainly and awkward, he was described by Santayana as a man whose "great head seemed too heavy for his small body."[6] Unthinking Dolores, full of animal energy, is in touch with her physical environment; Royce, full of thought, is so out of touch that he forgets his tie. Dolores is part of a noisy crowd; Royce is quiet and solitary. Both, however, are strippers—she by design, he by accident— and where she undoes the conventional formalities, he forgets to put them on. Here, in short, are Cummings' two worlds: the world of the mind and the world of the senses, high culture and the demimonde. That Cummings felt some comradery with Dolores and her sisters is evident from other poems; at the same time, however, he owed much to his own Cambridge upbringing and felt fondly toward Royce, who had introduced the young Cummings to the sonnets of Rossetti and who, perhaps, is being rewarded by this poem for making the introduction.[7]

The third word in "she being Brand" embodies another strand woven into these poems: the language of advertising, of "Brand" names. "POEM, OR BEAUTY HURTS MR. VINAL" ("One," II) is filled with trade names and slogans. The title is a slash at the secretary of the Poetry Society of America, who, nineteen years later, would announce the award of the Shelley Memorial Award to Cummings. A poem decrying the proliferation of "scented merde" circulating in the name of poetry, it suggests a connection between the commercialized sensibilities of America ("land of the Cluet / Shirt Boston Garter and Spearment / Girl With the Wrigley Eyes") and the insipid sentiments of the poets writing in "that and this radically defunct periodical." Here Cummings, riding out to do battle with the cliché, notes that "certain ideas gestures / rhythms" have reached their "mystical moment of dullness" and cannot be "Resharpened." The objects of his censure, here, are the "sweetly / melancholy trillers" of verse; and his final metaphor, of "americans . . . crouched . . . upon the / sternly allotted sandpile" who "emit a tiny violetflavoured nuisance," suggests that in such prissy verse even excrement has been sanitized into something resembling a commercial preparation. The poem raises to new heights Cummings' use of puns (on such trade names as Ordorno) and allusions; it remains, however, squarely within the range of his usual interest in praising the vital over the effete, the raw over the deodorized.

Similar in effect is "MEMORABILIA" ("One," xxvii), a blast at "the substantial dollarbringing virgins" who babble vacuously over Italy's tourist attractions each summer. The language, handled here with consummate deftness, moves the poem in and out of allusions, mock-serious tones of voice, and parody of conversations. His subject is the anomalous mixing of styles and lives wrought by such tourism. Like the memorabilia brought home by souvenir hunters who feel no respect for the traditions they are vandalizing, this poem, a pot-pourri of phrases and echoes, wrecks a number of literary conventions. It begins, conventionally enough, with several apostrophes. But the first, to an ancient city ("stop look & / listen Venezia"), borrows up-to-date language from American railroads, symbol of modernity and mechanization. The second addresses in Biblical language a modern "glassworks." The third speaks of an elevator in words from the opening lines of *The Divine Comedy:* "nel / mezzo del cammin," meaning *in the middle of the journey,* describes, in Dante's poem, the middle of the journey of life, while here it is

mistranslated, by a voice resembling that of the tourists, as "half-
/ way up the Campanile" or bell-tower. Even the "Battle
Hymn of the Republic" comes in for parody, in the ironic "mine
eyes have seen / the glory of / the coming of / the Americans,"
where "Americans" replaces "Lord" as image of omnipotence.
Perhaps to dissociate his background from theirs, Cummings
has these tourists come from the less eastern (in his view, less
sophisticated) reaches of America, from Omaha, Altoona, Du-
luth, and Cincinnati ("Cincingondolanati"). To sing the praise of
learning ("O Education") is for them to adulate "thos cook &
son," the English travel firm which, providing brief and superficial tours of famous places, gave us the term "Cook's tour."

Several of the shots in this volume are aimed at types who
would become, in later poems, his familiar targets. The rationalizations of society in refusing to come to grips with its derelicts
is the subject of "a man who had fallen among thieves" ("One,"
XXVIII), the opening line of which quotes from Jesus' parable of
the Good Samaritan. Jesus' point was not only that the most
respected members of society failed to respond to a wounded
man's needs; it was also that the man who did show his humanity and concern was of a race generally held in low esteem by
Jesus' audience. Here, too, the respected "staunch and leal /
citizens," like the Cambridge ladies, are "fired by hypercivic
zeal" but devoid of constructive action. Their excuse for avoiding the drunk is still in wide use today in rationalizing all sorts
of segregation: "he looked / as if he did not care to rise." It is
the poet—the "i," the man held in contempt by the society in
which he lives—who offers help, even though "in terror" of the
consequences. The simple act of charity has results far transcending the usual rewards of daily business. In a cataclysmic
transfiguration, the poet is "banged in terror through / a million
billion trillion stars." Perhaps he is suddenly elevated to his
place among the stars; or he is shoved light-years ahead of his

contemporaries in his understanding of man's divinity; or he simply fights his way through the coldly polite and famous "stars" of his society and on into the kingdom of heaven. It is an oddly compassionate poem. Although Cummings generally has little respect for the drab conventionality of "fifteenthrate ideas" such as this man espouses, the fact of his helplessness overrides the poet's critical disdain. Aloof intellectual superiority, says the poet, must give way to the demands of brotherhood in times of great need; men who think must give way to the man who feels.

Indifference to the plight of the common man was an extreme Cummings shunned. But its opposite—a fuzzy-minded elevation of the suffering of the proletariat into something altogether laudable—was equally reprehensible. Cummings is still several years away from his later excoriations of communism; but in "than(by yon sunset's wintry glow" ("One," xxv) he sharpens his claws for the attack. The syntax of the first four stanzas praises the "incalculable bliss!" of a "poorbuthonest workingman" supping with his loving wife and sixteen children on a cold night. But the diction, with its exaggeratedly archaic language ("quite ennobling forsooth") mixed with the crudities of contemporary slang ("One wondrous fine sonofabitch"), prepares the reader for the final ironic blow: "it's snowing buttercups." Those who sing encomiums to this sort of life, the poem says, must blind themselves to the realities of such things as the coldness of real snow. The satire blasts those who would idealize the life of the slums by making it appear rosy—by writing, perhaps, poems of the "MR. VINAL" sort—as though the harsh weather were inconsequential, and as though poverty, seasoned by family devotion, were in itself wonderful.

In two of the best poems in this sequence, Cummings again reworks the *carpe diem* theme. The frequently anthologized "(ponder,darling,these busted statues" ("One," xxx) urges the poet's lover to "instigate / constructive / Horizontal / business," and presents other sorts of constructed things—the statues, the "motheaten forum," the "ruined aqueduct"—as stern examples of the destruction wrought by "Them Greediest Paws of careful / time." Presumably the sexual and anatomical implications of the final image—the aqueduct that "used to lead something into somewhere"—are not lost on his lady. Worth noting here is Cummings' use of parentheses around passages describing the desecrations of time; the central lines, which declare in the face of all this decay that "Life / matters," are not parenthesized. It is as though the speaker begins in sotto voce, rises to open declamation, and returns to an intimate whisper in pressing his ultimate designs on the lady. Hardly a love poem, it touches only on promiscuity, on "a peculiarly / momentary / partnership."

The first line of "voices to voices, lip to lip" ("One," XXXIII), echoing the liturgical "ashes to ashes, dust to dust," fittingly begins this poem in praise of "undying." The line appears among Cummings' drafts on a drawing of a dancing couple, suggesting that the poem may have originated in a visual image.[8] The eight stanzas are constructed around images of opposition between imaginative, artistic articulations and dull but correct factual statement—between "sculpture" and "prose." This pair reappears as "flowers and machinery," "piston and . . . pistil," philosophy and roses, and even, perhaps, the "voices" of logic and the "lip" of feeling. Running throughout the poem, too, are various oaths: "by God," "Heaven knows," "give a damn," "son of a bitch," and "to Hell with that." These are variants of the initial stanza's "i swear," by which the speaker underscores his thesis: that the communication of "voices to voices" and "lip to lip" constitutes the only real life, whereas merely "to exist" is a counterfeit of living, a "peculiar form of sleep."

The fourth stanza presents a sobering realization: we must

always remember (since we are still in our "sleep" and not fully awake to our undying nature) that we are like machines, which "easily break / in spite of the best overseeing." Even so, continues the fifth stanza, the model for living fully will be found not in careful plans and solemn beliefs but in the unpremeditated growth of flowers: "not for philosophy does this rose give a damn." Very well, says the narrator, "bring on your fireworks," which, because they are mechanical devices resembling flowers in their explosions, are "a mixed / splendor of piston and of pistil." For all their splendor, however, they will not last; they cannot be "fixed" either like a culture on a microscope slide or like a piece of art ("any other pastel"). What matters, then, is something which is so alive that it escapes the "oneeyed" (and hence narrow) technician who, peering through microscope or telescope and trying to classify and measure the spontaneous, "invents an instrument to measure Spring with." Knowing that "each dream nascitur"—is born, rather than made—the narrator can assert (but only "perhaps") his final point: "the thing perhaps is / to eat flowers and not to be afraid." Enigmatic, this conclusion urges the reader not to fear beauty (and want the comforts of machinery and instruments to explain it), nor to fear the hygienic consequences of a diet of something so insubstantial, nor to fear the social condemnation attendant upon eaters of flowers. Perhaps this sort of eating is what lips are best at, in which case the pun in the first line on "to lip" (tulip) is not entirely irrelevant.

Like "(ponder,darling,these busted statues," this poem is ultimately a piece of high persuasion addressed to his lady: as long as we have lips and voices, "who cares"? Like that poem, too, it deliberately affects an undressed syntax and a conversational looseness. Such locutions, there, as "Them Greediest Paws," such mixed metaphors as "motheaten forum," and such blendings of diction as the formal ("ponder") with the colloquial ("busted") and the archaic ("yon") have their counterparts, here, in a language deliberately flat, inexact, execratory, and even trite—"this and that," "delivers the goods," "the thing perhaps is." Intentionally avoiding the careful flow of "logic," the poet affirms in style what he has asserted in idea: "what's beyond logic happens beneath will; / nor can these moments be translated." Cummings takes as his subject a topic which, since language requires some sort of logic, can barely be assimilated into words. And if the result is a poem whose arrangement seems less linear than spatial, less rational than organic, it is because, as he discovered in "Gert," "there's no sharpest neat / word for the thing."

War and its effects are the subjects of the ten poems in the next sequence, "Two." The first ("the season 'tis, my lovely lambs") begins with a fine sarcasm on topical allusions. "Sumner" was the secretary of the New York Society for the Suppression of Vice, who rampaged for censorship and hounded publishers of unseemly books; the Volstead Act established prohibition; and the Mann Act prohibited white-slave traffic. Cummings' objection here is not so much to the specifics of each sort of control (although he inalterably opposed literary censorship and prohibition) as to the progressive interference by government in the lives of individuals. He takes to task this intrusion in the rest of the poem, condemning the military and political elite who govern, from comfortable offices, the soldiers and the underprivileged who suffer. He also takes, along the way, a poke at Elaine Orr, who hailed from "Troy (N. Y.)."

The poems following develop the themes of war and its manipulation by politicians, who appear on newsreels with pictures of the eternal flame on the Tomb of the Unknown Soldier (II) or on platforms giving inane and cliché-ridden speeches (III). Their facile volubility counterpoints the inarticulate reactions of the soldiers in the next two poems, who can only observe that the sudden and inexplicable battlefield death of a companion ("old thing") is "jolly odd" (IV) or who, fascinated by the mangling of a body by the shell of a "75" millimeter fieldpiece, can only react by saying "funny aint / it." Poem VI, also examining the speaker's inarticulateness in the face of death, is either black humor or tasteless crudity. Poem VII draws the moral from this brief study of political chattering and front-line speechlessness: most people who have never been to the front not only "never / will know" but "don't want / to / no."

The tone shifts to high irony with poem VIII, which begins "come,gaze with me upon this dome / of many coloured glass." Quoting Shelley's "Adonais" ("Life, like a dome of many-coloured glass, / Stains the white radiance of eternity"), Cummings gives his own twist to *stains*. Here the "clean upstanding well dressed boy," who promises to go off to war and "do or die / for God for country and for Yale," is patterned after Emerson's "The Youth" ("When Duty whispers low 'Thou must,' / The youth replies 'I can!' "). It is a fine imitation of alumni-magazine verse, which Cummings, tongue in cheek, holds unsullied until the last word, when "the son of man goes forth to war / with trumpets clap and syphilis." Like the great heroes of history, he goes to war with trumpets and clapping; but (since "to war" may also be a verb) he also goes out to do battle with the common enemies of the trenches, "clap and syphilis."

"16 heures" ("Two," IX) is less notable for its quality than its subject; it suggests that even as late as 1926 Cummings still sympathized with the Communists. The suggestion may be misleading, however, for this account of Paris police brutality denounces the "flics" more than it commends their victims. The final poem in the sequence, "my sweet old etcetera" ("Two," X), is a nimble collusion of subject and style. Like "come,gaze with me," it contrasts the reality of a soldier's life on the front with

the fictions entertained by his family at home. His "aunt lucy" is
the newsmonger; his sister knits socks, shirts, and "fleaproof
earwarmers"; his parents tout such abstractions as courage and
loyalty; and all the while the soldier himself lies "in the deep
mud" dreaming of "Your smile / eyes knees and of your Etcetera." The repeated "etcetera" changes its grammatical role significantly as the poem progresses. First used to amplify adjectives ("sweet old"), it next amplifies the nouns in the list of
things his sister knits. It then modifies a verb ("my / mother
hoped that / i would die etcetera / bravely"). This gradual shift
stresses its use in the last line as a noun in its own right, where
"your Etcetera" stands for some noun or nouns which, if printed,
would call down the wrath of Sumner and his Vice Society.[9]

The poems in the next sequence, "Three," are interrelated by
their interest in distinctly European scenes and by their references to sunsets or sunlight. Each is in some way a meditation
on the significance of a natural scene. Typical of the sequence is
II ("Among / these / red pieces of / day . . ."). Standing on a
railroad platform, the poet muses on the sunset, in which the
local hills resemble paper scorching itself and curling up into
ash. He is suddenly recalled to reality by the announcement of
the train for Rome. Like Hemingway's prose, the poem gains
strength from what it does not say: as its numerous expositors
have discovered, it leaves much to inference. It also makes particularly good use of typography in describing the hills tortured
in sunset ("scorchbend ingthem / -selves-U / pcurv E,into: /
anguish . . .") and the train, which jerkily rushes ("jerk. /
ilyr,ushes") into the station.
   The following two poems come as close to the earlier satires
as any in the sequence. The first ("it is winter a moon in the afternoon," "Three," III) portrays a twilight street circus in front
of Notre Dame ("our lady"), and contrasts, in its last stanza, the

miracles of the "mysterious" animal trainer with the "mystery" which the cathedral is supposed to celebrate. In "candles and" (IV), tone and diction serve up an irreverently unceremonious version of a holy procession. The crowd falls to its knees in ecstasy as priests carry past "a glass box" containing "the exhumed / hand of Saint Ignatz." Cummings, a devotee of the comic strip *Krazy Kat,* no doubt chose the saint's name with more than a glance at Ignatz Mouse, one of the cartoon's central characters.[10] More pointed than his comments on the street-circus crowd, this satire is directed at those who expect miracles from traditional religion: where the animal trainer in the former poem played tricks, at least he used a real mouse.

The last three poems in "Three," in which the narrator questions the nature of existence and moves toward a tentative resolution, also form something of a set. Poem V asks searching questions about why the poet is where he is. In poem VI ("but observe;although") he considers the difference between an inner and an outer life, seen specifically in terms of a distinction between the poet and his lover, in bed at five o'clock on a winter afternoon, and the "stout fellow in a blouse" who lights the gaslamps outside their window. With his "magic / stick" that causes the lamps to "explode / silently into crocuses of brightness," the lamplighter brings a metaphor of springtime and sexual experience. The poet, looking beyond the confines of the bed to a larger world, would question the nature of life. But his lady, whose presence asserts the primacy of feeling over thinking, substitutes palpable experience for the asking of questions. The final poem ("sunlight was over," VII) sees in sexual consummation a kind of resolution: bright sunlight turning to sunset, two lovers becoming one, and "what had been something / else carefully slowly fatally turning into ourselves." These two last poems strike a significantly new note: without being sonnets, they praise sexual love with little of the undercutting so noticeable in ↳. In this way, they provide a fitting introduction to the fourth sequence.

The eighteen poems in "Four," a well-knit cycle of love poems, come into clearest focus when seen through the lens of Cummings' relationship with Elaine Orr, his former wife. They form a loose progression in subject (innocence through sexual experience and on to separation) and in imagery (night through daylight and on into evening), a progression which can be assessed by comparing the first and last poems in the sequence. Each is about window and moon: but the first ("the moon looked into my window"), making no mention of love, describes the movement of moonlight across the poet's bedroom in terms ("infantile / fingers," "playing") recalling his earlier "Chansons Innocentes." By the last poem ("i go to this window"), however, love has come and gone, and the poet looks "in fear" at the "new moon"—a moon changed by his shift in perspective. Reflecting on his lover, he finds that the moon now makes him feel "coarse and dull / compared with you"—an expression markedly similar in feeling to those in his letters home after his divorce from Elaine.[11] Between these boundaries, the poems appear to group themselves into an introduction (II), a series about their relationship together (III through X), and a series (XI through XVII) about separation and loss.

The only poem of any experimental tendencies here is the third ("here's a little mouse)and,"), which compounds the childlike tone with the *carpe diem* theme. It divides into two parts: the first fourteen lines devote themselves to a description of the mouse, who "drifts" across the floor like a "littlest / poem" and disappears with the word "(gonE)." In the last ten lines the narrator examines the significance of what he has seen. As he progresses, the objective fact of the mouse's appearance becomes less certain: as though to emphasize the mouse as idea rather than animal, as something quoted rather than original, he puts the word "mouse" in quotation marks and gives it a line to itself. Where the first part confidently called the mouse "he," the second part moves to "It" and wonders finally whether it really existed at all. The poem ends by identifying the lovers with the mouse, which "Disappeared / into ourselves." Symbol of the freely roaming individuality accountable to no one, the mouse has become part of the lovers, allowing them to put aside conventional restraints and kiss. After all, suggests the poet, the mouse may have been only an objectification of our own consciousness, "something we saw in the mirror," an outward sign of our inner liberation. In any case, the simile of mouse and poem suggests a further dimension: poetry, too, drifts into view, is hard to size up, frisks quickly past, and is gone, disappearing into ourselves. Here Cummings, with masterful economy, introduces a new range of meaning by the inclusion of a single word, "poem," without which this would be a much simpler piece. As it is, the poem takes poetry as well as love for its subject.

In "since feeling is first" ("Four," VII), Cummings brings to ripeness the ironic *carpe diem* mode in one of his surest pieces. Taking grammar as his metaphor, the poet notes that those who pay attention only to "the syntax of things"—the logic, the intellectual aspects of experience—can never involve themselves so thoroughly in love as to "wholly kiss you." Arguing against rigid adherence to syntax, the first stanza demonstrates its point by violating conventional grammar and leaving out the word *he* before the line "who pays any attention." Syntax gets further tangled in the next three lines: "wholly to be a fool / while Spring is in the world / my blood approves" is hardly a natural word order. Arguing for whole-hearted abandonment to intuitive impulses, the poet eschews the self-conscious distancing of "wisdom" and pleads instead for the direct experience of "kisses." By now, however, the ironic undertone has begun to make itself felt: "to be a fool," no matter how attractive an idea to lovers of the unconventional, is no very complimentary term, nor is the word "fate" devoid of complicating connotations. And his assertion that "i swear by all flowers" recalls Romeo's oath on the moon: Juliet chided him for swearing by "th'inconstant moon," and the lover here, were she alert to the irony of the argument, might note that even the most beautiful flowers wilt too fast for any but the most evanescent vows. Sensing his lady's reluctance, the poet urges her not to cry, assuring her that "the best gesture of my brain" (his best argument, his finest poem) "is less than / your eyelid's flutter"—an ironic simile, since eyelids are associated with little beyond mere flirtiness. His thesis is disarmingly simple: her actions are more significant than his poetry. Not unlike the speaker who placates his audience by well-turned words disavowing his skill at oratory, the poet feigns disdain for poetry while writing a carefully crafted poem. Returning to the metaphor of syntax, he rests his case with a supremely persuasive analogy. Life, he notes, is "not a paragraph," not a carefully composed articulation with a clear beginning, a thoughtful development, and an orderly completion; nor is death a "parenthesis," an interruption in the general on-going flow of thought which, while useful, can safely be ignored. Life is not ordered but haphazard, reads the argument; death is no dispensible insertion but an unavoidable fact. Therefore the only sensible course of action is to "laugh, leaning back in my arms"—a delightful image of trust, liberation, and affection—and abandon all concern for constraints. Feeling, for Cummings, may well be "first" over logic; but the poet in this poem bends this idea to his own ends with a logical skill carefully calculated to ensnare his prey.

Not seeing himself simply as poet, the narrator imagines himself as painter, sculptor, and musician in "some ask praise of their fellows" ("Four," VIII). The first stanza, noting that he is "otherwise / made" from the ordinary seekers of fame, presents in construction what it says in meaning. Deliberately avoiding conventional rhyme and rhythm—which might indeed have won praise from the public—Cummings breaks the lines in such a way as to avoid obvious end-rhymes (*fellows/yellows*) and the regular rhythm inherent in the arrangement of words. In poems IX through XII, the narrator comes to terms with the lady's effect on his life and prepares the way for "Nobody wears a yellow" ("Four," XIII). "Nobody" is the name of "a queer fellow" who "wears a yellow / flower in his buttonhole," who "frisks down the boulevards," and who generally behaves in ways that are youthful, incongruous, and bohemian. Like others looking from outside into Greenwich Village or Montmartre, the narrator is led to ask, "i wonder what he does." The narrator wonders, too, why he himself finds, buried in a trunk with other relics, "a dead yellow small rose." Here, narrator and "Nobody" share a common past. A bohemian anonymity permits "Nobody" to behave as he pleases; so, too, the narrator once wore the yellow rose of exuberant unconventionality. The poem leaves to the reader the inference that the narrator no longer wears the rose; no longer a "Nobody," he has become, in the terms of the distinctions Cummings would later make in "anyone lived in a pretty how town," a "someone," a responsible and well-known member of society, a poet of renown. All this happened "perhaps a year ago": the poem, published in *The Dial* for October 1925, looks back to 1924, the year of his separation from Elaine. For all the narrator's apparent detachment, the poem conveys more than a hint of remorse for the "dead yellow small rose" of a more simple past.

The last poems in the sequence, perhaps too full of sentiment to convey real feeling, suggest that "our separating selves become museums / filled with skillfully stuffed memories" (XIV), that the poet is a beggar appealing blindly for "a little love preferably" or even "a / plugged promise" (xv), that he walks the streets, battered by weather, as a ghostly rebuke to her unkindness (xvi), and that, living a friendliness and anonymous city existence of restaurants and dark streets, he suddenly remembers her "kissed thrice suddenly smile" (xvii). Taking themselves a little too seriously, they have neither the distancing self-awareness nor the grandeur of vision that inform his better poems. They are interesting confessional statements for the biographer; but even their convolutions of syntax and surprises of diction cannot overcome their somewhat soft-boiled moistness.

By contrast, the five sonnets composing the last sequence, "Five," are less mawkish and more resolved. All but the third predate by several years the poems in the previous sequence, having appeared together in *Vanity Fair* in December 1923. The first, "after all white horses are in bed," describes a walk through city twilight with "my very lady" and makes the point that "a suddenly unsaid / gesture" of hers is more meaningful to him than all the "white horses" of fable or the "heroes" who battle on "huge blue horses" in history. The theme is familiar: the poet once again claims to find more in the smallest facts of life than in the great images of literary tradition. The second takes a similar situation, an evening walk with the lover in the country. Frightened, the lady observes that in such curious light "everything / turns into something else" and that "leaves are Thingish with moondrool"—a wonderfully pregnant image for the biomorphic monsters of fantasy.

Poem iii ("along the brittle treacherous bright streets"), although poised dangerously close to sentiment, maintains its balance and evokes instead a genuine sorrow—largely because feeling is registered not as some uniform attitude but as a com-

plex interweaving of pleasure and regret, of lightness and sadness. The reader need know nothing of Cummings' aversion to
the "policeman" nor of his sympathy for drunks, derelicts, and
bohemians to understand his point in the opening sentence:
feeling goes on in happy abandon until reason intrudes and
explains away that happiness. Although the "dreams" of the
poet's past now "are folded," packed away or perhaps gone out
of business, life ("the year") goes forward. Reason forces the
poet to "awake," to recognize that those dreams are gone. Out
of these general statements a specific scene begins to coalesce:
the last half of the poem suggests that the particular "dream" he
has in mind is of a walk in a Paris park. Now, however, the park
has other lovers, whose evocative French conversation adverts
to their search for a place to make love. Their search, like the
narrator's, is frustrated by the cold—literally for them, figuratively for him. The image of the merry-go-round ("chevaux de
bois") which, like the drunk, is "Halfwhispering . . . . halfsing-
ing" and "always smiling," suggests pleasure incapacitated by
the season—a jarring irony for the poet. Only at the end do we
learn the cause of the narrator's "fear / and sweetness": "when
you were in Paris we met here." Nowhere does Cummings use
the word *sad;* nowhere does he connect his images together
with a commentary that busily informs the reader of the point
he wishes to make. He shows, rather than tells: he simply sets
out several ideas—drunkenness, lovers, merry-go-round—and
controls their order and force so that they produce the desired
connotations. It is a difficult effect to master, quite unlike that
of the more discursive sonnets; and only once, in the phrase
"the year completes / his life as a forgotten prisoner," does he
falter into an image which, though perhaps drawn from his own
days in an Enormous Room of an earlier France, is a bit too
vapid for impact.

The final poem in the volume, "if i have made,my lady,intricate," shows Cummings at his finest. Although written before his divorce from Elaine, it takes on an added poignancy by its placement at the end of a book dealing so centrally with that separation. Tinged with regret, it becomes a gallant valediction to a lady no longer his. Yet as an ending to the volume it provides resolution: it is, after all, a poem about poetry, a poem which redeems his experience by transforming it into art.

The draft versions suggest the serendipities out of which Cummings sometimes made poems. Here, he toyed with several phrases—"my lady intricate" and "my lady absolute"—as terms of address, only later adding the comma in a change that furthers the flow of the poem. Apparently, too, he came rather quickly upon the first and final lines, and spent the bulk of his energies in composing the twelve intervening ones. As in "some ask praise of their fellows," he originally began with metaphors not only of singer and poet but of painter as well: a line in the draft ("if i have failed to snare / the glance too shy for any painter's guile") identifies the "imperfect various things" not only as his poems ("songs") but also as his paintings.[12]

The poem is a plea for forgiveness. If (says the poet) I have failed to capture your beauty in my poems and paintings, if my creations "wrong / your eyes" (get them all wrong, as an unskilled portrait painter might; or look wrong to you), if the songs I write do not quite live up to the ideal vision within "my mind"—if I fail in these ways, then let us not object when the world judges my best works as lifeless, impermanent things incapable of capturing your real vitality and so saving it from death. After all, you are "so perfectly alive" that no poem could ever hope to take on such vibrancy; and no one will know (after your death) that I failed, because the only thing that could bring shame to my efforts would be a direct comparison between my creation and you, the subject of that creation. You, after all, are the one who, through the deep and delicate communications of your lips (both with words and kisses), brought to me the "clumsy feet of April"—my sense of renewal and freshness, as well as the poetic "feet" of my verse. And you brought them into the "ragged meadow of my soul"—into the natural and unkempt ambience of my inner feelings.

Even in such a poem, however, the underlying irony is apparent. I cannot write poems of praise, says the poet, who, saying so, manages to write one of the finest poems of praise in the century. And if the poem seems less than that, it is perhaps because of the success enjoyed by certain of its devices in more recent verse. The technique behind such phrases as "the ragged meadow of my soul"—the coupling of a concrete substantive with a modifying phrase containing an abstraction—has become the staple of current songwriters, and our sense of the purity of this poem may be a little jaded by jukebox verse built on such lines as "the bright illusive butterfly of love" and a hundred similar phrases.

Chapter 5

ViVa

Considering how rapidly Cummings had published his earlier books of poems—four volumes in less than three years—the five years between the appearance of *is* 5 (1926) and *ViVa* (1931) is notable. They were not idle years. He published a play (*Him*, 1927), an untitled book of oddly surreal short stories (1930), and a collection of ninety-nine reproductions of his own art (*CIOPW*, 1931), the letters of whose title stand for the media represented: charcoal, ink, oil, pencil, and watercolor. On May 1, 1929, he married his second wife, Anne Barton, and spent much of his time abroad with her and her daughter, Diana. As usual, he gave his energy to painting and sketching, and participated in exhibitions sponsored by the Society of Independent Artists, the Salons of America, and the Society of Painters, Sculptors, and Gravers. The summer before *ViVa* appeared he took a month's tour of Soviet Russia, observing the inhumanities he later recorded in *Eimi*.

Much of his life had changed in these years. His father had been killed in an automobile accident in 1926, and with him had gone, it seems, something of his son's need to rebel against the Brahmin ancestry and conservative traditions of his family. His mother, injured in the same accident, recovered with a strength and courage that astounded her children, to live for another twenty years in close and friendly contact with them both.

These changes in family attended changes in art: even before
the accident Cummings had written his mother that he planned
"to resume Painting but in a new direction," commenting later
that "I don't know myself what 'painting in a new direction'
means—since it hasn't yet begun. But it must mean something
new!"[1] The change, in fact, was not unlike that overtaking the
art of many of Cummings' contemporaries, a movement away
from the modernism that had come in on the heels of the 1913
Armory Show and toward a more representational work. While
Cummings never moved into the social realism so characteristic
of the thirties, he did turn away from his series of large abstract
works (of which *Noise Number 13* is the best known) and toward
recognizable portraits, landscapes, and still lifes.

Whether these developments are reflected in *ViVa* is open to
interpretation. The topics, to be sure, are characteristic: there
are love poems, portraits, impressions, low-life sketches, and a
generous helping of satires. The collection was similar enough
to his earlier volumes that William Carlos Williams dismissed it
as "definitely an aftermath" and objected that Cummings
sounded too much like Cummings, that he "reminds one very
much of him."[2] But Cummings, it now appears, had something
more in mind than simply the tone of individual poems. His
earlier volumes had been divided into sequences which gathered a number of poems under separate headings. *ViVa* rather
innocently numbered its seventy poems in a single sequence;
and, with one exception, neither the early reviewers nor the
more recent critics noticed any subsets within this overall
series. Malcolm Cowley, however, observed in passing that
"Every seventh page-picture, including the sixty-third, is a sonnet; the last seven form a group of sonnets."[3]

ViVa reveals, in fact, a great deal more patterning than at first
appears. The seventy poems divide evenly into two goups. In
the second half, poem xxxvi begins a series of seven-poem

sequences (each ending with a sonnet) that take up impressions of weather, sky, and landscape (XXXVI–XLII), studies of relationships among people (XLIII–XLIX), an extended *carpe diem* theme (L–LVI), praise of the lover and of love (LVII–LXIII), and transcendental examinations of the nature of life and the supremacy of love (LXIV–LXX). In general, these five sequences consider either nature by itself or man as an individual thinker and lover. The poems in the first half, by contrast, generally take up man as a social being: they satirize the foibles of society, paint some unflattering portraits, investigate some low-life (and some high-life) scenes, and direct themselves more toward city than country subjects. These first thirty-five poems, although marked off by every seventh sonnet, do not fall into the cohesive units characteristic of the latter half: there seems to be a good deal of overlap, and no clear topics emerge for each of the five separate groups. Cummings may have intended it that way. The design he builds into the second half reflects his tribute to the individual, and the lack of cohesion (indeed, even of coherence at times) in the first half manifests his low estimate of man as a social animal.

Problems of coherence arise immediately in *ViVa*. Poem I (",mean-") is certainly about humanity and about putrescence, two words whose elements, scattered among other words and letters, can be recomposed. It seems (not unlike poem XI, "a / mong crum / bling people(a") to concern itself with the idleness of the affluent interested only in "golf" and "bridge," those who live among elevators, rubber plants, and fancy hotel lobbies. They are, to paraphrase, the undead, the not living who can only stroll, spawn, and imitate. By contrast to these bridge players, the second poem ("oil tel duh woild doi sez") focuses on a group of poker-playing toughs from the opposite end of the social spectrum. Here the obscurity is less formidable, depending for its resolution only on the realization that Cummings is

writing a dialectical transcription of slang. Transliterated, the
first lines read, " 'I'll tell the world,' I says. 'Do you understand
me?' he says, pulling his mustache. 'I don't give a shit,' I says
. . . ," and the rest continues in the same vein. A surprisingly
apt *tranche de vie*, it depends on the dramatist's technique of
evoking an entire milieu from a few scraps of conversation.
Some years before, in a letter home, Cummings had hinted at
the place of subject-matter in his painting:

> Speaking of chasms,I am painting that—and bumps. Or what is
> commonly(obscurely may I add?)called "getting form by colour." The
> "helps" or "raw material" are occasionally "bodies," "scenes,"
> "faces," "naturae mortae." Other incidentals crop out I dare say or
> go under. That's my procedure,just as precisely as I can give it.[4]

Attempting a more complex statement of this "procedure" for
transforming " 'raw material' " into art, "the surely" (III) both
discusses and exemplifies the use of covert and ambiguous subject matter in poetry and painting. Three metaphors—of billiard
ball, hoop, and top—each suggest the way an object or a
"motif" impacts upon the artist's imagination, produces its effect, and then withdraws so that only the effect, and not the object itself, remains on view. The final product, like a work of
Analytic Cubism, has reduced what was originally a recognizable subject into a design all but free of representational reference. The last four stanzas present a verbal parallel for the effects achieved in some of Cummings' own "noisecoloured"
abstractions, those "Concentric geometries of transparency"
which he painted in the early twenties. Like the paintings, the
poem does not unlock itself to the casual glance: supplying a
period after "everywheres" and a comma after "gush" in the last
stanza helps resolve the obscurity. In his early paintings his intent is, perhaps, to portray "solids(More / fluid Than gas," to
make over the elements of the world into qualities of motion. As

one of the aims of Cubism was to present simultaneously the various viewpoints of a single object, so Cummings' purpose in his abstract paintings is to suggest a sense of matter in all three states—solid, liquid, and gaseous—at once. Those paintings translated the audible into the visible—a kind of parallel to this and other poems, which translate sights into the sounds of words.

The following poems are portraits: of neighbors in the city ("there are 6 doors," IV), of a panhandler whose "future" is reduced to "smoking / found / Butts" ("but mr can you maybe listen there 's," VI), and of "myself,walking in Dragon st" and being met by "i" (V). In the latter, "myself" asks "i" " 'how do you do' " and continues,

> "thought you
> were earning your living
> or probably dead,"

those two possibilities being, from the standpoint of the Bohemian poet, really the same. "Dragon st" (Cummings mentions "rue du Dragon" in Paris in his correspondence) stands for the menace of society to the individual: here even violence is routine and nearly anonymous ("Jones was murdered by / a man named Smith"). The "Dragon" of society in the first line suggests the poem's last word, "Leviathan"—a reference to Hobbes' *Leviathan* (1651), where the word also stood for the state. For Hobbes, life was "nasty, brutish, and short," and so society and sovereignty are formed in which man gives up certain freedoms in return for protection. For Cummings, the hypothetical benefits of the state were hardly worth the loss of freedom—a point he later made with some vehemence in *Eimi.*

The character portrayed in poem VII is created by the monologue. Trying to wade through a tome on relativity, the speaker begins bravely enough ("Space being(don't forget to remember)Curved"). But he (or she, perhaps) gets distracted, loses the place, and is finally content to "sum it All Up god being Dead" and praise the "Lord of Creation,MAN," whose dominion is registered by the fact that he can crook his "compassionate digit" on the trigger and reduce an elephant into ivory billiard balls. The poem is about many things: about a failure to think and a consequent contentment with oversimplified philosophical questions; about the blandly selfish views that reduce the best of modern scientific thought only to proofs that man, not God, is mighty; and about the willingness of society to supply its whim for games and pastimes by slaughtering the elephant, Cummings' favorite animal and, as he elsewhere put it, his "totem."[5] The final word "billiardBalls" also suggests the use of billiards as a metaphor for the random collisions of particles in space, an illustration not uncommon in discussions of physics.

In "(one fine day)" (VIII) and "y is a WELL KNOWN ATHLETE'S BRIDE" are two views of sexual activity. In the former "again" and "never" are lovers, "now" is raped by "was" (a compact image for the present being seeded by the past), and "thither" and "thence" both get together with "young fore'er." The second borrows Dos Passos' device of capitalized headlines ("WELL KNOWN ATHLETE'S BRIDE . . . SHOT AND KILLED") and uses dialect transcriptions ("hoe tel days are / teased" for Hotel des Artistes) and pithy neologisms ("an infra-fairy of floating / ultrawrists") to describe the sensational double suicide in 1929 of Harry Crosby and Josephine Bigelow. As with "Buffalo Bill 's," Cummings apparently wove the poem out of strands from newspaper accounts of the death and, perhaps, from Crosby's journal (*Shadows of the Sun*, 1928), in which Cummings himself figures.[6]

The "poor But TerFLY / . . . / from Troy, / n.y." (XII) is

Elaine Orr, Cummings' former wife, and the fact that she did indeed come from Troy, New York, serves to connect her with the classical Helen, who also eloped. Names have been changed: "one 'Paul' / a harvard boy" probably refers to Scofield Thayer, Elaine's first husband, who had married her in 1916. Some "seven years" later, around the time she finally (and so briefly) married Cummings, she became enamored of an Irishman named MacDermott and ultimately married him—a fact which accounts not only for the interweaving of the line "Ireland must be heaven, for my mother came from there" (from the popular lyric, "Did your mother come from Ireland?") but also for the rather nasty slashes at the older MacDermott as someone who "smelt rath / er like her fath / er." Even here, however, Cummings' virulence cannot keep down the poet's impulse for an exact recording of speech: the divisions of these words emphasizes the particularly Irish pronunciation of "father" as very nearly rhyming with the American "rather."

More fodder for name-hunters appears in successive poems. Poem XIII ("remarked Robinson Jefferson") winds its way through presidents (Jefferson, Wilson, Washington, McKinley, Buchanan, Lincoln, Cleveland, both Roosevelts, Grant, and Coolidge) and picks up Robinson Jeffers (a contemporary American poet) and Lydia E. Pinkham (a promulgator of patent medicine) along the way, depositing its own history of "Lays aytash unee"—*Les Etats-Unis*, the United States. Poem XVI asks someone to "tell me not how electricity or / god was invented"— these are comparatively simple questions—but how one can explain the confusions of current news and the presence of people like German War I General Eric Ludendorff, who in 1929 was being busily praised by the Fascists. And "FULL SPEED ASTERN)" (XVII) exemplifies its first line by moving backwards down the alphabet from *m* to *i* as successive stanzas are introduced. It brings in more names: Mussolini is disguised as *musilage;* Marx appears with his famous dictum that "religion is the opium of the people," written here as

"(relijinisde)o(peemuvdepipl);

J. P. Morgan and Herbert Hoover are in evidence; and finally comes "babbitt," perhaps in reference to the archetypal Philistine created by Sinclair Lewis, perhaps in reference to the conservative critic Irving Babbitt, more likely (such was Cummings' wit) in reference to both. The poem ends with his mocking salute to his home state, the Commonwealth of Massachusetts (the "UNCOMMONWEALTH OF HUMANUSETTS").

As though to present another extreme of style—for the first half of *ViVa* is filled with pairs of poems which contrast markedly with each other—the poem about Miss Gay (XVIII) recounts with prosy baldness Cummings' visit, some eleven years before, to the Bronx Zoo with a friend of his sister named Peggy Gay. Shortly after the visit in 1920, Cummings wrote his mother that "It was very sweet of Elos [his sister] to write explaining what an enjoyable time Peggy Gay . . . really had at the Bronx. I hope to have time to answer it soon. . . ."[7] His "answer" was to turn the experience into a poem in which Miss Gay, an unconscionable prude "unacquainted with the libido," is scandalized at the "uncouthly erotic" behavior of the zoo's inmates. Significantly, Miss Gay is a Radcliffe student: her response to the zoo is a telling comment on the great gulf fixed (in Cummings' view) between formal and informal education. "Miss Gay," the poet summarizes, "had nothing to say to the animals and the animals had nothing to say to Miss Gay." Not unlike Miss Gay is the dainty esthete of "i will cultivate within" (XIX) who asserts that "these unique dreams / never shall soil their raiment / with phenomena. . . ." In abrupt contrast, however, is "helves surling out of eakspeasies per(reel)hapsingly" (XXI), which, unscrambled, is a poem about selves being hurled out of speakeasies. Like "oil tel duh woil doi sez," and like Ash Can painting, it contents itself merely with presenting a brief sketch of a saloon scene without comment. So, too, does XXIII, about a bunch of rowdies from the Athletic Club beating up a sentimental drunk.

In poem XXIV, Cummings carries the fallacy of imitative form to its extreme. By way of suggesting that the "cognoscenti" of the "radarw leschin" or revolution—those who foment Communist activity—are incomprehensible in their arguments, he writes a poem which is apparently intended to be uninterpretable. Like Gertrude Stein's *Tender Buttons* (a work Cummings mentioned in his 1915 graduation address), it flows along with interesting words aptly joined together but devoid of syntactical order or apparent meaning—except, perhaps, at the end, where the writer of this letter signs himself "truly pseudo yours podia." Pseudopodia, here, suggests the ameboid activity of the Communists, who would engulf and digest the world. It also recalls the literal meaning of the roots of the word: *fake foot*, after all, may suggest the clay foundations of these idols.

The remaining poems in the first half are, with few exceptions, satirical portraits of known or anonymous figures. One of the more ingenious is poem XXV ("murderfully in midmost o.c.an"), which details the poet's desire to launch in midmost ocean a luxury liner (the "S. S. VAN MERDE") which, being a "superseive," will promptly sink. The passengers are to be "all . . . / wrongers who write what they are dine to live"—creators of pulp fiction, who are dying to live, vicariously, the stories they tell, and who literally can "dine" off the proceeds of their successes. That the target of the poet's censure is the detective writer is made "right sleuthfully" clear by another sense of "dine." The popular fiction of S. S. Van Dine (*nom de plume* of Willard Huntington Wright) was especially repugnant to Cummings. After writing *Modern Painting* (1915) in his own name (punned on here as "right" and "write"), Wright had forgone a promising future as an interpreter of modern art to write such things as *The Benson Murder Case,* which Cummings evidently took to be nothing short of literary prostitution. He must have objected to its quality; he also, as a struggling artist, must have envied (cf. "Hyperluxurious") the money it made. And he must have been offended by the fall of an idol: for *Modern Painting* was the book which to Cummings had been the Chapman's Homer of avant-garde art, a book which, according to his biographer, he "marked and annotated like a textbook" while still an undergraduate.[8]

One of his best-known portraits is "i sing of Olaf glad and big" (XXX). Adopting carefully metrical rhythm and perfect rhyme, as he often did for explicit and unambiguous satires, he tells with great narrative economy the story of Olaf, the "conscientious object–or" who was treated, as the latter word implies, less as person than object. The tale is a grim one of vengeance and torture inflicted on a draftee whose "heart recoiled at war." Yet the tone is everywhere light, an effect achieved less by the narrative presentation of incongruities—a common enough device in humorous writing—than by the use of poetic techniques that create a sense of parody. Imitating the grand style of Virgil, the poet begins not with "I sing of arms and the man" but with "i sing of Olaf." The relentless rhyme scheme and tetrameter pattern lend a singsong effect, driving the poem gaily forward no matter what the words are saying. The words themselves are incongruously drawn from various sources. Using his typical blend of stuffy formality ("our president, being of which / assertions duly notified"), colloquialism ("the yellowsonofabitch"), obscenity ("your fucking flag"), and archaisms ("anent"), Cummings also mixes straightforward word order with the most ludicrous rearrangements designed to bring a word into rhyming position. These, along with a generous sprinkling of clichés ("nation's blueeyed pride"), redundancies ("bayonets roasted hot with heat"), and echoes of an earlier poetic language ("Christ(of His mercy infinite / i pray to see;and Olaf,too"), combine to create a poem whose delight is not in untangling the ambiguities but in riding the abrupt shifts of diction and surprising conjunctions of tone, and whose skillfulness is revealed in descriptions of singular aptness ("trig / westpointer most succinctly bred") which draw the most unexpected words into effective relationships. Not unlike Picasso's *Three Musicians* (1921), which as Alfred Barr noted is a happy subject full of bright colors that nevertheless produces a most somber tone, Cummings' poem makes of the most somber subject a poem which, true to the satirist's art, has about it an astringent humor.

The final poem of the first half (xxxv) weaves together an obscure veil of allusions to Robinson Crusoe and his green-feathered parrot finding "a recent footprint in the sand of was." If its first line is any indication, the poem is meant to focus on the fact that only what actually exists can ever die ("what is strictly fiercely and wholly dies"), a statement that accords with much of Cummings' praise of dying (see "dying is fine)but Death," *Xaipe*, 6). Dying, after all, is a sign that something has actually been alive. Perhaps Cummings means to say, by this poem, that the thirty-five-poem section it summarizes has been concerned with grim realities. For he now turns toward the less unpleasant qualities of experience.

The second half opens with a group of seven impressions (xxxvi–xlii), brief renditions of natural scenes involving sky, weather, or landscape. The first of these ("sunset)edges become swiftly") describes the effect of city twilight as the office-workers "spill . . . / out of final / towers" into the late fall weather, "the season of / crumbling & folding / hopes." The second poem ("how," XXXVII) moves from autumn into winter. Trees lose their leaves ("shout appalling / deathmoney into / spiralS") and "Now)comes" the "season . . . of him(every) / who does (where)not / move." Perhaps "him" is simply winter. But it may also refer to Jesus, whose "season" is Christmas. If so, the entire fabric of the poem takes on a Joycean density: "deathmoney" becomes a reference to Judas' betrayal and, obliquely, to Easter, and the final lines become a description of Jesus' crucifixion by the spirits of anti-nature ("the shrill / Nonleaf daemons") and the life-suppressing gods of imprisonment—"The downlife gods of / shut." The poem ends on this isolated word, whose connotations of imprisonment and oppression will later make it the appropriate first word of *Eimi*.

The third poem ("n(o)w," XXXVIII) is one of Cummings' most successful experimental ventures. A happy conjunction of subject (a violent thunderstorm) and style (a violent fracturing of words) allow the poem to illustrate itself as it proceeds: the world

iS Slapped:with;liGhtninG
!

in a manner that makes capital letters flash out to the noise of a "THuNdeRB / loSSo!M." Toward the end a ray of sun ("s / U / n. . .") breaks through. For the energetic reader, the poetic devices display a tireless inventiveness. The darkness before the storm covers the "dis(appeared cleverly)world"; the phrase suggests not only the gradual disappearance of the landscape but its sudden, intriguing, and almost parenthetical reappearance in the lightning. And "starT" suggests both that the sun is a star and that, after the storm, it will "start" anew. Here the words, even when reorganized and stripped of their visual design, retain the lift and ingenuity of his best poetry. "Jumps of thunder-blossom invisibly among fragments of sky" shall "pounce and crack up," reads a reconstruction; "What meaninglessness unrollingly strolls; whole overdomains collide." Here, perhaps, is the poem to dumbfound the Babbitts, who would assert that such modern verse either is devoid of worthwhile verbal content or is obscured by gratuitous typographical tricks. Fortunately, "n(o)w" is neither.

The following poems describe a sunrise or moonrise ("An(fragrance)Of," XXXIX), the appearing of a first star ("thou," XL), and a twilight full of birds and bells ("twi-," XLI); the latter contains an apt conjunction of chuckling, clucking, and luck in the letters "c(h)luck / (l)ing." The final sonnet of this sequence ("structure,miraculous challenge,devout am," XLII) sets itself the task of describing attributes without naming its subject— and succeeds in spite of the fact that the reader is never exactly sure of the object of the poet's apostrophe. Perhaps the poet has in mind the moon, or the sun, or the sky, or a cloud, or a landscape: a case can be made for each. Whatever the object of his praise, it has no traffic with the "noisy impotence of not and same," of negation and conformity. Blending disparate elements—impressions of landscape with satire on humanity—the poem also sounds the note of transcendental worship absent from the first half of *ViVa*.

Cummings' well-known eulogy to his mother, beginning "if there are any heavens my mother will(all by herself)have / one" (XLIII), opens the second sequence, which portrays individuals alone or in intimate relationships. This first poem captures much of the tenderness Cummings felt for his mother; the unembarrassed honesty of his feeling is attested by the fact that the poem was published while she was still very much alive. Cummings, who wrote her hundreds of letters and made numerous pencil, oil, and watercolor portraits of her, did not need (as one commentator assumes) the pressure of her accident to

call forth this affection.[9] It seems unlikely that, had he written
the poem in direct response to her recovery in 1927, he would
have delayed publication until its 1931 appearance in *This Quarter*. Reflecting less a specific incident than a lifetime fondness,
this poem of praise proves both that feeling is first and that its
unironic expression in poetry does not necessarily produce
mere sentimentality. His mother's heaven is neither "pansy"
nor "fragile," neither insipid nor delicately feminine: instead, it
is a "heaven of blackred roses," of flowers whose archetypal
beauty is made majestic and powerful by the surprising use of
the word *black*. In this imagined portrait, his father will be
"standing near my"—the phrase is left incomplete, trailing off
into quietness without pronouncing the understood word
mother. Later the father whispers, "This is my beloved my," again
suppressing the identifying word as though the name were too
holy or the power of articulation too impotent to reach it. Indeed, the phrase is holy. In the Biblical account of the transfiguration of Jesus, the voice of God is heard to say of His son,
"This is my beloved," continuing—as the poet's father no doubt
would about his wife—"in whom I am well pleased" (Matt.
17:5). Turning from words to action, his father "suddenly in
sunlight / . . . will bow, / & the whole garden will bow)," as
man and nature do obeisance to the woman. The image fits his
mother: his portraits show her quiet and bookish, usually sitting
outdoors among gardened (rather than natural) vegetation. The
poem captures the same serenity, the same sense of inner resil-
ience, and, especially when read aloud, the same sense of love.

Less moving are the remaining poems of the sequence. In
xliv the poet thinks of "things / which / were supposed to / be
out of my / reach." The poem may take its genesis from his
courting of Anne Barton, who, when he made her acquaintance,
was still married and so presumably "out of . . . / reach." A
sequel to it may be the final poem in the sequence ("a light Out)

/ & first of all foam," XLIX), a poem describing his sexual adventures with a "queen" who, like Venus, "out of deeplyness rose
to undeath."

The poems of the third sequence, taken together, form a kind
of extended *carpe diem* argument to the poet's lover. The major
strands of that convention—the imminence of death, the self-
pitying complaint, the suggestion that feeling is better than
thinking, the insistence on the transforming power of love, and
the proposition—are here sorted out into separate poems. The
first three poems (L, LI, and LII) establish the threat of death:
the poet in the first (beginning "when hair falls off and eyes blur
And / thighs forget") tells his lover that "then [,] dearest," all
the beauty of nature and life "matters / nothing." Poem LIII
("breathe with me this fear") urges the lover to forget "what's to
know" and "only consider How." The theme reappears in LV
("speaking of love(of"), which moves from knowing (stanza 1) to
thinking (stanza 2) and on to "let's feel" (stanza 4). The poem
separating these ("if i love You," LIV) portrays love as the translator, making over the natural world into a place of dreams and
"faeries." The final poem, beginning "lady will you come with
me into / the extremely little house of / my mind" (LVI) is a
proposition which, although veiled in *chanson innocente* diction, is really no more innocent than Marlowe's "The Passionate
Shepherd to His Love."

The most curious of the sequence is "a clown's smirk in the
skull of a baboon" (LI). Reverting to rhymed iambic pentameter
stanzas with a common last line ("I have never loved you dear as
now i love"), the poem would seem, except for certain devices
of style and facets of subject, something left from his undergraduate days. It depends, a little too glibly, on easy associations of
the sort favored by song writers: the poet complains that he is
but "a hand's impression in an empty glove, / a soon forgotten
tune, a house for lease." Yet it includes the makings of a sur-

realistic image in the second stanza, which pictures the poet rising toward the planets in a "tight balloon / until the smallening world became absurd," only to be shot down "into the abyss." The line "—and wonderfully i fell through the green groove" could almost have come from Dylan Thomas, except that Cummings resolves the ambiguity by adding, in the next line, the explanatory words "of twilight." Those who think Cummings had categorically abandoned the upper-case "I" will find both forms of the pronoun in this poem, suggesting, it seems, that the proud declaimer of the refrain in the first three stanzas (where the capital letter appears) is reduced to lower-case humility at the last. It is a competent piece of versifying; but it demonstrates, by contrast to his finer work, how far Cummings had to go to circumvent such conventional approaches to poetic complaint and unrequited love as he wanders into here.

The sequence which comprises poems in praise of love and lovers (poems LVII–LXIII) opens with the justly famous "somewhere i have never travelled,gladly beyond" (LVII). A complex piece, it depends on an appearance of simplicity. Using commonplace diction ("intense" and "fragility" are perhaps the only words an elementary-schooler might pause over), Cummings builds the poem largely out of monosyllabic words either by themselves or attached to ordinary suffixes. The subject, too, is uncomplicated: images of eyes and hands interweave their themes of opening, closing, and touching. Rhythmically, the poem is probably best construed as free verse lines gathered into stanzas, although a case can be made for sprung rhythm pentameter. The last stanza locks into perfect rhyme; previous stanzas conform to no rhyme scheme, although occasional hints ("enclose me" / "unclose me"; "descending" / "breathing"; and the anticipatory "and" and "rose") prepare for the last stanza's rhymes on the significant words "closes" and "hands."

Part of the poem's success lies in its skillful assimilation of complexity into an easily apprehended structure. Not unlike the poetry of the Psalms, it has both the initial appeal and the lasting resonance of carefully crafted workmanship. It is built, in fact, on many kinds of subtle paradox. The first two lines seem simple enough: your eyes, says the poet, have a depth to them far beyond any experiencing, an inexhaustible (and so "gladly" constant and trustworthy) inner stillness which is beyond reach. But in context (especially given the "voice of your eyes" in the penultimate line), the "silence" takes on a new and less positive meaning: the unpleasant possibility of a loss of that "voice" is gladly so remote as to be beyond "any experience." Seemingly contradictory, the two meanings here are resolved by providing two meanings for the key word. If "silence" means muffled suppression, the lines deny its power; if it means quiet peace, they affirm its value.

Another sort of paradox appears in the third and fourth lines:

> in your most frail gesture are things which enclose me,
> or which i cannot touch because they are too near.

One has only to work with tools in a tightly cramped space, or to try to touch one's elbow with the fingers on the same hand, to know that nearness and untouchability are compatible attributes. Cummings also planted in "touch" the less physical meaning of *comprehend* or *come to grips with:* your very nearness, the narrator says, shows me how much I am missing.

Punctuation provides paradox in the next stanza. Its second line functions so smoothly as an extension of the first, and so well as an introductory clause for the next lines, that the reader tends to move right through the stanza without pausing to determine where the full stop should fall. The paradox is that our sense of grammar insists on punctuation, while our sense of semantic continuity ignores such restraints.

The paradox of the third stanza is that an inanimate object can be endowed with foresight. The flower, says the poet, need not wait until it *feels* the snow; because it can imagine the future, it closes up in anticipation of bad weather. The fourth stanza hangs its paradox on the standard technique of oxymoron: "the power of your intense fragility" combines strangely dissimilar ideas into an effective characterization of a rose. The lines continue by fusing the usually distinct effects of "texture" and "colour." The last line—"rendering death and forever with each breathing"—takes a universal symbol of life (breath) as a source of death. But it does more: "death and forever" suggests an eternity beyond mere physical dissolution; and "rendering," among its many meanings, means to melt oil out of something, or (in this case, figuratively) to break down and annihilate the structure and substantiality of "death and forever" by the presence of life.

The final stanza admits (as Cummings' poems often admit) to ignorance: "(i do not know what it is about you that closes / and opens." The poet does understand, however, that a comparison between "all roses" and "the voice of your eyes" proves the supremacy of the latter. The last line ("nobody,not even the rain,has such small hands") summarizes in the word "rain" his ideas of fragility and frailty blended with efficacy and life-giving force.

It is worth noting what is missing here. Like the earlier poem for his mother, there is no trace of irony: the praise is unabashed, unmitigated. Like the more satiric and witty early poems, there is an appearance of formal patterning in the layout of the lines on the page; but unlike them, there is no tight adherence to rhyme and rhythm. Neither is there any attempt at profound philosophic insight. Yet the very simplicity of the idea—that you have the power to control me just as naturally as the weather controls the flowers, and that ultimately you are even more effective than nature—is knitted into a tight web of theme and variation, of progression from images of spring through winter and on into spring again, and of depths that reveal themselves as individual words are plumbed.

The last poem in this sequence on love and lovers begins "be unto love as rain is unto colour;create / me gradually" (LXIII). It concerns both love and poetry. "Wait / if i am not heart,because at least i beat," the poet entreats: if I am not the embodiment of profound affection (to the lover) nor the expression of pure feeling (to the reader), let me develop and progress. The progress—of both love and poetry—takes place quite apart from critical judgment and public views: "nor has a syllable of the heart's eager dim / enormous language loss or gain from blame or praise." The three adjectives here are telling: the language of the heart (which Cummings was always trying to write), while enthusiastic and vast, remains dimmed, obscured by other languages, faint from lack of proper nourishment. The narrator's redeeming faith, as old as poetry itself, is in the immortality of his words: "though wish and world go down," he concludes, "one poem yet shall swim."

The final sequence contains seven sonnets which are, superficially at least, less about lovers than about love, less about psychology than ontology. The first three poems are arguments aimed at eliciting the lady's sympathy. The most complex is the first ("granted the all / saving our young kiss only," LXIV), which probes the consequences of the insubstantiality of matter. "Granted," says the poet, "that everything except our love has no reality, but only seems to exist by dressing its unreality in isolated molecular vibrations"—granted that matter, as contemporary theoretical physics demonstrates, is nothing but states of energy—"we dive, nakedly and perfectly, out of the limitations of temporality into everpresent infinity, aiming for the essential creative spirit that underlies everything. As we dive, we find that memory"—which, depending on time, has no place in everpresent *Now*—"falls away from us as we search successfully for new attributes of infinite being. Nor, as we search, can our fixed and defined conceptions of the term 'truth' expand enough to include what really is true." Thus far, the metaphysical tenor is conventional: love plunges us right through matter and human logic and time into an apprehension of ultimate reality. Such a reality is less mundane than spiritual, as suggested by the conjunction of *nakedness* (which in biblical language often means stripped of all vain worldly possessions) and the deific connotations of "essential flame." But the final couplet shifts the tone. Paraphrased, it tells us that all this is happening "while your 'contriving' fate and my 'sharpening' life are (behind every prohibition and negation) reaching deep affirmation and positive goodness." The key word, "contriving," means scheming or plotting; the poem, although appareled in the highest sort of language, may after all be simply another *carpe diem* proposition. It addresses his lover; it suggests that she, too, lives by a kind of scheming; it makes use of connotations ("truth opening encompass true," "sharpening," "touching," and the more common meaning of "nakedest") which, taken together, hint at the sensual. And, as though to render moot the question of whether these lovers have world enough and time, it argues that time and matter do not exist. All of which is not to deny the religious fabric here: Cummings, like Donne before him and Dylan Thomas after him, interwove the sensual and the religious to great effect.

The fifth poem ("but if a living dance upon dead minds," LXVIII) moves to more explicit religious statement. Love, says the poet, is what causes the smallest spark of life ("a living," with proper emphasis on the article) to resurrect "dead minds," to turn off stars, to make stones talk, and to make "one / name control more incredible splendor than / our merely universe."

The "one name"—which later becomes the capitalized "Who" and "Whom"—seems to be the Logos, the Christian God, Who (according to John) is Love. It is the power which harrows the "weird worlds" of hell; more significantly for Cummings, it is the power whose characteristics are neither humanly comprehended ("does not forget,perish,sleep") nor scientifically measured by "the trivial labelling of punctual brains." The final poem ("here is the ocean,this is moonlight:say," LXX) builds on the conceit of the moon's influence on the sea to suggest the lady's influence on the poet: "only by you my heart always moves." It is a fitting ending for the volume, which rises from the sordid to the joyful, from satire to praise. It is also an ending in keeping with the other terminal poems in his volumes since *is* 5, which end in unqualified praise of either his love (*is 5, 50 Poems, 1 x 1, 95 Poems, 73 Poems*) or of celestial bodies (*No Thanks, Xaipe*). Here these two topics mingle.

Chapter 6

No Thanks

Cummings' sixth volume of poems, *No Thanks*, was his most difficult to publish. When it was finally printed privately in 1935, it had already reaped fourteen rejections from the publishers whose names appear after its title page. That poems should be difficult to publish is not surprising; but that a poet of Cummings' stature, with thirteen books of various sorts already behind him, should be without a publisher demands some explanation. That explanation probably resides in the combination of two things: the radical politization of literature since the end of the twenties, and the appearance, in 1933, of *Eimi*.

It was a matter of course that a young American writer in the thirties should be a supporter of the Left. Socialism, as Alfred Kazin remembers, was "a way of life." No longer a matter of "personal assent or decision," it had become a religion.[1] Those who frequented the campuses or wrote and read books and reviews were socialists as unthinkingly as, in previous decades, their ancestors had been Christians. Not that writers had been without causes in earlier decades. But the causes were different, more often matters of individual than political compulsion. "When you thought of the typical writers of the Twenties," Kazin recollected, "you thought of the rebels from 'good' families—Dos Passos, Hemingway, Fitzgerald, Cummings, Wilson, Cowley."[2] Standing against the old conformities, they also resisted new ones: "to be a writer in the twenties," Kazin wrote in *On Native Grounds,* "was to be an enemy of the Herd State."[3] Cummings, surely, was that, and continued to be throughout his career. But the times shifted around him. Kazin recalls that "the Thirties in literature were the age of the plebes—of writers from the working class, from Western farms and mills," who shared an "angry militancy" and "wore a proletarian scowl on their faces as familiar as the cigarette butt pasted in their mouths."[4]

Not only were the writers' backgrounds and predilections different in these two decades. There was also a discernible shift in what Fredrick J. Hoffman has called "the consequences of free discussion."

> From 1915 to 1930 the writer seemed at home in his world; even the interference of World War I did not long discourage him in his freedom. He was afraid of little because he saw little to fear. Least of all was he afraid of seeming inconsistent or illogical in his exchange of ideas. Fear of ideas, and of their consequences for persons and personalities, seems to have begun in 1930, when ideas became weapons.[5]

How a man wrote, then, became of less consequence to readers and reviewers than what position he espoused in the war of ideas. Literature was becoming less an art of words than a commerce of arguments.

The literary community in which Cummings lived in the early thirties had, almost to a man, sworn allegiance to socialism. It was fascinated by the great Soviet experiment. It had heard too many hymns of praise to Russia, to the proletariat, and to salvation through revolution to resist the blandishments of communism; and it had expended too much of its own rancor in denouncing capitalism to listen openmindedly to alternatives. Into this context came *Eimi,* Cummings' account of his thirty-six-day trip to the Soviet Union. There, for those willing to unravel its remarkable prose, was a report of the grim inhumanities of the Soviet system, of repression, apathy, priggishness, kitsch, and ennervating suspicion.

Shortly after its appearance there came, to various publishing houses, a manuscript of poems by its author. The rejections that followed could hardly have been based on quality alone. *No Thanks* is no less competent a collection than *ViVa*. It makes more progress toward experimental forms; but it provides nothing so radically different nor indefensibly bad as to justify rejection on merit. It is, in many ways, standard Cummings: the age, not the man, had changed.

Like *ViVa*, *No Thanks* is designed on a numerological pattern, with sonnets occurring at regular intervals. The pattern is more complex, however, and it is not surprising that none of Cummings' reviewers or critics noticed it—with the possible exception of his typesetter, S. A. Jacobs, who merely observed that the book had an exact center (poem 36 out of the seventy-one) marked by a poem "where the poet imagines himself dead and buried."[6] The design radiates outward from this point. Flanking the central poem are two sonnets (35 and 37); after 37 every fourth poem (41, 45, 49, 53, 57, 61, 65, 69) is a sonnet, until the pattern runs out as it butts up against the final poem, also a sonnet. And before the center, beginning with poem 3 and ending with 35, every fourth poem is a sonnet. Like *ViVa*, then, the volume divides evenly in half. Unlike the earlier volume, however, there seems no clear identity to most of the sequences embraced by these boundary sonnets. There is, however, a general thematic development throughout the volume, which progresses in the first half downward toward the poems of defeat at its center, and thereafter moves upward into more transcendent ideas.

The opening poems move from impressions of restful nature

("mOOn Over tOwns mOOn," 1) toward an imagery of social turmoil. The second ("moon over gai") describes an outdoor circus, perhaps a Bastille Day celebration ("juillet moon over s / -unday") like the one of which he did a small oil painting. The third, a sonnet, echoes a standard Christian sentiment in its closing lines: "that which we die for lives / as wholly as that which we live for dies." Its first line ("that which we who're alive in spite of mirrors") may suggest not only that life goes beyond visual self-assurances but also that it transcends the cheap trickery of illusionists: "It's all done with mirrors" was a quip which, according to Edmund Wilson, Cummings used regularly.[7] The poet then visits low-life scenes: a men's room where "a)glazed mind layed in a / urinal" vomits wine ("vino") and spaghetti (4), and a boxing match ("i," 5). The latter poem, after twenty-seven lines of rather violent dislocation describing this fight, ends by telling us that Mr. Jeff Dickson organized it in 1932. Dickson, an American, went to Paris in the late twenties and, according to a *New York Times* account, "has promoted most of the boxing staged in Paris since that time."[8] Cummings, an enthusiast for the sport, had already done a line drawing in *The Dial* ("Knockout," August 1921) to accompany an article by Scofield Thayer on the Dempsey-Carpentier fight, and had published an oil rendition of the Greb-Flowers match in *CIOPW*.

Scorning the inflated pomp of commercial self-esteem, the portrait (6) of "little / mr Big / notbusy / Busi / ness notman" notes "you / are dead." Here are the people—sons at Yale, wives in hell—who, according to the poet, run the world and do it rather badly. The companion poem, fittingly, is "sonnet entitled how to run the world)" (7). Built on what Friedman calls a "mock-agenda format,"[9] the poem advises (point "A") "always don't," since (point "B") there is "no such thing" as a world to run. Cummings paraphrased the poem himself in a letter. Commenting on the line "highest fly only the flag that's furled," for example, he writes, "treat your true(*h*ighest)self as something sacred—never flaunt it in public,like a flag,for everyone to see." Of the final lines he writes, "I owe death one life,the mortal part of me,& bequeath all the(immortal)rest of myself to these children;whom I see building,out of snow,the figure of a man who'll melt away in the rain(become a rainman)."[10] In pursuit of the theme of death-in-life comes "the(/ Wistfully / dead" (8). The poem needs to be read straight through its parentheses; a colon at the parenthesis in line 3, and periods at the parentheses in lines 9, 12, and 16, aid the sense. Noting how kind the dead are to each other, the poet enumerates, by implication, all the meannesses of the living. The idea of death does not attack the dead, he says; it attacks the living, whose habits destroy them. More of these habits—the American penchant for baseball and movies—appear in "o pr" (9), whose initial letter *o* must be added to the beginnings and endings of the succeeding lines to recreate whole words. It is a poem about the president of the United States (apparently displayed, in the third stanza, on a stuttering newsreel) opening a game by throwing out the first ball. It is also a poem tacitly calling attention to the things that are left out (like the *o*) in the clamber for progress, and to the ways in which society is going to hell, a place "from which" (in the words of the Latin tag) "they refuse to send back anyone."

A similar linguistic play attends "r-p-o-p-h-e-s-s-a-g-r" (13), Cummings' famous experiment in exploded verse. It offers three cryptogrammic rearrangements of the letters in the word "grasshopper" before arriving at the standard spelling. These variants are meant to suggest a grasshopper leaping wildly and suddenly about, landing in unrecognizable positions, and escaping before the eye can surely identify it. The first variant ("r-p-o-p-h-e-s-s-a-g-r") is spread out and perhaps relaxed; although it is not readily pronounceable, it does group the letters from the two parts of the word together, ending with the five letters of *grass* and beginning with the six of *hopper*. As we look, the insect gathers itself for a leap. Before we expect it (right in the middle of the word *gathering*, in fact) it explodes into the capitalized and more easily pronounceable "PPEGORHRASS." Here the letters have drawn closer to their final form: the word begins with three properly ordered letters from *hopper* and ends with four from *grass,* but the two parts of the word are still inverted. The insect then jumps, a motion indicated by the spread letters of the word *leaps,* and settles solidly on the word's final S, so far toward the left that it is actually a space beyond the margin line, as though the insect overshot. A long pause seems indicated by the distance from the S to the *a* beginning the next word (*arriving*) at the extreme right, and once again the grasshopper hops and lands in a different position (".gRrEaPsPhOs"). Here the letters are beginning to sort themselves out: the lower-case letters (leaving out the *h*) spell *grass,* and the capitals (read backwards and restoring the *h*) spell *hopper.* While the alternation of lower case and capital letters suggests the jumpiness of the insect, the word has a less violent sound than the previous one. At last the insect shifts again, "to / rea(be)rran(com)gi(e)ngly" (to rearrangingly become) ",grasshopper;."

The poem is a skillful one: Cummings paid attention not only to the major passages but to the lesser details. The insect at first is not defined by an article: lacking *a* or *the*, it is simply the essence of grasshopperhood, albeit disarranged. But "a)s w)e loo)k"—as we peer about in a disjointed and interrupted search for the insect's identity, with pop eyes shaped like parentheses—we come upon the articles "aThe):l." Misplaced though they are, they give us the choice of identifying the insect as *a* or *the* grasshopper—or as *one* grasshopper, if the "l" in the series (which actually begins the word "leaps") is taken as a digit. The poem, finally, is about many things: about the way the mysterious resolves itself into the mundane; about the way we, as readers, unscramble and decode the messages sent to us by nature and by language; and about Cummings' own poetry, as if to say, "That which looks most unlikely is simply rearranged; be patient, let it leap, and it will suddenly and gracefully appear to make perfect sense."

The next few poems back away from such carefully crafted experimentation. But by the time we reach "who before dying demands not rebirth" (19), Cummings is at his most elliptical. The syntax may best be understood by adding a "He" before the first word and by recognizing the parallel clauses beginning in line 5 (*he whose life is never proudly swallowed by* . . .) and continuing with "nor . . . breathes" in the fourth stanza. The poem is one extended periodic sentence, whose main clause may be paraphrased "neither precision nor fate shall touch such a person." The poem condemns "such a person" as one who cannot think metaphysically. The man who stays "far from tangible domains" of "soul," although he may believe in "brains" and biological life, can have no grasp of "mind" and the more transcendent capacities of perception.

The tmesis of "go(perpe)go" (20) provides little difficulty once it is noted that everything within parentheses describes ants, while the words outside address the anteater in a parody of Proverbs 6:6 ("go to the ant, thou anteater"). The poem, as Nat Henry has observed, expresses Cummings' "contempt for the convention of approving compulsive diligence as an end in itself."[11] That sort of diligence surfaces in the next poems. Poem 21 is a memorial for those who "got / athlete's mouth jumping / on&off bandwaggons," and seems aimed at the vigorous but diseased mouths and the conventional political leanings of Cummings' literary contemporaries. The politics becomes more explicit in "when muckers pimps and tratesmen" (22), a poem whose first line appears to offer Cummings' definition of the proletariat. The folks with "missians" will, warns the poet, do their best to turn us into Russians. But they are, in fact, "fools," for they cry, "god help me it aint no ews [use] / eye like the steak all reid / but eye certainly hate the juse." The poem turns on the neatly juxtaposed interpretations of "reid" and "juse." *I like the steak, all right,* notes the poet, but the *juice* is intolerable—a statement which becomes even more paradoxical if "reid" means red or rare. But if "juse" also means Jews, the redness may refer not only to meat but to Russia: I like the grand equality of the working classes preached by revolutionaries (says the "fool"), except that I hate Jews. Here Cummings notes the illogical position of an ideology which in theory approves all workers while in fact persecuting some. He also may hint at the curious paradox in Russia's apologists: although praising Communism, they behave, because of their prejudices, like Fascists. However it is interpreted, the poem is hardly anti-Semitic; it is, rather, a satire on anti-Semitism. That the poem was pointed at the Left was no doubt perfectly clear to its first readers: it appeared in company of the scathing "kumrads die because they're told)" (30) in the January 1935 issue of *Alcestis.*

More slender and pointed is " 'let's start a magazine" (24). Here he satirizes the literary magazines of his day for their ridiculous standards ("fearlessly obscene / but really clean / get what I mean") and their idolatry of the "genuine" (which, as he notes, is also a character of "a mark / in a toilet"). Such writing is akin to the tough-talking of Hemingway; and "what does little Ernest croon" (26) volleys a derisive quip at Cummings' famous contemporary. Hemingway, here, comes out little better than Longfellow, a poet whom Cummings despised. In *A Psalm of Life,* Longfellow had written "Dust thou art, to dust returnest, / Was not spoken of the soul"; Cummings' last lines, restored to standard English, read, *"Cow thou art, to bull returnest, was the words of little Ernest*." In such masculine instinct, Cummings may be saying, is Hemingway's entire philosophy, a philosophy he characterizes as "bull."

More portraits follow. Cummings' friend Little Joe Gould (poem 27) was a Greenwich Village fixture who made it known that he was writing a voluminous book entitled *An Oral History of Our Time*. He was actually (as Joseph Mitchell has made clear) doing nothing of the kind, but cadging drinks.[12] Cummings may have divined the secret: as he observes in this sonnet, "a myth is as good as a smile." The following poems satirize various things: the barroom sentiments of those who scorn "famous fatheads" (28), the attitudes of "most(people)" who, rather than dying, simply become buried (29), and the "kumrads" of the revolution, who hate "because they are afraid to love" (30). These first two poems present an unmistakable context for the "kumrads": like the scoffers at "famous fatheads," they have emotions without compassion and rancor without critical analysis, and like "most(people)" they are abject conformists.

The last five poems in the first half (poems 31 through 35) also form a sequence: the first and last are sonnets on failure, while the intervening three are lyric impressions dealing with snow. Of these middle poems, the first ("numb(and," 32) describes snow which slides from a statue in a park and scribbles "lonely truth" on the ground below. The statue ("this serene / mightily how rooted / who of iron") awaits "this alive secretly i," the poet and interpreter who can decipher the message of the winter. The "who of iron" may be Alexander Lyman Holley, a nineteenth-century industrialist; his bust, erected in 1889, stands where Cummings would have seen it in Washington Square Park, with an inscription noting his contribution to "the manufacture of Bessemer steel." An obscure individual memorialized by a bust whose inscription is fading and difficult to read, Holley has become a "who," an appropriate subject for the relative obscurity of this poem. The landscape speaks a similar message in "emptied.hills.listen" (33), where rain mixing with snowflakes produces "r / hythms." The third poem ("snow)says!Says," 34) seems so purely lyric that paraphrase is impossible: more like a painting than a poem, it makes its point almost independently of linear syntax, setting out images and playing on their variations.

Snow, here, becomes a fitting symbol for defeat, and the two sonnets that embrace these snow poems explore, in a way peculiarly appropriate to Cummings' own reputation in the *No Thanks* years, the nature and lessons of failure. The first ("does yesterday's perfection seem not quite," 31) is a periodic sentence, a stack of four conditional clauses resting on the bed of its conclusion. The clauses may be paraphrased as follows: if yesterday's perfection does not seem quite "so clever as the pratfall of a clown"; if, that is, everything whose sweetness was once recognized and renowned should "stink of failure" more than wars stink of feet; if all dreams suddenly unmake themselves, due to the fact that in a smashed world there stands one who has not learned that if anguish once touched him he might live (and who, therefore, resists that anguish); if a star in "edgeless" space could only make room for such anguish, although it can't, since the only thing that likes anguish is the "mere one bursting soul" of man—if all these things obtain, then "comes peace unto men": failure brings peace, a resignation and humility where the assertive IS of existence becomes "I the lost shoulders S the empty spine." In a poem as complex as this one, even paraphrase needs explication. If two conditions are fulfilled, says the poet, men will have peace. First, public praise and self-congratulation must turn to failure. Second, one's dreams of glory must vanish because one finds himself in a "smashed" dreamworld, destroyed because one did not recognize the importance of *anguish*—the deep, sustained effort and privation involved in poetic creation—as a means for producing something that really lives (rather than something that is merely "unslain"). All this is true, and it is further true that no undefined ideal ("star") could give room to (find a place and purpose for) anguish, since our ideals generally envision only the glory, not the anguish, of our endeavors. In fact, the only thing that likes anguish (or that takes it into consideration) is this "soul," so filled with its creative urge that it is both an "eternal" being and a "mere" mortal doomed to burst. Given all this healthy destruction of false ideals, men who really are men— the truest poets—will attain peace. For a real man shall be, as a god sometimes is, an active (not merely conditional) verb, an *is*—even though that isness produces a look (because of the anguish required) of slouching cowardice, a look that is anything but the world's ideal of a man (or god) who squares his shoulders and stiffens his spine to cope with difficulties. Like Yeats in "To a Friend Whose Work Has Come to Nothing," Cummings draws lessons from rebuffs. Looking back on his early poems as "things whose slendering sweetness touched renown," he had reason now to learn what lessons he could from his recent defeats.

The final poem in the sequence ("how dark and single,where he ends,the earth," 35) addresses the problem in more explicit terms. Noting how bleak and lonely the coast looks as the tide covers it—or perhaps how dark the earth looks as night overtakes it—the poet draws many morals from the land's graceful resignation, from the natural ease with which "he comes to his disappearance." That the enormity of this failure has to do with poetry is made clear in the next lines: as opposed to the "dark and single" earth, the "bright and plural tide" takes the measure of the earth "as critics will upon a poet feast." The "stink" of "renown" in the previous sonnet here becomes the more poignant "hurt of praise": beyond praising, the poet is also beyond hurting, for he is drowned, like the land, in "the unimaginable night not known."

From such defeat the poet begins to chart his way to triumph. The poem at the center of the book ("into a truly," 36) is no less central in Cummings' development. Significantly, it speaks of a kind of salvation. The poet's soul enters "a truly / curving form" and feels "all small / facts dissolved"—all the trivia departed, all the things gone which in the previous poem he called "life's busy little dyings." In that poem "this ghost goes under"; but here the "ship lifts." The metaphor of a nighttime storm at sea concludes grandly:

> and through only this night a
> mightily form moves
> whose passenger and whose
> pilot my spirit is.

The "form" on the water, the word "spirit," and the familiar metaphor of the pilot as the Savior recall the description (Matthew 14) of Jesus walking on the sea. The salvation here, however, is probably less religious than poetic: the "form" of poetry carries the spirit along and is guided by it. Leaving behind the mundane world (where critics devour poets), the narrator is now ready to ride through any roughness on the ship of poetry filled with "soul" and "spirit"—on poetry that deals, as his increasingly does, in metaphysics.

As though to illustrate, Cummings follows the poem with a sonnet ("conceive a man,should he have anything," 37) which describes his ideal individual. Given the context, it seems less probably a poem about his father (as some have thought) than about himself. Imagine a man (says the poet) who, if he had anything, would give it and more away. For him the grim expectation of decline followed by barrenness would transform itself into a promise of fullness and would set aside time. Imagine this man, from whose memory (or history or example) no ordinary "unstrange" mind could learn (nor could all the world's pedantry make an educated guess) that life is not to be reduced to rules: one doesn't discover rules simply by living, because there are none. This discovery will not be made even if "loud" (obtrusive) "most howish" (concerned with methods and modes of operation) time interferes with and tries to upset the natural causes ("whys") that underlie his immortality. (Time, in other words, tries to reduce all things to temporal phenomena. But it fails to get at the real principles, especially for the man who sets aside all laws of seasonal cause and effect.) Simple folk and scholars also will not learn or guess that what they consider to be "dark beginnings" (primary causes shrouded in mystery) are in fact the whole purpose and goal of such a man's life and are completely lucid to him. It is as impossible to think of such a man being lonely as it is to think of cool fires. He takes for his companions all natural phenomena. So have, world (the poet concludes), intercourse with fate and conceive such a man—but in order to do so you will need to get rid of selfishness and withhold nothing.

These three central poems (35–37) were immediately preceded by ones which dealt with snow imagery. The first poem following the central group ("SNOW," 38) returns to the same image, but in a strangely distorted manner. Much of the poem's meaning can be pieced together by recombining words: it seems to describe a late snowfall coming upon birds who perch on "SCARCELYEST . . . FLOWERING" trees in early spring. Ultimately, however, the grammar eludes the meaning, and the poem seems more a set of related ideas spread in a painterly way across the page than a linear development of meaning. Poem 39, beginning "move / deeply,rain," advances the season beyond snow. An apostrophe, it urges the rain to "strike / into form" the "realness" of things by killing the "known" and establishing the new; its thesis is a blending of ideas from "Spring is like a perhaps hand" (&, "N," III) and "be unto love as rain is unto colour" (*ViVa*, LXIII). The following poems support the spring metaphor: "as if as" (40) is an experimental typograph describing the world coming into view at dawn, and "here's to opening and upward,to leaf and to sap" (41) praises spring, joy, laughter, and drunkenness while applauding "a disappearing poet of always,snow."

From natural impressions the tone shifts suddenly to the lively arts of dancing and burlesque: "out of a super-metamathical subpreincestures" (42) lauds Sally Rand, who (according to Barry Marks) was a 1930s fan dancer and who (according to Cummings) was incomparably more alive than anything captured by phonograph, radio, or movies.[13] The next two poems also concern dancing: "theys sO alive" (43) reworks the cliché of the black dancers' natural rhythm into a poem that arranges words into a visual counterpart of the subject. Readers familiar with Cummings' art will find in this poem and in "ondumonde' " (47) a sinuous and vertical line similar to the design underlying many of his drawings of dancers and dancing couples.[14] Dancing continues in "the boys i mean are not refined" (44), a poem so frank in its obscenities that it appeared only in the nine copies of the holograph issue of the book, where Cummings inscribed it himself on a page left blank for the purpose. For all its profanity, it seems at first blush the poem of praise which Friedman calls it.[15] In contrast to the mock-prissy speech of its first line, the rough language of most of the poem recalls the poet's often articulated preference for vigorous vulgarity over social refinement. For these boys, sex is all; and, while "they cannot chat of that and this," they do by their dancing "shake the mountains," the symbols of traditional and enduring stability. Surely Cummings would approve the fact that

these boys "speak whatever's on their mind." but to judge by
the treatment sex receives in the imagery of his other poems,
his applause for those who "do whatever's in their pants" was
not unqualified. The apparent celebration of those who "do not
give a fart for art" and who "kill like you would take a piss"
comes, it must be remembered, from a man whose entire life
was given to art and whose central theme was love. The poem
is, after all, not so much a panegyric as a highly literate and
skillful parody of outhouse verse.

A sequence of particularly fine work begins with "what a
proud dreamhorse pulling(smoothloomingly)through" (53). As
archetype of returning spring, the poet uses the flower-seller
with his horse-drawn cart—an image he may have appropriated
from the painters, who have used it frequently. The choice is a
particularly happy one for Cummings, who once theorized on
the "Colours & Shape & Form" seen in "the banks of hues" at a
flower market.[16] What a proud horse this is (says the poet),
pulling "wonderful / flowers" through the "crazily seething" and
"screamingly" "raving" city street, stepping "smoothloomingly"
as he goes. The light from the flowers "opens / sharp holes in
dark places": it "paints eyes" and "touches hands with new- /
ness," and it pierces clothes and thoughts, kisses and wishes
and bodies. The children (the "startled whats" and "whiches"
who are "small / its") are intensely ("squirm-of-frightened")
timid at its approach. But these "its" (not yet individualized
enough even to be called *whos*) are "hungry for Is" and for
"Love" and for "Spring." They are also "thirsty" for three corresponding terms: "happens" (the "Is" of experience), "only" (the
uniqueness of "Love"), and "beautiful" (the loveliness of
"Spring"). The poet then tells us, with effectual ellipsis, that
"there is a ragged [man] beside the [horse] who limps"—a line
which, if read with slight pauses where the interpolated words
are missing, captures the pace of the man's limp. As he goes, he

is "crying silence upward," as though the silence had settled to the bottom of the street canyons and his voice, as he cries his wares, had driven it upward like oil lifted by water poured under it. "Beautiful," "Only," and "Happens" reappear, having borrowed capitalization from the three terms they paralleled, and the man urges the "kids" to "skip," "dance," "hop," and "point" at the flowers, at the "red blue yellow violet white orange" colored "green- / ness." Green, the final term, is nature's basic color, and the six-color compound adjective describing it suggests the modification (as adjectives modify nouns) of that green by the flowers' colors. As though to emphasize the intensity of this epiphanic experience, the poet recapitulates by noting that the horse's feet "almost walk air." The rhythm, like the horse and like the poem, slows down and comes to a standstill: "now who stops. Smiles.he / stamps" are the final words, as the horse becomes again a real animal with feet stamping the ground.

Like his later poems in *Xaipe* about tinkers and scissorsgrinders ("who sharpens every dull," 26, and "in," 62), "what a proud dreamhorse" elevates a common figure from the street into a symbol of universal import. The horse, after all, is a "dreamhorse"—both real beast and fanciful animal who, like the horses of Phoebus pulling the sun out of the night, pulls the essence of spring and nature into the gloom and violence of the city. The effect is complex: it brings to the children a promise of the individuality which (as mere pronouns) they are missing until the man calls them "kids"; and it brings to the narrator, who watches the kids watching the man and horse, a sense of epiphany which literally elevates his conception of the horse into a transcendent being walking above the ground. Nowhere, however, does the poet explain: he simply shows us the scene and brings us so deeply into it that our response must be akin to his own. Here, perhaps, is the metaphor for the effect of poetry on humanity, for the effect of the "tulips" of praise that have such transforming power among the "chimneys" of civilization.

The ensuing poems slide from praise into vitriolics. The best is the first ("Jehovah buried, Satan dead," 54), a poem whose "argument" (according to a note Cummings penciled on a manuscript draft) is that "man fancies himself god but has become base;what's needed is a(god who dares to be a)man."[17] A kind of double sonnet—three "quatrains" of eight lines followed by a "couplet" of four lines—the poem develops a parallel construction as it lists the objects of its invective. Now that the standards are gone and society is godless, there are no worshippers but only "fearers" who idolize "Much" (material abundance) and "Quick" (speed and busyness). In this world, both joy and pain are pawned and unredeemed; "dreamless knaves" have no inner vision; "Gadgets" such as radios "squawk"; Jews turn to rapacious stereotypes of themselves ("kike") in order "to kiss the mike"—to win fame by worshipping the microphone, perhaps, or to befriend (and presumably cheat) the stereotype of the gullible Irishman. In such a world, "who dares to call himself a man?" Cummings usually associates this idea of *daring* (a word appearing some thirty-eight times in various forms in his poems) with the bravery of those he applauds. Here the only salvation is in "King Christ," the one man "Who dares to call Himself a man" and who can save us from sinking.

A similar invective begins "worshipping Same / they squirm and they spawn" (55). Where "Jehovah buried" decried conformity ("the cult of Same is all the chic") and posited salvation in a man who could rise above it ("King Christ"), the sequel suggests that "his birth"—the birth of the nonconformist whose cry is "a thousand dreams thick," whose "laugh is a million griefs wide," and whose shoulders are "a hundred joys high"— may again be Jesus, whom the "cowards" label "fiend" and scheme to trap. Denying merely rational answers ("dancing isn't on why"), this savior may also be the poet. In any case, he has the courage to proclaim that " 'the harder the wind blows the / taller I am' "—the more he encounters flattening resistance and leveling sameness, the more he stands up to it. The third poem in this series of satires ("this mind made war," 56) is also about the savior (here clearly the poet) who resists conformity. Perhaps intended as a self-portrait, it praises the poet who has the courage to write vitriolic satires, and who "laughed and spat" when "on him they shat." Supplying terminal punctuation (after lines 1, 3, 4, 6, 8, 10, 11, 16, 19, 23, 26, 30, 34, 36, 40, 48, 65, and 68) and quotation marks (in lines 6, 7, and 31) clarifies syntax.

One of Cummings' most appealing sonnets is "love's function is to fabricate unknownness" (61), a poem he chose for inclusion in *100 Selected Poems*. In general and particular ways, the sonnet recalls Shakespeare's sonnet 116, which it resembles in more than rhyme scheme and use of paradox. Like that poem, it discusses the attributes of love by beginning with a brief assertion, exploring the counterfeits and opposites, and then moving to the true view. Even the diction echoes Shakespeare: "love may not care / if time totters" recalls "Love's not time's fool"; "all measures bend" echoes "Nor bends with the remover to remove"; the idea of weighing a star has a parallel in Shakespeare's image of "the star to every wandering bark" whose "height" is taken; and the line "—dreads dying least;and less,that death should end)" recalls Shakespeare's love that "bears it out even to the edge of doom." Cummings, however, brands the poem as his own in such deft plays as "fish boast of fishing / and men are caught by worms," which is both a paradox illustrating the idea that "life's lived wrongsideout" and a surprisingly apt image for dissolution in the grave. Typical of Cummings, too, is the last line, "while the whole moves;and every part stands still." For all his scorn of physical science,

Cummings picked up from its teachings enough to be familiar with the molecular model of a seemingly stable object in fact composed of constantly moving particles. Here he simply reverses the model: since the spiritual universe—the universe of love—must be the reverse of the material, it manifests overall movement even while it maintains individual peace and stillness.

By contrast, the poet in Poem 67 issues a dashingly defiant challenge to the "mischief- / hatchers" to "hatch / mischief" and "throw dynamite." None of these antics will destroy life and being: "Is will still occur" and poems will still be composed—not merely in order to come to terms with "harm" (evil and pain), nor to comprehend natural disasters such as "earthquakes," nor even to apprehend such symbols of ideal beauty as "starfish." Real poems will be composed simply because "nobody / can sell the Moon to The)moon"—because we who are of a piece with transcendence can't be sold some conventionalized (note the capital *M*) version of reality. Let the worst come, says the poet here: those at one with the eternal are ready.

The last four poems in the book attain the transcendent temper on which his volumes usually end. Number 68, beginning "be of love(a little) / More careful / Than of everything" (68), urges us also to "guard" love less than we guard "Nothing"—or, in other words, to refrain from impounding love in such a way that we can not "give entirely each / Forever its freedom." The following poem, a sonnet, is again best in its first two lines ("reason let others give and realness bring— / ask the always impossible of me") than in its entirety. Offering an obscure vision of heaven, it prepares the way for one of the most carefully wrought poems in the entire canon, "brIght" (70). Here, as McIlvaine has noted, is a poem of only eleven words, each repeated as many times as there are letters in the word—so that "yes," "big," and "who" are repeated three times, "star," "soft," "near," "calm," "holy," and "deep" four times, "alone" five times, and "brIght" (in its various manifestations, some of which replace individual letters with question marks) six times.[18] In addition, Cummings designs progressions of capital letters as words repeat, and increases in succeeding stanzas the number of lines, the length of lines, and the number of words. The poem concerns the appearance of a star (beginning as "s???" and ending as "star"). The word "holy," the emphasis on unusual brightness, and the particular context of the poem—flanked as it is by a poem about heaven and another about a star—suggest the star of Bethlehem.

Turning from impression to apostrophe, the volume ends with "morsel miraculous and meaningless" (71), a poem addressed to a "fabulous crumb" of a star. Delaying his main verb until line 12, the poet ranges through an extended parenthesis describing the star before calling upon it to "honour this loneliness of even him / who fears and eyes lifts." Unlike the emboldening but aloof star of Williams' "El Hombre," this star is to "nourish my failure with thy freedom"—a most appropriate ending for a volume that, in poems such as "how dark and single," probed deeply into Cummings' feeling of defeat. Here, however, there is a redemption for failure, an aspiration to fix upon. Here, too, in what must not have been a wholly unpremeditated gesture, is the final wry twist of the wit that led Cummings to title the volume as he did. All his earlier volumes had ended with sonnets; this poem, apparently a sonnet, in fact has fifteen lines. Here, as though in quiet defiance of the critics who "will upon a poet feast," he upset expectations and then waited to see if anyone would catch him at it. So far, no one has: the poem is generally numbered among his sonnets, and Cummings, bidding "no thanks" to critics as well as publishers, has laughed last.

Chapter 7

New Poems

(from Collected Poems)

Collected Poems (1938), on which so much of Cummings' early popularity rested, in fact is more selection than collection. It is tempting to regard the book, even though truncated, as a repository for all that he thought worth saving. But Charles Norman's account of its genesis and publication, including some of the letters through which Cummings and Charles A. Pearce of Harcourt, Brace hammered out the contents, suggests otherwise.[1] While Pearce was later to recall that "e. e. c. made the decision to limit," the letters themselves indicate that Cummings, given no carte blanche to select, had to adjust and compromise with others' choices. He may have viewed the book, at its inception, as a collection of his best things: sending a list of poems to be excluded, he remarked that "What I don't like is,naturally,whatever I don't feel to be myself." The discrepencies between his original list and the published volume, however, are too large to justify the view that the selection was all his own.

As published, *Collected Poems* includes, as a percentage of the original, more of *is* 5 than of any other volume—a representation in keeping with Cummings' initial choice. Obviously feeling that his recent work was strongest, Cummings had at first proposed keeping *ViVa* and *No Thanks* intact; the published collection, however, deletes sixteen poems from the former and twenty-two from the latter book, reducing by more than a quarter the representation of work during the previous twelve years. In making these compromises, Cummings expressed surprisingly little stubbornness, giving Pearce a good deal of flexibility in deciding which poems to omit. He was, in fact, more insistent on format than contents, writing Pearce that "what I care infinitely is that each poempicture should remain intact. Why? Possibly because,with few exceptions,my poems are essentially pictures." What he wanted was such a "combination of typesize and papersize as will allow every picture to breathe its particular life(no 'runover' lines)in its own private world." Pearce, having so much to do with the selection, may also have been left the task of determining sequence. For whatever reason, the order of poems in *Collected Poems* represents a wholesale departure from the arrangement in the individual volumes and in fact seems to have been made in ignorance of the carefully developed patterns so evident in the earlier sequences. Only with *Poems 1923–1954* was a collected edition available which accurately reproduced the earlier volumes.

Collected Poems begins with an introduction, a prose statement akin to but much more extensive than the one introducing *is* 5. Here he identifies his villains, the "mostpeople" who prefer inertia to activity. Describing them, he happens upon a word for their essential attribute—"passivity." The metaphor characterizing their behavior is of the womb. What "mostpeople" want is "a guaranteed birthproof safetysuit"; what they fear most is being born. For "ourselves," on the other hand, "birth is a supremely welcome mystery," and "We can never be born enough." The entire introduction is built on this opposition—as, indeed, are many of his poems. Apart from the diction (which is his own particular invention) and the sometimes pretentious or condescending tone (which is his own occasional failing), the piece has an odd flavor of the pulpit. The language insists on miracles and on love; it presents the ideal man in the Christlike attitude of a "citizen of immortality" who is "a little more than everything," who is "alive," and who is "ourselves"; and its central argument is not far from Jesus' insistence that "Ye must be born again." Even his comment on the "anaesthetized impersons" looking for a "cosmic comfortstation" has about it the same bravura he would later recall about the sermons preached by his father, who one day "horribly shocked his pewholders by crying 'the Kingdom of Heaven is no spiritual roofgarden:it's inside you.' "[2] The introduction builds to its culmination in reaffirming the poet's commitment "never to rest and never to have:only to grow." And it ends with an ambiguity worthy of his poems—"Always the beautiful answer who asks a more beautiful question"—a sentence which means both "[there is] always the beautiful answer [for him] who asks a more beautiful question" and "the beautiful [people, ideas] always answer [the person] who asks a more beautiful question."

The "New Poems" section in *Collected Poems* contains twenty-two previously unpublished poems. It begins with "un," a poem about the transforming magic of fog, under whose influence "whichs / turn / in / to whos" and "people / be / come / un." Segmented by fragments of the word "slowliest," the poem ends as it began, with "un" circling back on itself in imitation of a self-contained world hemmed in by fog. Cummings, whose verse is generally a good deal less free than it looks, devises still another form of circling within this poem. Grouping his very short lines into stanzas, he includes in each a single two-syllable line. It appears as the second line in stanza 1; as stanzas progress, it shows up as the third, then the fourth, until at last it circles back to the first line in stanza 4, as though to begin the process anew.

A lecture on science sponsored by the YMCA-YWCA provides the subject for "kind)" (2). Mystified by this talk on the nature of the universe, with its mathematical examples trickling harmlessly over the audience, the narrator takes delight in the contrast between such stale analysis of the heavens and "the not / merely immeasurable . . . / dear beautiful eternal night" into which he at last escapes. The poem captures the embarrassing attempts of a befuddled lecturer to amuse his audience with his own tedious insights. Concision being essential to wit, the lecturer's pointless tale fails here: strung out through various detours, and interrupted by pauses, coughs, and "uh," it produces only the reaction noted by the poet: "(&so on & so unto canned / swoonsong."

A sketch of the seasick idle rich and the dangers of surfeit (3) leads easily into "(of Ever-Ever Land i speak" (4), a satire in the mocking sing-song Cummings reserves for his sharpest barbs. Blending diction from the nursery rhyme and the come-all-ye, the poet pretends to praise, not Never-Never Land, but the land of "Ever," of full realizations, of the New Deal where all will be "measured and safe and known." Here the refrain is "down with the human soul," "down with hell and heaven," and "down above all with love"; these, after all, are qualities that endanger the collective by promoting individuality. A focus on individuality would insist that some are different from others and that differences are worth preserving. Here, however, opposites are reconciled—"the hitler lies down with the cohn"— without any attempt to distinguish good from evil. And here love is seen simply as a perversion "which makes some feel more better," when, as Cummings sees it, the goal of Roosevelt's programs was simply to be sure that "all . . . feel less worse." Rephrasing Kipling ("A woman is only a woman, but a good cigar is a smoke"),[3] Cummings ends with "a bad cigar is a woman / but a gland is only a gland": in Ever-Ever Land, poorly manufactured products replace humanity, and love is reduced to mere glandular reactions.

With "this little bride & groom are" (8), he undertakes an equally searching social probe in an entirely different language. Describing a wedding cake topped with bride-and-groom figurines, the poet offers a comment on the sugary view of love. The poem saves its barb for the end: "everything is protected by / cellophane" because "nothing really exists." Sealed off from reality, protected from "anything" harmful but also from everything meaningful, the cake symbolizes the complex of feelings which Cummings—twice divorced and never officially married to his third wife—may have associated with the traditional views of marriage. As though to isolate his own editorial comment in the final four words, he separates them by a parenthesis. His comment has many meanings. In the first place, the imitation bride and groom on the cake do not "really" exist. Then, too, the thing they stand for—the traditional views of marriage— needs the protection of the cheaply commercial cellophane, since without defense it would be found to be unreal and would go to pieces. Finally, the thing they stand on—rings of cake— are insubstantial. Only in the last stanza is the word "cake" used: until then, the idea of the bride and groom standing on "a thin ring" suggests the wedding ring, which, another symbol, is at least more substantial than what really supports them: cake. A simple poem, it achieves its depth by describing an image and then connecting it in the last four words with a highly abstract statement designed to make us consider the image as symbol.

The three following poems are of a piece. Jimmy Savo, an entertainer who, as Norman recalls, "strewed the stage with bits of paper in gestures extremely birdlike," is portrayed in the picture-poem "so little he is" (9).[4] Like Cummings' line drawings of male dancers, this poem is tall, thin, and balanced on tiptoe on its final comma. Like the drawings, the poem captures him in midair as the final punctuation, moving from period to colon to semicolon to comma, becomes progressively less conclusive. The next poem ("nor woman," 10), recounting an unspecified incident in a park, again pictures the vertical sinuous line so typical of his drawings and paintings. Recomposed, the words in parentheses tells us that "just as it began to snow he disappeared leaving on itself propped upright that (in this otherwise how empty park) bundle of what man can't hurt any more hush." One commentator sees this as a nefarious act in which a murderer dumps the sacked body of a young girl.[5] More probably, however, the poem is designed to be humorous. The "he" may even be a dog, and the shape of the poem may stand for what Cummings elsewhere calls "spontaneous twurls-of-excrement" (&, "Post Impressions," VI). More probably, however, the "he" is a bum and the propped-up bundle is his drunken companion. The poet has prepared us for this low-life vignette by focusing our attention on the dance-hall comedian in the previous poem. He follows it with "my speciality is living said" (11), a portrait of Little Joe Gould or his bohemian ilk who, refusing to "sell his head" and prostitute his literary skills, preferred a derelict's life among lice and dead trousers. It is a portrait of someone who could well have been mistaken for a bundle in a park.

On his trip to California in 1935, Cummings and Hollywood finally encountered one another. "The Mind's(" (12) is the poet's report of the meeting. He fixes upon a director coaching his actress on the set; transcribed, the director's comments read, "I said beauty, Miss Isaacs, and you can tell Finklestein it stinks. You ready? All right, let's go. Action. Camera. They're turning." Within the poem's parentheses is his picture of Hollywood "nonexistence," and outside ("The Mind's . . . Ah, Soul") is his comment on it: the mind's asshole.

With "beware beware beware" (16), Cummings moves from the raw to the gnomic in composing one of his most cryptic satires on science. Punctuating the material outside the parentheses produces the sentence "Beware *beware; beware *because*, because *because* equals . . . *why*." Beware (in other words) the warnings to beware, for they are not to be trusted; and beware the word *because*, since *because* is the logical result of *why*, and *why* is a question scientists use. Reading through parentheses, *because* also equals *transparent*, or something whose deception is not even successful. As an example of such deception, he notes that "science must / bait laws with / stars to catch telescopes." The phrase, if inverted, would make more sense, telling us that science baits stars with telescopes—coaxes stars down into their observatories—in order to catch and define the laws of the universe. For Cummings, however, science works in reverse: having imagined fanciful laws to explain away the heavens, it surrounds its fancies with attractive pieces of evidence (stars) in order to persuade the world to build more telescopes. Just as he must labor to untangle the complexities of this poem, so the puzzled layman, like the baffled listener to the YMCA lecturer in "kind)," must also struggle to ferret out what science is really saying. The enigmatic last lines—"only fishermen are / prevented by cathedrals"—suggests more than it explains. If the scientists who "bait" laws are the fishermen, they are prevented by their enemy since before Galileo's time—the church—from discovering too much about the laws of the universe; Cummings may be noting an earthly war raging between the institutions purporting to represent reality and divinity. On the other hand (given his emphasis on "patience," a quality needed by the fishermen), Cummings may be distinguishing fishermen from scientists here, and may be thinking of Jesus' promise that "I will make you fishers of men"—an outreach resisted by the synagogues of Jesus' day much as, for Cummings, real love is resisted by the cathedrals and wedding cakes of his own.

From science and cathedrals, the poet turns to a dense and abtruse love poem in "only as what(out of a flophouse)floats" (17). Here the "flophouse," and the "death's dollhead" (doll's death's-head?) who wanders out of it at dawn to peer into pawnshop windows at "much soundless rubbish of guitars / and watches," are the backdrop for the poet's expression of feeling for his lover. The message is unexceptional; the presentation is complex, however, and demonstrates yet one more strategy through which Cummings saves the poem of praise from slipping into the conventional jingling of sweet sentiments.

The final poem, as usual, is a sonnet: "you shall above all things be glad and young" (22). Insisting on his lover's youth, the poet develops at greater length the idea presented a few poems earlier in "may my heart always be open to little": whatever birds sing "is better than to know / and if men should not hear them men are old." This sonnet depends on some deftly handled double meanings: "above all things," meaning *most importantly*, also means *in a category above all mere objects;* and "become," which means "complement" in line 3, means *change into* in line 4. That "Girlboys may nothing more than boygirls need"—that *hoi polloi*, sexually indistinct and genderless, may be content to take mirrored images of itself as lovers—is a matter of indifference to the poet, who loves only "her" whose mystery makes him expansive ("put space on") and immortal ("take off time"). The following quatrain slants several allusions at Shakespeare. The line "that you should ever think, may god forbid," a typical Cummings animadversion against reason and "to know," echoes Quince's confusion in *A Midsummer Night's Dream.* Hopelessly enmeshed in mistaken punctuation, Quince murders the sense of some verse he reads as prologue to the wedding play, construing his lines as "That you should think, we come not to offend, / But with goodwill." Cummings counts on us to anticipate a relative clause after "that you should ever think"; as in Shakespeare, the humor comes not only in the abrupt termination of our expectations but also in the surprising rightness produced by the distortion. Several lines later Cummings echoes Lear's "that way madness lies" in the phrase "for that way knowledge lies"; here the line depends, to some extent, on the reader recognizing a synonymity between "madness" and "knowledge" as equally destructive conditions. Like Sidney, who exulted that "two negatives affirm," Cummings presents, in "negation's dead undoom," a compound of reversals which ultimately means deadness. The final lines summarize the poet's increasingly acute sense of the ways in which the "knowing" of science—here, of astronomical calculation—destroys the poetic mysteries of the universe. They provide the poem, and *Collected Poems*, with a memorable close:

> I'd rather learn from one bird how to sing
> than teach ten thousand stars how not to dance.

Chapter 8

50 Poems

"As Plato forgot to say to Aristotle," wrote Cummings to Sibley Watson in February of 1939, "I'm trying to borrow money."[1] These were slender years for a poet trying to support himself and his wife solely by writing and painting. Yet he was convinced of the value of the life-style he had espoused, and the specter of penury never prompted him to look for more lucrative endeavors. Thanking Watson a few days later for "the 300," he wrote: "am literally American enough to hope I'll be able to 'make my own way' 'some day' 'soon.' Seem to remember mon père telling me the best thing which could happen to you would be that what you want to do most should give you a living;anyhow, feel this is so. . . ."[2] In a letter at the end of the following summer he thanked Hildegarde Watson for the "good time Estlin and Marion had this summer [at Joy Farm],thanks to SW," and noting what their beneficence had engendered: "some paintings and poems may(here's hoping)have made themselves."[3] Making his way, for Cummings, meant earning a living through painting and writing—a state he was only to achieve late in life, after the munificence of the Norton Lectureship at Harvard started him on the road to a modest kind of financial security.

The very years in which his struggle for funds tended toward the acute, however, were the years in which his scorn for socialism deepened. Unlike the bulk of his contemporaries in the arts, he never saw in government subsidies an answer to his problems, but felt instead that the preservation of individuality and the acceptance of New Deal handouts were irreconcilably opposed. This opposition is the burden of *50 Poems* (1940), which contains some of his best-known poems praising individuality and condemning the state: "as freedom is a breakfast-food," "the way to hump a cow is not," "anyone lived in a pretty how town," and "my father moved through dooms of love." Like his recent books, it mixes sonnets with other forms; unlike them, however, it makes no attempt to organize the contents through a pattern of recurring sonnets. Unlike earlier books, it moves farther away from free verse. Most of these poems employ a recognizable rhythmic or stanzaic pattern; there are only three (9, 30, and 48) in which structure conforms to the demands of intuition rather than convention.

The first poem ("!blac"), an apparently random littering of letters, actually groups its lines into alternate one- and four-line stanzas. Recomposed and slightly rearranged, it reads: "black against white sky; trees from which a dropped leaf goes whirling." More than a simple Imagist sketch, it is an experiment in fragmentation. Commenting on the initial "!" Cummings explained that it "might be called an emphatic(=very)."[4] The poem has been seen as describing a flash of lightning; more probably, however, it describes a scene in Washington Square Park where, walking after dark, the poet sees a tree silhouetted against the cloudy sky bright with city lights. Arguing for this interpretation is the arrangement of "whirling," which surely suggests the slow and reflective rather than the violent and explosive. Several of Cummings' volumes begin in this way: the opening poems of *1 x 1* ("nonsun blob a") and *95 Poems* ("1(a") are similar to "!blac" in subject, style, and quietly meditative tone. Message, here, justifies the experimental pattern: far from adding confusion, the arrangement of words reduces ambiguity and points toward proper meaning.

A similar typograph ("fl," 2) describes the derelicts whom Cummings no doubt encountered on his daily sojourns to the same park. These bums are less like real beings with manhood "in" them than like "flattened" cardboard cutouts, "on" which the delineations of mankind have been drawn. The quietly measured pace ("sh sh," says one line) suggests the poet's compassion for these creatures. In particular, the reduction of the word "men" to "me" ("ccocoucougcoughcoughi / ng with me") suddenly brings their broken health into touch with the poet and indicates a kind of unity between him and these outcasts.

Bums or bohemians reappear in "If you can't eat you got to" (3), a poem about progressive inanition. And in "nobody loved this" (4) the poet portrays still another denizen of the park who, apish in appearance, is condemned to a loveless existence. Concluding these visions of autumn and decaying humanity, the fifth poem ("am was. are leaves few this. is these a or," 5) is a sonnet which runs through a jungle of syntax in its octave. It seems to be about autumn ("scratchily over . . . earth dragged / . . . leaf"), the disappearance of individual being ("am was"), and the onset of winter's first snow flurries ("colding hereless," "float silently down . . . / snow"). The sestet suggests dangers to nature and individuality by noting that "cities" can destroy "grassblades," that "five / ideas" (perhaps the five senses?) can "swallow a man," and that "three words" (probably "I love you") can "im- /prison a woman for all her now." Ending with affirmation, however, the poet distinguishes between those people and "us": like spring, which will come forth out of the wintry desolation of the first eight stanzas, we have "so / much greenness only dying makes us grow."

Decrying another sort of social decay, the sixth poem, published as "Dirge" in *Furioso* (1939), comments on the visit to

America of two homosexual British leftist poets named "flotsam and jetsam" (6). With their socialist dicta, their primly British speech which pronounces "poets" as "ppoyds," and their formal dress and demeanor ("senectie"), they capture the hearts of "our spinsters and coeds"—the same ones who in later years would be transported into ecstasies by the American tours of Dylan Thomas. The words "neck and senecktie" are borrowed, as Gary Lane explains, from Horace's ode on death.[5] Cummings evidently knew the poem well, for he had used its first line ("Eheu fugaces, Postume, Postume") some years earlier in describing "Mr Do- / nothing the wellknown parvenu" (*is* 5, "One," VII). Here the point is clear: such verse as these Britishers affect is, like their political and sexual affiliations, deathly.

Cultural annihilation is also the subject of "the Noster was a ship of swank" (8), a poem about a luxury liner which "hit a mine and sank / just off the coast of Sum." The "Noster"—Latin for "our," and suggesting the collectivism which Cummings found so abhorrent—sank by coming too close to the coast of "Sum," Latin for "I am." The immediate cause of the sinking was a "mine," suggesting both bomb and possessive pronoun. Disaster came to the collective, in other words, when it encountered the individual. It went down "precisely where a craft of cost / the Ergo perished later." This ship (the "Therefore") is named with a term appropriated by scholars, logicians, and other analytical minds whom Cummings mistrusted. All hands were lost in that accident, "including captain Pater." The reference here may be to Walter Pater, the Victorian essayist whose excessive refinement of style and championship of art and poetry brought him into favor with nineteenth-century esthetes. More obviously, the reference is to the first words of the Lord's Prayer ("Pater Noster . . ."), and suggests that what sank was "Our Father" and that God is now dead. Intertwined throughout the poem is the allusion to Descartes' famous statement of rationalism ("Cogito ergo sum"), which has also gone down with the ships.

While meaning can be erected fairly clearly here, significance is ambiguous: and in fact the poem may be taking two sides at once. If "Noster" stands for the collectivist activities of the socialists, then it (along with rationalism and oversweet prose) come to grief on the protective defenses of the self, the individuality preached so insistently in Cummings' poetry. But if "Pater" has overtones of something Cummings admired—a sense of tradition, an interest in things religious, even a commitment to classical languages—then the poem may have another thrust. "Noster" may suggest not collectivism but a sense of community, of sharing, of love for one another. This sense of love is destroyed by the "mine" of possessiveness, the selfish hoarding of those things, like money, which the world of commerce values only in "Sum" as arithmetic totals. If "Noster" is love and "Ergo" intelligence—a word which, for Cummings, was by no means the equivalent of what he usually derided as "thinking"—then these grand things have been destroyed by selfishness. The Father, trying to steer the ship of the intelligence past the dangers of egoism, has perished along with humanity. Read in the first sense, the poem takes its place nicely among a number of similar poems praising the individual; read in the second, it rises to a power recalling "Jehovah buried, Satan dead" (*No Thanks*, 54) in its warning against selfishness.

With "red-rag and pink-flag" (11) the poet turns to political invective. Some years later he commended the poem to his German translator, "lest anyone suppose that . . . I was a 'fascist.' "[6] The poem, as Friedman notes, parodies nursery rhymes, echoing "Hark, Hark, the Dogs Do Bark" and "Pease Porridge Hot."[7] Excoriating Communists ("red-rag"), Socialists ("pink-flag"), and Fascists (Italian Blackshirts and Nazi Brown-shirts), the poet jeers at the "strut-mince" of Fascists, proud of their elitism, and the "stink-brag" of Communists, proud of their unwashed proletarian earthiness. For all their apparent distinctions of symbolic color and political platform, however, they are disgustingly alike, concerned only with the violence that ends life and the lust that begins it. Such selfish concern is likewise the subject of "buy me an ounce and i'll sell you a pound" (27), which comments on the self-justifying arguments of those who assert that "mine is yours." After all, proclaims the ironic voice of the narrator, we have every right to get back at "them," for "we / order a steak and they send us a-pie." And "they" are so rich that we may as well take whatever we need, for "a / hole in the ocean will never be missed." The poem is one of Cummings' most subtle castigations of the sort of New Deal mentality which looks to government for salvation. Those who espouse these programs are unreceptive but vocal: "either was deafer than neither was dumb."

The great American philistine is the subject of "proud of his scientific attitude" (13). Various puns—"comma" for coma, "sic" for sick, "period" for menstruation, and "colon" for rectum—suggest the man's wife, teenaged daughter, and homosexual son. Everything is controlled and dehumanized by the "scien-tific attitude": even the potential tragedy of a wife who "wants to die" (of sickness, and of boredom) is prevented by "doctors" who "won't let her." The man considers Freud "mistaken," probably because he thinks of him as preaching the ascendancy of erotic impulse. Ignoring such teaching, he fails to recognize how much of his own experience—a wife ignored, a son per-verted, and a daughter who recalls the "unscented shapeless" daughters of "the Cambridge ladies"—is affected by uncon-scious sexual urges. His hobby gives him away: he likes photog-raphy, which in his hands is no doubt a scientific and impersonal way to record the objects of the world. He never has "plumbed / the heights" of Proust, but he certainly has freely mixed his metaphors. Cummings' point is that this man, worshipping at the altars of "scientific" objectivity, superficial views of art and letters, and self-importance as a financier or politician dealing in "the paper destinies of nations," is godless. Even in such a context, however, the summary comment—"the godless are the dull and the dull are the damned"—comes as a surprise. We expect godlessness to be damned. But we are accustomed to having our twentieth-century writers accept such damnation as the price of wicked excitement. So we are not prepared to have godlessness equated with dullness. Here, however, as in "the Noster was a ship of swank," the "scientific attitude" of the rationalists, which precludes the godliness that invests life with transcendence, drowns "Pater" on the "Ergo."

The speaker of "the way to hump a cow is not" (14) is, as Friedman observes, "an old-time political hack telling an aspirant the secrets of successful electioneering."[8] The six ballad stanzas, locked together in the perfect rhyme Cummings reserved for satires, divide into three pairs. In each, the advice is not to act but to discuss, comment, admire, equivocate, and finally fail to accomplish anything. The second stanza of the first pair needs quotation marks around "because," "why," "thens," "nows," and "and": paraphrased, it explains that success comes by providing a plethora of rationalizations, by reducing the potential of the past or future (the "thens") to the limits of the present (the "nows"), and by tacking on plenty of extraneous verbiage (the "ands"). The second pair of stanzas urges the vicarious action of the erotic peep show ("drop a penny in the slot") as a replacement for real action, and touts a mindless respect for the traditional ("ancient" Greece) that lauds the safe and unfeeling ("insulated brows") while scorning things of real value by "tossing boms at uncle toms." Here Cummings may have been thinking not only of hypocritical political stances towards the blacks but also of the public neglect of his own ballet based on *Uncle Tom's Cabin* (*Tom*, 1935), which has to date not been staged. The speaker in the last pair appeals for the vote of "all decent mem / and wonens": transposing letters, he mixes up genders in a way that, presumably, could not happen if normal sexual relationships replaced the sodomy suggested here.

Marion, bedridden with a cough, is the subject of "harder perhaps than a newengland bed" (20). Filled with unflattering imagery (hands that "died / squirming," a "gnarled" unself that "vomits a rock of mindscream," and a voice "with the splendor of an angel's fart"), the poem suggests the enforced celibacy overtaking the lovers during the seige of sickness. Watching her lying in the uncomfortably Puritanical "newengland bed," the narrator feels his own voice "darker than a spinster's heart." Yet the "lady's small grin" redeems the situation. With a simply spoken " 'thank you' " for his concern, she sets aside all the harshness of imagery and the potential frigidity of sexual isolation "with more simplicity than makes a world." Unlike a number of Cummings' poems, in which love and the physical expression of affection are intertwined, the power of love here "makes a world" in spite of all difficulties—and in spite of the unpromising language used at the outset. For all its quizzical humor, it marks a new sense of mature marital affection, a sense wholly foreign to the Cummings of the twenties.

Three poems toward the center of the volume share a common interest in form. The first ("six," 21) constructs by a kind of theme-and-variations technique the impressions of a room in which three dancing couples, five flowers, and perhaps a fire in a fireplace are seen as though reflected in various mirrors. The third ("a pretty a day," 23), has a marvelous lyricism which demonstrates the impertinence of paraphrase. It "says" simply that maids are like flowers, men like mowers, and days to be seized. The beauty resides in the music: words, here, are treated more as notes, chiming against each other in delicate tones as the pattern of rhyme and near-rhyme progresses. Between these two is "nouns to nouns" (22), a poem about two nuns in springtime. In the first five stanzas, repetition produces complex patterns: in one-line stanzas the line begins and ends with the same word, and in the two-line stanzas words are repeated vertically. A pattern also emerges in the changes rung on the word which starts as "nouns," becomes "nons" and "nuns," and ends as "known" in "untheknowndulous." For Cummings, "nouns" is a derogatory term: where verbs, as he said elsewhere, are "crisp," nouns are "soggy," and their "agglomeration constitutes the mechanism of Normality," of mere conformity to convention.[9] Locked into such conventionality, these sisters are "wan," again a derogatory term from a poet so deeply interested in color and vitality. But "wan" and "wan" make "too," and these two "nons"—a word best paraphrased as "nothings"—are extraneous, for "too" means "in addition, also," and suggests how thoroughly out of place they are in the lushness of spring. Like Hopkins, who labored to reconcile his asceticism with his sensual response to the "long and lovely and lush" weeds of spring,[10] these nuns experience a season which, "untheknowndulous," is both unknown and undulant, surging with a mysterous life. It is also "singular"; unlike these nuns, who seem to require companionship and can exist only as each other's double, spring is self-existent, single. It is also singularly and intensely itself, in contrast to the nuns' uniformed drabness. And, due to the fracturing of "singular," it is in their eyes perhaps a time of "sin," of an unholy luxuriousness. In such a spring the nuns are "w an d / ering": tainted by the proscribed magic of spring's "wand," they are "erring" in their aimless wanderings. The enjambment of the last word ("s / pring") (which, as John Clendenning has observed, imitates the season which "silently approaches at first and then suddenly bursts into life"[11]) parallels the movement of the whole poem, which starts in excessive restraint and explodes into strangeness. Carefully structured, it moves from the monosyllabic starkness of the first lines to the glorious abandon of a five-syllable nonce-word as the only fitting description of the season.

In contrast to the musicality of these three poems, "these people socalled were not given hearts" (24) is relentless in its logic. Full of conditional clauses introduced by "but if," the poem is largely given over to describing what Cummings in his introduction to *Collected Poems* called "mostpeople." It comes to its conclusion, however, in a brief assertion of "your" and "my" separation from this mass. In a similar way, "as freedom is a breakfastfood" (25) spends most of its length castigating the emptiness of modern society and turns only in its last lines to the salvation implied in "i am for you." Resembling "a pretty a day" in its recurrent syntactical structure, it also recalls "these people socalled" in the density of its statement and in its use of hypothetical impossibilities. As long as "freedom is a breakfast-food" (a typically American product, cheap, synthetic, and basically for the unadult); as long as "truth can live with right and wrong" (by contrast, Cummings explained elsewhere that joy is "a mystery at right angles equally to pain & pleasure,as truth is to fact & fiction");[12] and as long as grand things ("mountains") are minimized into "molehills," then "just so long" will other self-evident contradictions have the appearance of rightness. The same logic recurs in subsequent stanzas. The repeated line ("long enough and just so long") draws closer to the end of the stanza each time, as though ominously reducing the amount left to be said to balance the evident impossibilities articulated in preceding lines. Finally, at the end of stanza 3, the strategy shifts: the line "tomorrow will not be too late," not patently

paradoxical on the order of "as hatracks into peachtrees grow"
or "robins never welcome spring," is only contradictory in context. It also serves to prepare the *carpe diem* theme, which
emerges unmistakably in the final stanza's reference to
"worms," "breasts," "thighs," and "love is the sky and i am for
you."

In poems 28 and 29, Cummings pursues his explorations of
the relation of the individual to society. As Eleanor Sickels has
observed, the sonnet (28) owes its idea that there are only "2½
or . . . 3 / individuals every several fat / thousand years" to
Emerson: "In a century," he wrote in *The American Scholar*,
"in a millennium, one or two men; that is to say, one or two ap-
proximations to the right state of every man."[13] If, says the narrator here, "something more small occurs" than the current
state of "mankind," then "i'll kiss a stalinist arse / in hitler's window. . . ." As in "red-rag and pink-flag" and "the way to hump
a cow is not," the purpose here is more than obscenity: just as
"the hitler lies down with the cohn" to produce the pseudo-
utopian "Ever-Ever Land" (*New Poems*, 4), so here the only
way to produce a state worse than the present one would be for
the warring ideologies of the twentieth century to come
together—and for the poets and individuals to do obeisance to
them. Contemporary political events may figure here: the poem
was published in the January 1940 *Furioso*, only three months
after Germany and Russia had agreed to divide Poland between
them. In 1940 the specter of an alliance between these two
powers may have seemed less improbable than it could in later
years.

Probing similar themes, "anyone lived in a pretty how town"
(29) creates a different diction for its parable of individuality
hounded by Babbitry. Avoiding topical reference to political
events, the poem also avoids proper names. The "pretty how
town" in which the nonhero lives is, by rearrangement, "how

pretty a town." More significantly, however, it is "pretty" in a superficial way, as he used the word in "O Distinct" (*Tulips and Chimneys*, "Amores," VII) for the consciously trite and conventional. And it is a town focused on the "how," the method and rule, of things, as he used the word in the phrase "loud most howish time" (*No Thanks*, 37). Stripped of originality, the town tinkles with bells and watches the seasons pass in a kind of stupor. Meanwhile, the protagonist ("anyone") "sang his didn't" and "danced his did," entering heartily into things both unpleasant and pleasant. The aptness of Cummings' choice of pronouns as names is evident in such lines as "they cared for anyone not at all": not caring for him, the townspeople also cared for nobody at all in their loveless selfishness. Sowing nonexistence ("their isn't"), they "reaped their same." Reaping the same thing they sowed, as the Apostle Paul assured us they would, they also harvested a sameness, a dull conformity, from their crop of negations. The town's children sense the love of the character "noone" (no one) for "anyone." But they also sense that nobody loved anybody in this town, and like the children in the slightly foreboding poems of Cummings' earlier "Chansons Innocentes," they grow up into forgetful adulthood.

Repeating throughout the poem the pattern of the first three stanzas—a quatrain devoted to "anyone" followed by one on the townspeople and a third on the children—the poet returns, in stanza 4, to the relation of "anyone" and "noone." On the analogy of the later phrases "side by side" and "little by little," he sets up similar terms ("more by more," "when by now," "tree by leaf") which function in complex ways in describing the lovers' feelings. Where "side by side" evoked two separate entities united by the word "by," and "little by little" suggested progress through accretion, "more by more" takes on overtones of both of these as a variation of the expected "more and more." In this way Cummings wrings multiple senses out of single phrases, compelling the tale to say, as good parables must, many things in few words. The phrase "someones married their everyones" suggests the French *tout le monde,* which, literally meaning all the world, or everyone, actually comes to mean *those who really matter:* the real "someones" of the town married, and "everyone" was there to see. Significantly, "anyone" and "noone" never marry, never involve themselves in what, for Cummings, is too much the "candy" and "cellophane" institution suggested in "this little bride & groom are" (*New Poems,* 8). In contrast to the humane and sympathetic "noone," who "laughed his joy" and "cried his grief," the townspeople "laughed their cryings," covering deep feeling in a shallow joviality. Then they "said their nevers" (their negations of prayer) and "slept their dream"—while the lovers, rather than sleeping right through their dreams, "dream their sleep" into something much more than mere unconsciousness.

The last three stanzas break from the rest with the authorial intrusion of "one day anyone died i guess." Far more than a needed slant-rhyme for the word "face," the phrase "i guess" presents narrator as raconteur. Suddenly deciding that the tale he is spinning needs to be drawn to a close, he emphasizes thereby its purely fictional, and therefore allegorical, character. He tells us that the "busy folk" of the town bury the lovers "side by side" and (as they progressively forget this example of tenderness and caring) "little by little." The narrator then takes off on a flight of inventiveness which, producing strange mutations of these phrases, ultimates in grand affirmation:

> all by all and deep by deep
> and more by more they dream their sleep
> noone and anyone earth by april
> wish by spirit and if by yes.

The last stanza concludes with the children, who "forget to remember / with up so floating many bells down." They have become the "Women and men(both dong and ding)," conventional people like the "dingsters" who, several poems earlier, "die at break of dong" (25). Unchanged by what they have witnessed, they "went their came" without altering course. The refrain of bells, seasons, and weathers echoing through the stanzas recalls a similar metaphor in Dylan Thomas' "I see the boys of summer," where

> seasons must be challenged, or they totter
> Into a chiming quarter
> Where, punctual as death, we ring the stars.[14]

In Thomas' poem the feisty boys at least gave the lie to social conformity. Here the children simply grow up to accept the circularity of seasons, habitual changes in weather, repetitions of bells, and, by implication, the tradition of lovelessness. Even the form, which gives every third stanza to the townspeople, dictates that this nine-stanza poem is to end not with "anyone" and "noone" but with "dong and ding," not with the bang of exemplary self-sacrifice but with the whimper of timid decorum.

If this parable presents a nonhero, the other justly famous poem in the volume—"my father moved through dooms of love"—presents a figure expressly heroic. Like "anyone lived," it too is introduced by a poem ("one slipslouch twi," 33) which anticipates some of its themes and prepares the way. The song by a black guitar player is about "dis / dumdam slamslum slopp / idy wurl"—this sloppy world, which evidently needs redemption. The singer can only note its existence; he has no power to save it. His attitude is one of laissez faire: "it's their pain [or payin']," reads the last stanza in transcription, "theirs and nobody else's, and it's their joy." He admits the world's wickedness; but who, he asks, can hate it? His dialect introduces further meanings: asking "hooz / gwine ter / hate / dad hurt / fool wurl," he asks also who can hate Dad—a question answered without hesitation in the following poem.

What the entertainer could only point at, the father can overcome. The world, in "my father moved through dooms of love" (34), needs redemption: it is a place of "scheming" and "passion," of stealing, cruelty, fear, and doubt, and of "maggoty minus and dumb death." Unlike some of Cummings' poems, however, this one emphasizes not primarily this corruption but the nature of the individual who redeems it. And unlike other poems, this one presents an individual who finds answers not in transcendent escape but in direct engagement and correction of the world's wrong. It is a poem about love. But like the Gospels—in which the word "love" appears with surprising infrequency—the poem does not so much explain as demonstrate. Defining the attributes of love not in exposition but through narrative, it echoes the technique of the Gospel writers by showing how love is exemplified in the works of a single man. Fittingly, the word "love" occurs only twice in the poem—in the first and last lines.

Commentators have generally assumed that the poem is biographical. That Cummings had deep respect for his own father is born out by their voluminous correspondence in the decade between Cummings' graduation and his father's death in 1926. Too independent to be merely submissive, and too affectionate to be merely rebellious, Cummings shows himself sometimes bemused at his father's advice, sometimes bristling at its implications, and consistently friendly and appreciative. The tone of the letters resembles that of the affectionate portrait of his father in Cummings' first Harvard non-lecture in 1953. There he elevates his father to the status of Renaissance man, marking first his skills in the practical arts ("a crack shot & a famous fly-fisherman," a woodsman, taxidermist, carpenter, and plumber) and then his talents as professor, preacher, and public servant. Noting that acting was one of his hobbies, he observes that "my father's voice was so magnificent that he was called on to impersonate God speaking from Beacon Hill."[15] The father in the lecture and the poem is indeed a godlike man. But whether he is more closely allied to the real-life model than any of America's folk heroes are to their originals is a matter best left to biographers. Certainly the poem describes in some ways the Reverend Edward Cummings. Essentially, however, it describes qualities of feeling and habits of mind which have fathered Cummings' own mental set. Not simply recording the ideals of a real man, the poet chooses to embody his own highest ideals in a fictionalized character, describe him in action, and claim a sonship with him which makes clear his own intellectual and spiritual heritage.

This lower-case poem is divided into four parts, each marked with an initial capital. But, like a fifteen-line sonnet—and like its larger-than-life hero—the poem exceeds itself, and is perhaps best described as a sixteen-stanza piece that has seventeen stanzas. The first three groups of four stanzas blend seasonal reference (from "april" through "midsummer's" into "octobering") with images of growth (from birth through strength and into harvest). The first stanza of each of these parts defines what his father moved through and sets out the subjects for the stanzas immediately following: "dooms of love" (stanza one), "griefs of joy" (stanza five), and "dooms of feel" (stanza nine). In each part, three stanzas describe the father, while the fourth focuses on his effect on those around him. Toward the end of the third part the seasonal metaphor accelerates: the harvest imagery of stanza 12 ends with the "snow" of winter. By stanza 13—the beginning of the fourth part, in which we might have expected winter imagery—spring has already come. The strategy then shifts quickly, reducing the description of his father to one stanza and following it by the four-stanza climax which, delineating the characteristics of the world he wars against, ultimates in grand affirmation.

Where some of Cummings' poems are aggressively complex and others patently simple, this one erects a smooth facade which, significant in itself, reverberates inside with more profound meaning. Apparently simple, it nevertheless rewards close reading. The phase "moved through," as Lane rightly notes, "means 'travelled amidst,' 'passed beyond,' 'was animated by,' and 'expressed himself by means of.' "[16] So "my father moved through dooms of love" suggests not only that he espoused love as his fate or fortune but also that he overcame the notion of love as his demise. Similar multiplicity of meaning surrounds "sames of am," "haves of give," and "depths of height," each of which can mean something positive which he welcomes and something negative which he resists: "sames of am," for example, suggests both a slavish conformity and a wonderful consistency, one of which he would overcome and the other embrace. In his presence, "this . . . where" turns to "here," and "that if" (a conditional sense of things which is "so timid" that by contrast "air is firm") begins to "stir" with life. His "april touch" awakens the lethargic and comforts the sorrowing: and "no smallest voice" would cry in vain (and, as Lane observes, with vanity) to this man who, one with nature, redeems the meek while deflating the proud. A story of creation, the first stanzas parallel Genesis while overturning *The Waste Land*. Assembling a number of words echoing the first six lines of Eliot's poem ("forgetful," "stir," "april," "roots," "unburied," and "sleeping"), Cummings reverses the thrust of Eliot's despair and restores April to its more traditional place. With stanzas 14 the poet shifts into a denser syntax. As though to slow us down and insist on our attentiveness—as though to prevent us from hastening in with our own preconceptions about meaning—Cummings describes the world of evil in a compact and eliptical style:

> then let men kill which cannot share,
> let blood and flesh be mud and mire,
> scheming imagine, passion willed,
> freedom a drug that's bought and sold
>
> giving to steal and cruel kind
> a heart to fear, to doubt a mind. . . .

The first couplet is clear. Thereafter words must be inserted regularly: let men, scheming and willed by passion, imagine that freedom is a drug; let them imagine that giving is to steal, that cruel is kind, that a heart is made to fear and a mind made to doubt. Let them imagine that the world is really as bad as the poet described it in "as freedom is a breakfastfood" (25) or "(of Ever-Ever Land i speak" (*New Poems*, 4). Let them imagine what they will: for "though hate were why men breathe"—the summary phrase for these lesser and more specific evils—the point is not these imagined lies but the reality of love. It is not an abstract love. It is not, as it was not in the poem to his mother ("if there are any heavens," *ViVa*, XLIII), a "pansy heaven." It is a love embodied in the works of a man who "lived his soul," not of those who, like the townspeople in "anyone lived in a pretty how town," "slept their dream." Not the stuff of romantic attachments, it is the love which, in the New Testament, is the basis of Christianity and which is the only explanation for the events reported there. Here, as there, the validation for the final absolute statement—"love is the whole and more than all"—is the particularity of the life already described.

Most of the remaining poems develop themes raised in "my father moved through dooms of love": individuality, love, and redemption from the world's assertive evils. The portrait of "goldberger" ("i say no world," 36) describes a Jewish tailor in terms which leave little doubt about the poet's sympathy for this remarkable individual. Eschewing the world of ready-to-wear, Goldberger resists, thereby, the wholesale conformity of "mostpeople." A poem demanding some attentive reading (lines 10 through 27, for example, record the tailor's rushed and gnomic speech), it was apparently too profound for the rabble of commentators who, in a 1951 issue of *Congress Weekly,* ignored it as they lambasted Cummings for a fancied anti-Semitism.[17] Another sort of individuality—the "eachness" of aerialists who blend into "ex / quisite theys" during their performance—draws praise in "mortals)" (48). "These extraordinary creatures," wrote Cummings in a letter, "appear together on the tanbark as mere 'mortals'(like you or me)but then 'climbing' up high 'into eachness begin' their amazing 'trapeze' act—becoming 'things'-which-'swing' & turning 'somersaults' & 'swoop'ing far away only to 'exquisite'ly 'return'—& afterwards 'drop' into a net 'fall'-ing with 'dreamlike'grace . . . transformed from 'mortals' into 'im'mortals because they risked their lives to create something beautiful. Finally they all disappear into the place from which they appeared;just as the last syllable '(im' of my poem goes back to the first word 'mortals.' "[18]

Relating individuality to love, poem 49 ("i am so glad and very") emphasizes the power of love to enrich the individual: "i am through you so i." For love, as he says in "hate blows a bubble of despair into" (43), is what "makes the little thickness of the coin"; an interesting study in the strategy of his sonnets, this poem starts bravely enough in the metaphors of its octave but goes to pieces in the sestet. Two very good love poems, however, are "love is the every only god" and "love is more thicker than forget." The latter (42) is a carefully proportioned lyric whose ideas are conveyed in a succession of one-line state-

ments. Like "as freedom is a breakfastfood" in technique, it
demands that the reader pause over every line, each of which finally yields up significant meaning. The third stanza, for example, describes love as "less always than to win"—less permanent than goals or successes, a statement in accord with the
poet's preference for *making* over *having*. It is "less never than
alive" (more permanent than life) and "less bigger than the least
begin"—smaller, and so more fundamental and basic, than the
tiniest beginning. And being "less littler than forgive," it is
larger than mere pardon, presumably because love does not
simply overlook but completely undoes the offense. Playing on
the syntax of the adage that blood is thicker than water, the
poet capitalizes on the typically hyperbolic language of love
poems, so working it to his advantage that he is able to say, with
some freshness, such common things as that love is "deeper
than the sea" and "higher than the sky." Cummings makes a
similar point in the unabashedly Christian "love is the every
only god" (38), which needs some rearranging in order to make
it paraphrasable. The third and fourth stanzas, restored to standard word order and punctuation, read: "for love, 'beginning'
means 'return': seas, who could sing one queerying wave so
deep and strong, will whitely yearn from each last shore and
home come young." Seas, sending their waves out like radar
pulses, will bounce them off the far shore; yearning for their
place of origin, the waves will come home again as fresh and un-
dissipated as when they left. Breaking "whitely" into foam, the
waves will also be white-haired with age; but the homecoming
will restore their youth. Hence what appears as a "beginning"—
as a new wave breaking on the shore—is only a "return" of a
wave from another shore. For "beginning means return," as
must be the case in a universe which, eternal and forever preex-
isting, could have had no beginning. This metaphysical point is
brought to earth in the last lines, which assure the lover that

every star, incomplete in itself, "completes its brightness with your eyes."

The world needing redemption is charted in "denied night's face" (39), where the "shadowless they" of mob conformity destroys all individual things. The answer to the "grey snow / of mothery same" is, once again, the power of the individual, the "i" or "sun of whom" who, like the Son of Man, comes to save the world. The sonnet following ("a peopleshaped toomany-ness far too," 40) cries out in disgust at the "notalive undead toonearishness" of the same mob. Perhaps a reaction against the ugliness of city life in the winter, the poet turns to what is becoming his standard solution: since the lust for "having" and for material gain plagues humanity, "we'll / not have . . . and we'll make." And what we will make is "yes," the affirmative word of concord which, for Cummings as for Molly Bloom, is "the only living thing." The volume ends, typically, with a sonnet ("what freedom's not some under's mere above," 50) tying up these various themes. Its first line states the Hermetic argument (as above, so below) with a deft twist. Playing on paradoxes and impossibilities ("does mask wear face?have singings gone to say?"), the poet again engages in the strategy of asking how bad the world has become and offering his own antidote in consolation. Occasionally the language is dense: "any was a glove / but i'm and you are actual either hand" suggests that "any," a word which indiscriminately describes similar things, was merely the conventional conformity hiding the real life beneath. But the poem ends with a statement both lucid in its structure and typical in its assertion of the relationship between love, individuality, and the natural universe of "under" things which reflect things "above":

> nor a first rose explodes but shall increase
> whole truthful infinite immediate us.

Chapter 9

1x1

With the publication of *1 x 1* [One Times One] in 1944, Cummings' format returns to the explicit divisions that marked his first four books of poetry. The fifty-four poems in this volume are grouped into three sections, titled "1," "X," and "1," and arranged in progressive seasonal imagery. The sixteen poems of the first section begin with images of autumn and loss and continue with satires and diatribes against what man has made of man. The two final poems, Janus-like, both summarize the first section and anticipate the change of tone to come; still urging us to "beware of heartless them," they add a note of affirmation in suggesting salvation through love and natural beauty. The second section, introduced by a poem about snowflakes, develops a winter imagery, but treats winter less as a season of harshness than of stillness, recuperation, and consolidation. Where the temper of the first section was characterized by sardonic reaction to external events, the mood here turns toward contemplative introspection; and where the first section remained impersonal, the last nine poems in "X" are about the "us" who are lovers. The section closes with metaphors drawn from a "wintry" landscape where "all ignorance toboggans into know." Again the last poem anticipates, in its recurrent line "but if a look should april me," the spring that will follow. The imagery of the third section, which opens with a poem about a tiny white-petaled plant, embraces spring, birds, flowers, and greenness. The mood here tends toward the exultant, with poems of love and praise predominating.

While using this seasonal framework as a strategy for organization, Cummings was not enslaved by it: several poems in the second section ("dead every enormous piece" and "when god decided to invent" come to mind) seem equally at home among the satires in the first section. Generally, however, the sense of direction here is more evident than in earlier volumes, which either had no obvious structural scheme (as in *50 Poems*) or a pattern of recurrent sonnets (as in *ViVa* and *No Thanks*) sometimes more ingenious than helpful. The volume demonstrates that Cummings, having outgrown the simpler divisions ("Post Impressions," "Portraits," "Sonnets—Realities," and so forth) in the original manuscript of *Tulips and Chimneys*, now focuses his discernment more finely. Earlier, for example, his "Portraits" sections lumped together descriptions of disparate character types, setting poems of praise side by side with satiric barbs. In *1 x 1* he also describes individuals: the "blond / job," "mr u," "old mr lyman," Sam Ward, the Greek flower-seller, and others. But their common denominator as portraits no longer justifies their being grouped together, and they now appear in different sections according to message, mood, or metaphor. Cummings' antipathy for floozies and literary opportunists leads him to include the first two among his satires; his respect for Yankee self-reliance places the next two in the second section; the imagery of flowers qualifies the latter for the final section.

This same sense of direction underlies the mathematical metaphor suggested in the title. The closing poem of the first section ("one's not half two. It's two are halves of one:") treats "one" as the sum of halves. The closing poem of the final section, ending "we're wonderful one times one," advances from addition to multiplication in what is metaphysically an even more interesting analogy for the oneness of two individuals. Behind these poems lies Cummings' evident interest in arithmetic significance. Throughout his work he pays great attention to numbers, letting them determine the formats of some of his volumes and founding some of the poems on a strict counting of lines and even, at times, of syllables. This volume, in fact—the work of a poet generally thought of as rebelling against the restraint of reason—includes no completely free verse. Even poems whose lines appear most casual—"a-," for example, or "ygUDuh"—are arranged in stanzas. It is perhaps this achievement of design in matters large and small which leads Friedman to assess *1 x 1* as "a distinctively crystallized book, both in art and in vision—a highly-wrought and mature achievement."[1] Where the earlier Cummings was satisfied by gathering poems into self-contained sections, the poet here interweaves the sections themselves, anticipates and recalls their images, and appears to conceive of the volume less as a bricked accretion than as a fluid whole.

The volume opens with "nonsun blob a." While complex, it is hardly as troublesome as some commentators have thought. The poem, listed among Cummings' notes under the heading of "Portraits—Nature,"[2] makes good sense when seen simply as a brief description of a cloud-covered day in late autumn. The "blob" of "nonsun," sticking coldly to the "skylessness," describes the sun's appearance faintly discerned through overcast. The syntax of the second stanza, truncated and compressed in now-familiar ways, suggests that "my birds, your birds, our birds are one and all gone away." No longer seen as individuals, the birds have conformed to the demands of migration, gathered themselves into flocks, and merged their identities into "the they," the amorphous mass analogous to the undifferentiated crowds of what Cummings earlier called "mostpeople." All that remains are a few scattering leaves: transposed, the final stanza simply reads "some few ghosts of leaf creep here or there on unearth." The poem nicely captures the congealed chill of late autumn—the sense of slowed motion, of emptiness, of the loss of things bright and cheering and colorful. Sobering in itself, this loss is more serious as metaphor for a greater deprivation, that of individuality.

Significantly, the term signaling this loss—"they"—is repeated in similar usages in the two following poems. In "neither could say" (ii) the "my" and "your" of the first poem become the "they," the two lovers who, weighed down by this general atrophy, lose love without even knowing why it has gone. Confusion of syntax nicely parallels the confused thinking and feeling that dooms this relationship. The situation is "not false not true"; the blame is not to be put on "you" nor "i"; yet the end clearly has come. Autumn as a time of harvest justifies the placement of "it's over a(see just" (iii), in which the real culprit is "someone called they." A curious and intriguing parable based on the tale of Adam, Eve, and apple, it suggests more than it specifies about the way temptation is rationalized and justified. The apples here are "gravensteins," a name Cummings chose perhaps for its inclusion of the words "grave" (as in serious, or dead) and "graven" (as in images). They are, paradoxically, both "as red as to lose" and "as round as to find": although symbolizing spherical perfection and completeness in their shape, they are of a color associated with devils and destructive violence. The middle group of three stanzas, which begins with a capital and ends with a period, tells the tale of temptation and fall. The tempters here are not snakes but leaves, and the gist of their argument is the inevitability of sin: "what must . . . be must / be." The second and third stanzas present other arguments: that *doing* ("you're he as to do") is what individualizes while *dying* ("you're which as to die") is the attribute of the impersonal "which," and that stealing is more lively than giving. These persuasions convince "our thief," the "you" and "i" of the poem, to go over the wall. And for this sin "someone called they / made him pay with his now." Seizing the moment, in other words, results in immediate punishment—a significant point when raised by an author famous for *carpe diem* poems. The final stanza, beginning anew with a capitalized "But," tells the other side: if temptation is resisted and the apples left unpicked, they "fall / with a kind of a blind / big sound on the ground." To pluck the fruit is to incur the wrath, not of God, but of "they," of outraged social convention; to leave it is to watch it fall unused and wasted. The frustration at such a world recalls that of Hardy's Jude, railing against the injustices of both nature and society, and damned whichever side he espouses. Cummings, however, locates the cause of such injustice not in a mechanistic and indifferent deity but in the traditions and notions of men. The poem is a parable on the nature of temptation: plucking fruit may or may not be wrong, depending on the circumstances.

Hereafter the bulk of the poems in the first section are satires, appropriately introduced by "of all the blessings which to man" (iv). This poem is almost archetypal in its inclusion of the now-standard objects of Cummings' loathing: the "collective pseudobeast" of society, the "scienti / fic land of supernod" where "only man is god," and man as the "an / imal without a heart." It is also typical of his satires in its sing-song ballad stanza and ludicrously forced rhymes. Its target is "kind progress," the sort of polite and conventional improvements in creature comfort that reduce man to a thing "so kind it wouldn't like a soul / and couldn't use a mind." Two of the satires concern the war with Japan. Typically, however, the barbs are directed not at the declared enemy but at the hawkish and burtal ignorance of Cummings' own countrymen. The first, "ygUDuh" (vii), needs only transliteration to make plain the viewpoints in this

pothouse argument. " 'You got to!' 'You don't!' 'You understand'
. . . ," the poem begins. It ends with the grimly ironic reason
for the war—"Them goddam little bastards, we're going to CIV-
ILIZE them!"—where the verb implies something a good deal
more violent. The other war poem ("plato told," XIII), a nice
balance of stanzas and punctuation marks, is also an astute comment on the purposes of war. Plato has warned us against war;
so has Jesus, Lao-tsze (the founder of Taoism), and General
Sherman ("War at best is barbarism"); and so have "you," "i,"
and "we." But "he"—the professional war-maker akin to the
"trig / westpointer most succinctly bred" (*ViVa*, XXX) and allied
to all the other war-loving soldiers and politicians in Cummings'
earlier poems—refuses to heed the warning. What finally convinced him—and destroyed him—was "a nipponized bit of / the
old sixth / avenue / el;in the top of his head." Scrap steel from
this demolished elevated railroad in New York, which had been
sold to the Japanese, was now being returned as pieces of shrap-
nel: and it managed to penetrate where no merely verbal argument could. To judge by a letter referring to this poem some
twelve years later, Cummings viewed this irony as a just punishment. "When 'America' cheered wildly for Finland," he
writes to his German translator, "while secretly selling gasoline
to Russia so Its tanks could murder Finns,I ceased to be—in
the only true sense,that is spiritually—an 'American.' "[3]

The spiritual revulsion against America also finds articulation
in poems directed against other aspects of the nation. Roosevelt
("who always nothing says") and Churchill come in for their
share of criticism in "it was a goodly co" (XII), a poem surmised
by one commentator to be about the meeting that produced the
Atlantic Charter in 1941.[4] Political rhetoric, so precisely characterized in " 'next to of course god america i" (*is* 5, "Two," III),
comes in for an even more condensed comment in "applaws)"
(VIII). The division of the phrase *fellow citizens* " 'fell / ow / sit /

isn'ts' ") into words suggesting falling, pain, immobility, and negation is paralleled by the suggestion of animality in the pause—"(a paw s"—following the speaker's introduction. In "a salesman is an it that stinks Excuse / Me" (IX), Cummings berates those salesmen who, along with "snakeoil" and "vac / uumcleaners," also hawk "hate," "terror," and "democracy." And two short epigrams lambast politicians in general: "a politician is an arse upon" (X) and "mr u" (XI). The latter is directed at the anthologist Louis Untermeyer, who managed to include in his editions not only his own but also his wife's poetry.

Just as the section began with three poems introducing the body of satires, so it ends with three that, in various ways, summarize the section and look forward to the next. Most notable is the well-known sonnet beginning "pity this busy monster,manunkind, / not" (XIV). This unkind man (the word originally meant unnatural), finding that "Progress is a comfortable disease," evokes no pity after all. Noting recent advances in technology (through which a razor blade under an electron microscope appears a mountain range) and in theoretical physics (where the space-time continuum, or "wherewhen," is found to be curved and to return on itself), this man, playing god, is playing with "the bigness of his littleness." Pity, says the narrator, the elements of the natural world over which this man has such disastrous command; but surely, he notes with heavy irony, there is no need to pity this "fine speciman of hypermagical / ultraomnipotence." Central to our understanding of the poem are the final lines. The narrator, identifying himself as one of "We doctors" who are capable of identifying a hopeless case of inhumanity, addresses us in a kind of aside: "listen:there's a hell / of a good universe next door:let's go." The line break parallels that of the first line: each calls attention to a condition reversed by the continuing syntax, so that the imperative "pity" is countermanded and the word "hell" is seen to be merely an intensifier of something good. In each case, however, we are left with a significance which, although denied by syntax, is affirmed by context. We *are* to pity such a state of man, for the situation he is in now—as well as the one next door—may well be "hell." Cummings the man is not to be confused with the doctor-narrator here. Like Cummings, the narrator scorns "manunkind"; but Cummings would hardly counsel a simple-minded escape to another "universe next door" as an answer. The problem, as he perceived it, was not merely in places but in attitudes. Even through interplanetary travel those attitudes could hardly be escaped, especially in a situation where space curves in upon itself and brings such travels, ironically, back to their point of origin. Perhaps, however, the "universe next door" refers to the next sections of *1 x 1*, where attitudes do change and possibilities for redemption do occur.

Such, at least, is the promise offered by the masterful sonnet concluding the section, "one's not half two. It's two are halves of one" (XVI). A love poem, it draws its mathematical metaphor out to suggest that the two lovers, as "halves reintegrating," become one in a union surviving both death and mere human quantification. Cummings here takes over an ideal central to Christian monotheism: that oneness, "the song which fiends and angels sing," is the salient attribute of Deity. Dualism, the contrary view, is a mortal invention. Jesus spoke of the devil as "a liar and the father of it" (John 8:44); this poem, noting that "all murdering lies by mortals told make two," equates such lies with dualism. We lovers, "by a gift called dying born," experience a kind of rebirth also taught by Jesus. We "must grow," in deep darkness, "least ourselves"—least like the old man which Christianity urges us to put off. Alternatively, but with the same ultimate effect, we must grow "deep in dark least" (deep in the dark negation, the *leastness*, of this dying) into our real selves. In any case we must remember that "love only rides his year," that love alone is the governing power in its own existence. The result is the simply stated "All lose,whole find." Losing allness—the sense of quantity that would build completeness out of a sum of parts and a totting up of "numerable mosts"—we find the "actual more" of perfect reintegrated wholeness. Here, too, Jesus' words are not inappropriate: "He that loveth his life shall lose it; and he that hateth his life in this world shall keep it unto life eternal" (John 12:25). For Cummings, the "life eternal" involved real love; and the "life in this world," especially as depicted in the satires of this first section, might after all not be so hard to lose.

The first poem of the second section ("one(Floatingly)arrive," XVII) describes the arrival of snowflakes. These snowflakes are "vivid anonymous / mythical guests of Is"—the primary verb of being—and they bring "a whole / verbal adventure" to the "dull / all nouns" of the world. So the poem is also about poetry. Like snowflakes, verbs are active and evanescent. Without them the things of the world, represented by nouns, are dull. The "verbal adventure" of poetry, then, only happens when the nouns are overlayed by the verbs that arrive silently, a few at a time, in the process of poetic inspiration.

Snow, here, is a peaceful process; but in one of the central poems of the book—"what if a much of a which of a wind" (XX)—it is a symbol of devastation that "flays," "strangles," and "stifles." The three stanzas parallel one another in developing a single argument: let the worst happen, let everything go to smash, argues the poet, and man's immortality will still survive. Cummings occasionally writes poems whose roots reach out and draw sustenance from many other poems in his canon: this is one. It recalls the much quieter one addressed to his lady in the middle of this section beginning "let it go" (XXIX). Asking "what if . . . wind / gives the truth to summer's lie," the poem begins with imagery of the onset of autumn, when red leaves blown helter-skelter bloody the sun. "Blow king to beggar" suggests Shakespeare's Lear, an allusion made specific in the following poem, which ends with "the five nevers of a lear" (XXI). Lear, himself victim of a storm such as this, is reduced to beggarly status and ends his life with a speech including the line "Never, never, never, never, never!" Cummings balances the phrase "Blow king to beggar" with "blow queen to seem," as though to suggest that even so fixed a reality as royalty is reduced to mere illusion by such a storm—as, indeed, Lear's majesty seemed often illusory on the heath. The wind also operates in a physical way on the words here: in "blow friend to fiend," it blows the *r* away to create the opposite. Let these things come, says the poet: "the single secret will still be man," the individual who, inhabiting a transcendent universe ("tomorrow is our permanent address," as he says a few poems later), is unscathed by the vicissitudes of a merely physical universe.

Just as the first stanza moved from summer to autumn, so the second moves from winter to spring. Beginning with a description of physical devastation, the stanza invokes the worst sort of mental depravity: "blow pity to envy and soul to mind." But though compassion shades off into jealousy and intuition into mere rationality, those "whose hearts are mountains, roots are trees"—who are at one with nature—will survive and "cry hello to the spring." The seasonal metaphor concluded, the poet moves beyond the earthly into the cosmic in the final stanza. What if the beginning of the end of the dream of earthly existence destroys the entire universe and, harrowing hell, "peels forever out of his grave / and sprinkles nowhere with me and you?" We continue to live, even though the universe is bitten "in two," and "never" is blown into "twice"—even though the "single secret" of man is transformed into a dualism. The line recalls the imagery of dualism in "one's not half two," a poem which directly preceded this one in its first appearance in *Poetry* (July 1943). Another line from that earlier poem—"we by a gift called dying born"—seems to lie behind the last line here: "the most who die,the more we live." We who die the most, who experience the worst that this universe can hand us, live all the more. Involving Christian ideas, the poem deals with them only in a thematic way; avoiding direct reference or allusion to the Bible, it nevertheless is informed throughout with a Christian eschatology.

The sonnet "no man,if men are gods;but if gods must" (XXII), an indifferent piece with an interesting rhyme scheme, illustrates the dangers of self-parody. The idea that the "depths of horror" need to be "solved" like a troublesome equation is the only spark in these lines, which are withal too damp to ignite. The following three poems address themselves in various theoretical ways to love. Love is a spring on a mountain (XXIII) and a meeting of strangers (XXIV); it is also an act of intercourse performed by "what over" and "which under" (XXV), which is redeemed from merely hollow sensuality (where "dolls clutching their dolls wallow") and from fearful obscenity by the "beautiful most is now" of fulfilment. The tone changes with "when god decided to invent" (XXVI), one of the most deft of Cummings' short poems. God, says the first stanza, invented everything in one huge breath, the spirit or *pneuma* which, as Jesus said, "bloweth where it listeth" (John 3:8) and is the creative force mentioned in Genesis 1:2. Man, however, "determined to destroy / himself." To do so, he "picked the was / of shall": he chose (or, as did Eve, plucked) the past tense of future promise—history rather than prophecy, the dead in place of the vital. All he found was "why," a mystery. And given his penchant for the scientific and his revulsion at uncertainty, he "smashed it into because": he forced upon natural mystery a comprehensible cause, explaining away everything. Man destroys himself, that is, not by physical weapons but by mental attitudes, by a brutal self-will that will not "let it go" and accept love (XXIX) but instead insists on rationalization.

The two poems that follow portray denizens of the Joy Farm area. "Old Mr. Lyman" is a character appearing in *Adventures in Value* (1962), a book of photographs by Marion Morehouse with text by Cummings; he is also the subject of "old mr ly" (XXVII). In *Adventures in Value* Cummings writes that "During fifty years he worked—when loafing wasn't mankind's sole aim—hard & well,on behalf of a railroad which no longer feigns existence" (IV, 6). Lyman stands for a complex of values that the country and the individual maintain in contrast to the city and the mob: " 'this world's made 'bout / right it's the people that / abuses it,' " says Lyman in this poem, and the poet in *Adventures in Value* welcomes the opportunity to refresh himself, "when urbs has murdered me," by strolling through Lyman's barn. The other portrait, cast in the local Yankee dialect, is a tribute to Sam Ward, for many decades the caretaker at Joy Farm.

Like "man" in "when god decided to invent," the "maid" and "man" in "Hello is what a mirror says" (XXX) assign meanings to objects around them which in themselves convey no meanings. Answering a request from an inquirer puzzled by this poem, Cummings wrote, "all a mirror says is *Hello*:nothing more. It's a young girl who,looking in it & seeing her reflection,asks *Who*(can this be)?" Similarly, the man with the gun, because he is "full-of-hate," adds meaning to the weapon. Seeing the good, he will "curse the living something" and kill. If he kills "in a socalled war,the killer will suppose he's triumphed over an 'enemy.' He doesn't realize that *true wars are never won*;since they are inward,not outward,and necessitate facing one's self."[5] The commonplace incident of a girl looking in a mirror, then, betrays an attitude which, seemingly harmless, is the same one that engenders war. Once again Cummings insists that it is thought, not things, that determines our individual and collective experiences.

Like the opening poems of 50 Poems, 1 x 1, and 95 Poems, "a- / float on some" (XXXI) is a brief impression of a natural event seen sharply, presented in a slender and fragmented form. It introduces a sequence of love poems. Nearly all of them are addressed directly to the lover, and they abound in such appellatives as "dear," "my loveliest," "my lovely," and "darling!" This first poem is about a crescent moon, "an in / -ch / of an if," visually signified by the isolated parenthesis in line 13. A symbol of promise—a crescent moon at dusk is on the wax—it is, paradoxically, "more / dream than become" (more a figment of imagination than a promise of some future reality), yet "more / am than imagine"—more a part of individual being and identity than of imagination. The same moon appears in the following poem, "i've come to ask you if there isn't a" (XXXII). Here the crescent will "be a canoe / and a whole world and then a single hair / again" as it waxes and wanes, proving that "everything beautiful can grow."

Several of the sonnets in this sequence address themselves to the more metaphysical issue of love. In "nothing false and possible is love" (XXXIV), the "possible" is the "false," while the "imagined" is the "limitless" and hence the real. Love bears the same relation to "giving" as "give" does to keeping ("love's to giving as to keeping's give"). Love, then, is the source of giving, as giving is the source of keeping; so loving transcends mere giving. And "as yes is to if"—as the definite affirmative is to the conditional—so "love is to yes." Must, however, the word for obligations and entanglements, is "a schoolroom in the month of may," a trap, an irrelevancy that substitutes humanly devised education for nature's teaching. There, "all now turns when" as the vitality of the present is subsumed into mere history. Love, on the other hand, is "a universe / beyond obey," beyond the necessity for adherence to such commands. It is also (and here the poet enters an entirely different order of thinking) beyond "reality or un-." That love far exceeds giving, affirmation, and duty is only to say that love either reverses these things or outruns them on the same scale; to say that it is beyond both reality and unreality, however, is to declare for love an entirely different order of existence. Such transcendence is an idea that shimmers at the fringes of much of his later poetry. Having touched on it here, he moves back to the more conventional metaphors, praying that we will "continue to outgrow" ourselves. For only if we have known all our "mosts," or achievements and capabilities, can we "begin to guess" at our "least"— at the things we lack, or at the humble simplicity which worldly achievement ignores.

The metaphysics is refined in "true lovers in each happening of their hearts" (xxxvi). This slant-rhymed Shakespearean sonnet suggests that even such opposites as fear and hope, "doubts" and "certainties," are figments of "the mere mind's poor pretend," the dream that appears to deluded humanity as real life. Only love "immortally occurs beyond the mind," in a universe quite apart from the temporality of "duration." As in "what if a much of a which of a wind," the lovers here are proof against catastrophe: they would grow "even more true" if "out of midnight dropped more suns than are." And "even if time should ask into his was / all shall, their eyes would never miss a yes": even if temporality, like a spider, should ask into his historical parlor (his "was") the flies of the future ("all shall"), the lovers would never overlook a single possibility for affirmation.

Points similar to those in these two sonnets are raised in "yes is a pleasant country:" (xxxviii), which, praising the affirmative, notes that "if's wintry." Anticipating in its last line ("april's where we're") the spring poems to come in the third section of this volume, it again makes the point that "love is a deeper season / than reason": not different, but simply deeper. The winter imagery leads naturally into "all ignorance toboggans into know" (xxxix), in which love does not simply exceed but wholly transcends conventional thought. The "ignorance" here starts at the height, "toboggans" down into "knowledge"—a pointed comment on the place of "knowledge" in the poet's scale of values—and "trudges up to ignorance again." The cycle suggests history, the mad dashes toward what seems, to a particular society, to be knowledge, and the laborious climb out of that knowledge. Winter, however, is "not forever," and spring—intuition instead of rationality, feeling rather than thought—will come to "spoil the game." This "shrill collective myth," the myth that what matters is *to know,* swoops into the grave and, like the tobogganers, must again "toil the scale to shrillerness." All these permutations, however, cannot affect "us." We live elsewhere, in a transcendence far beyond these cycles, where "tomorrow is our permanent address." And if "they" find us there, "we'll move away still further:into now." To conventional thought, "now" (the present) would be closer, not further, than "tomorrow." To the poet, however, the reverse is true, perhaps since we spend so much time speculating on the future that we miss the present. The capacity to live in the present moment, something Cummings had been preaching from the beginning of his career, comes much less easily, it seems, than a penchant for procrastination.

The section ends with "darling!because my blood can sing" (xl), a poem whose conventional structure belies the complexity of syntax within its lines. The four stanzas deal respectively with four states of mind that threaten love—fear, doubt, hate, and death—and find the resurrection from each in the "look" from the lover that can "april" the narrator, wake him up to the rejuvenation and release of spring. Cummings, not usually an epigrammatic poet, includes a quotable line here ("doubting can turn men's see to stare"); for the most part, however, the complexities are not so immediately resolvable. The third stanza, paraphrased, tells that armies—larger than hate, and never too small for the slightest act of meanness—can meet other armies for centuries and win nothing. And the last stanza includes an ambiguity Empson would have envied. If we imagine commas after "such" and "despair," "such" may refer to the look, which "completely strikes" at the vastness of mind and soul, just as only "perfect hope" can feel unmitigated ("only") despair. Without the commas, "such" may be "those who," individuals like the narrator who because they can feel "perfect hope" are also capable of being struck by despair. Possibly, however, the stanza is highly elliptical, so that the third line, as though it were repeated, is meant to go both with the second line and, quite independently, with the fourth. The general sense, however, is that even though, being perfectly hopeful, the poet is subject to a despair that could wipe out forests of thought and mountains of feeling, nevertheless the "look" resurrects him and slays death. The result is the renewal of April itself: "Hills jump with brooks: / trees tumble out of twigs and sticks." Not simply a poem of affirmation, it is rather one that vigorously denies negation—an appropriate conclusion for a section of winter poems.

The final section emphasizes the lyrical, and the poems, not as thoughtful, are also not as good as those in the second section. Winter, a time for quiet meditation, was the time for coming to grips with difficulties which could be passed off perhaps too glibly in spring. With the coming of spring imagery, the poems become, in general, less penetrating. This section begins with a poem ("how," XLI) whose form nicely matches its content. Addressed to a tiny flower squirming between two stones, the poem is itself a narrow and brief thing in which meaning wriggles through the disordering of words. The flower, first addressed as "you," becomes "thou" at the end: the tone moves from formal to intimate and from modern to archaic as the poet comes to terms with this "mysterious" epitome of spring. Like the seasons, the poem itself is circular, beginning with "how" and ending with "t / hou." A poem of praise, it inaugurates a series of poems where the ominous is all but banished, where life, beauty, and spring are in ascendency.

Flowers, not surprisingly, are the central image in this section. Cummings' handling of the image ranges from the generalized to the particular. At times he is guilty of the kinds of usages objected to by Blackmur, who charged that "flower" for Cummings had become "a maid of all work . . . an idea . . . deprived of its history, its qualities, and its meaning."[6] So indeed it seems to be in "if(among" (XLIII), where flowers and leaves are little more than sentiment. One of the most effective flower poems, however, is "these(whom;pretends" (XLIV). It is also one of the most obscure, until the missing referent for "these" is supplied. As "petals" which "swim / snowing / ly upward with Joy" against the "blue nothing" of the sky, "these" are probably apple blossoms on trees at Joy Farm. Leaving out the central clue, Cummings compels the reader to work out the particulars of the situation without having the convenience (and the limitations) of a simple name. A similar ambiguity pervades "i think you like' " (XLV), which turns out to be a poem about a Greek street vendor with "a strawberry / bang" of hair and a mustache of "wintry / handlebars." Cummings, who seemed to have great difficulty avoiding the blandishments of flower-sellers, here reports an encounter with one who, diving into his wares and emerging with a bouquet of jonquils, bows and says, "I think you like my flowers. My home [is the] Ionian isles." Here he avoids Blackmur's blight: for the weight of the poem's meaning is carried less by the flowers than by the particulars describing the man. As in "what a proud dreamhorse" (*No Thanks*, 53), the significance resides not in the flowers but in the circumstances of their sale.

Another major image in this section is the bird. At times the poet mentions particular birds ("might these be thrushes climbing through almost(do they," XLII); and his poems make it clear that he had observed their habits at first hand. His letters, too, indicate an interest in bird life that was more than merely poetical. Writing to Pound in 1950 about "birdsters," he included some extended quotations from various bird guides.[7] At other times, birds enter his poetry less as particularities of the landscape than as metaphors for poetry and art: "until and i heard / a certain a bird," says the poet, "i dreamed i could sing" (XLVII). Here the emphasis seems almost on song for song's sake. The poem, like a bird's song, is less expository than lyric, and even the "and" in the first line, like the "and" in Shakespeare's "When that I was and a little tiny boy," is meant less as a conjunction than an expletive, a word to absorb a beat in the rhythm of the song. The purely lyric impulse informs several more poems here. Arranged to resemble free verse, the three stanzas of "trees" (XLIX) nevertheless follow a careful pattern. The poem, like the work of an analytic Cubist, may well have begun with a much more recognizably rhythmic line—"Trees were in bud / when to me you made love," for example—and then moved into its present distortions. Lyricism also predominates in "which is the very" (L), a poem praising the lover and dismissing mortality, and in " 'sweet spring is your" (LX). The latter, as Wegner notes, bears affinities in rhythm and subject to Nashe's "Spring, the sweete spring, is the yeres pleasant King," a poem Cummings was later to read as part of his second nonlecture at Harvard.[8]

This thrust toward pure lyricism is interrupted by a sonnet

near the end of the book: "life is more true than reason will
deceive" (LII), antiphonal in some of its repetitions of ideas,
nevertheless demands a soundly rational exploration. The first
three lines suggest that life is "more true" than rationality and
"more secret" than insanity, "deeper" than loss and "higher"
than possession. Beauty, however, is "more each than living's
all": it outdoes life in each of these categories. The second
stanza includes the much-quoted lines "the mightiest meditations of mankind / cancelled are by one merely opening leaf."
Unfortunately, the quoters generally bypass the following
lines—"beyond whose nearness there is no beyond"—which, to
the familiar sentiment of the preceding lines, adds an uncommon twist. Beyond the actual presence of the leaf—beyond the
power of the natural world to unfold and recreate itself each
spring—there is, says the poet, nothing more. We should look
not at distance but at nearness, at the present which, unlike the
"beyond" of past and future, has an existence that is more than
merely speculative. For, as he says in the third stanza, "futures
are obsolete;pasts are unborn." Reversing the expected conception of obsolete pasts and unborn futures, he provides a paradox
that introduces his main, and quite Christian, point: "here less
than nothing's more than everything." Not surprisingly, the
poem moves in its final couplet to a consideration of what Paul
calls "the last enemy that shall be destroyed" (I Cor. 15:26).
Death, here, is seen as a merely relative term, a conception in
the minds of men. Indeed, the very idea of manhood is only a
conception, for "death,as men call him,ends what they call
men." Beauty, however, survives by its omnipresence the mere
temporality of dying.

As though to blend the two modes of poetry in this section,
"o by the by" (LIII) fills a lyric form with a more profound message. Like "these(whom;pretends," this poem about a kite
never uses the identifying word. The protagonist, "little you-i,"

is flying his "wish" in the sky. The wish flies highest when it is neither "my" nor "your" but "our": and "what a wonderful thing / is the end of a string / (murmers little you-i," as, swept up into the sky, the lovers watch the world below recede. The poem, if not the lovers, comes back to earth in the final couplet: "and will somebody tell / me why people let go." These, the only unrhymed lines in the poem, "let go" of structure just as "people" let go of their ideals. Why is it, muses the poet, that in the face of such obvious ascendant beauty people remain earthbound? Why do we lose the promise of our wishes? The answer may be implied in the language: "you-i," the union of individuals based on love, can achieve things which "my" and "your," alone, cannot. And the distinctly identified "you-i" is worlds apart from mere "people." *1 x 1*, then, returns at its end to its beginning: "the they" in the opening poem absorbed the identity of the birds, just as the "people" here—"mostpeople," "manunkind," "what they call men"—let go of transcendent potential. Why? The implied answer is simply "because they cannot love."

The final poem ("if everything happens that can't be done," LIV) restores the lyric to its predominant position. Natural process, whereby things simply "happen," asserts itself over the human "doing" of things. If miracles arise, that only proves that the lovers are "one times one." Each of the five stanzas puts down "books" as it sets up experience: not unlike the Wordsworth of "Up, up, my friend, and quit your books," the poet here notes that "anything's righter / than books / could plan." The irony, of course, is that he says so in a book; but a deeper irony may be directed at the reader who fails to notice that this is the last poem before the book quits. Having come through poems of autumn, winter, and spring, through satires, meditations, and lyrics, the poet closes the book and sings the praises of the world beyond books, the summer itself where life is not for reading but for living. The deepest irony of all, however, is that even this exhortation to plunge into experience is made through words. Our very capacity to experience life, after all, is conditioned by the language through which we come to terms with life. And if we have in any way absorbed Cummings' poems, we are to that extent incapable of putting aside the book: some part of us will see experience through his insights. The "we" in this poem, then, refers not only to the lovers. It may also stand for the reader and the poet, "one times one" in their common outlook.

Chapter 10

Xaipe

"I spent several months," wrote Cummings to Ezra Pound in August, 1949, "persuading . . . 71 poems to make 1 book who called himself Xaipe. Now . . . The quote Oxford unquote Press registers alarm nudging horror;poems are nonsellable enough . . . without calling the poem book by some foreign word which no Good-American could either spell or pronounce."[1] *Xaipe,* a Greek word meaning "rejoice" or "greetings," is pronounced (as he wrote to another correspondent) "KAI(as in Kaiser)rea(as in ready)."[2] Oxford, swallowing its horror, published the volume in March 1950. The title is an appropriate one, for the book registers a decrease in poems that scorn and satirize and a corresponding increase in poems of praise.[3] Here, for the first time, is the Cummings who writes of the religious and transcendent not as an antidote to the evil of the world but because it alone is coming to seem the most real. The change in emphasis affects his choice of subjects. Of the seventy-one poems, only one addresses itself directly to the "infinite jukethrob" of seamy city life. The values and images of country life are increasingly attractive to the poet, who confessed to Hildegarde Watson in a 1949 letter from Joy Farm that he had "stopped pretending I don't dread(it's the first time in all my life!)returning to nyc. I do."[4]

The change in outlook affects the overall pattern of the book.

The seasonal structure is subdued: not until poems 27 and 28, when "summer is over" and things are "autumnal," are the seasons mentioned. Then, without pause, come six winter poems. The volume ends, as usual, with images of spring, but not before some eighteen unseasonal poems have intervened between the thrown-away Christmas tree (34) and the coming of the "mender / of things" in spring (62). As in *50 Poems*, the structure is open and fluid, only occasionally organized into sequences of portraits (7–9 and 12–21), satires on war (42–45), insights into religion (49–54), or poems about Joy Farm (55–60). Even the nineteen sonnets (or, with 14, twenty) are interspersed at random, forming no sequences.

The significance of this shift away from a rigid seasonal pattern is apparent in the poem which first raises seasonal themes, " 'summer is over" (27). The three stanzas present three arguments about the nature of reality: by the voices of reason ("mind"), romantic fancy ("heart"), and visionary transcendence ("soul"). Reason argues that, summer over, " 'it's no good pretending' " that permanence is an attribute of reality: now that autumn is imminent, it is evident that " 'all / sweet things are until' " and nothing is forever. Heart counters with the suggestion that " 'spring follows winter' " and that the " 'thorniest question' " will be answered by " 'roses' " and the inevitable return of spring. This answer of the heart is as far as the logic of Cummings' earlier volumes usually went: reason typically argued for autumnal gloom and wintery death, but a more-or-less romantic spring generally reasserted itself in the last pages. In this poem, however, mere romance is not sufficient. At the end of heart's argument, mind asserts its simple authority with the words " 'but dying's meanwhile.' " What good, after all, is returning spring if death has intervened to destroy life? Stanza three, however, denies both of these approaches: "soul," having the last word, argues that " 'truth would prove truthless' " if it could be proved that " 'now' " were not greater than " 'forever.' " Far beyond the merely seasonal metaphor, the transcendent fact of *now* sets aside the petty bickering between mind and heart and supersedes all time; eternity, for the visionary, is ever present. This idea Cummings has raised before. But here he links it clearly to the seasonal metaphor; and with this volume, by reducing the effect of the seasonal metaphor on his structure, he suggests its consequences. The pattern of decline followed by redemption is still here; but the emphasis shifts from the former to the latter.

Where other volumes begin with images of the end of the year, this one begins with a poem about the end of the day. The second poem describes the "citi / zens of / (hush" who come out "in the gloam / ing"; the third ("purer than purest pure") notes the appearance of the first star. The diction conspires to make this, like the earlier "brIght" (*No Thanks*, 70), a poem suggesting the star of Bethlehem: the words "forgivingly," "glory," "miracle," "childfully," and "holiness," and the phrases "big with innocence," "a pilgrim from beyond," and "the shadow / of love himself," make it not improbable that Jesus is as implicit here as he is explicit in 50, "no time ago." Twilight continues in "this out of within itself moo" (4), but tone and setting shift from country quiet to city music with this image of the organ-grinder "who is eye." Another in a long history of poems and pictures of organ-grinders,[5] this one makes the metaphor explicit: the poet, like the hurdy-gurdy man, is public entertainer, a maker of strange music "like nothing verdi" knew, a man subsisting by the charity of his listeners who now and then throw "six cents" into his Y-shaped, why-shaped hat.

With "dying is fine)but Death" (6), Cummings produces a brief masterpiece. Summing up several of his familiar ideas— that feeling is better than thinking, that verbs and verb forms ("dying") are better than nouns ("Death"), and that lower-case

humility is more natural than upper-case abstraction and pom-
posity—the poem also contrasts, as Lane notices, the fluid
rhythms of lines like "perfectly natural;perfectly" with the rigid
and abrupt meter of "strictly / scientific / & artificial & / evil &
legal."⁶ Central to the poem's success is the juxtaposition of contrary ideas and the continual surprising of our preconceptions.
The first surprise is the statement that "dying is fine"; the second comes on learning that the poet intends a distinction between "dying" and "Death." The third comes in the phrase "i /
wouldn't like / Death if Death / were / good." Implying all that
could be said by such a phrase as "I don't like Death because it
is bad," these lines do more. Asserting that the narrator is prepared not to like something even if it be good, they surprise us
with hyperbole and with a consideration of the impossible. The
fourth surprise comes with the apt replacement of the idea of
stopping to think of it with *stopping to feel of it:* addressing us
rationally, the poet nevertheless wants us to apprehend his
meaning not through reason but through intuition. The fifth
surprise is simple paradox: "miraculous," a word more commonly applied to the processes of life, is here an attribute of
dying. The sixth makes this paradox even more explicit: dying is
"lively." By contrast, however, "Death" is described in odd
collocations of words which normally remain apart from one
another, for the next surprise is in finding that "scientific" and
"artificial" go together, and that "evil" and "legal" cooperate.
Depending on our sense of the way prayers ought to be, the
poem surprises us yet again with "we thank thee / god / al-
mighty for dying," where we should expect at the end the word
"living." By now, however, the final line comes as no surprise:
"forgive us,o life!the sin of Death" summarizes the iconoclasm
that precedes it.

The ensuing poems, as though to illustrate his premise that
"dying is fine," are elegies for three acquaintances: Peter

Munro Jack, a friend who had reviewed Cummings' work in the *New York Times Book Review;* Paul Rosenfeld, the "round / little man we / loved so," author of *Port of New York* and fellow-contributor to *The Dial;* and Ford Madox Ford, British novelist and editor of the *transatlantic review*. These are sympathetic portraits; Ford, the object of a good deal of scorn by Hemingway and others, wins praise as "that undeluded notselfpitying / lover of all things excellently rare," a man "too gay for malice and too wise for fear" (9). Such a man might comprehend the poem that follows ("or who and who)," 10), which (to paraphrase roughly) tells us that there is a great gulf fixed between artistic beauty and obvious commonplace things, between the ordinary life and art, but that the smallest rose can travel this distance as can you and I or any real lovers ("who and who").

More portraits are coming: of two old men who sit, look, and dream (12); of Charles Sing, the Chinese launderer who does not do what his last name suggests but instead smiles (13); of the narrator and his lady (14); of the lady alone (15); of a woman undressing and a woman dancing (16 and 17); of an old man walking bowlegged down Conway Street (18); of Aristide Maillol (19), the sculptor whose work, represented in *The Dial*, had about it a massive stability and balance suggested by Cummings' phrase "growing stones"; of "nic" the "ice / coal wood / man" (20), who is to reappear as "dominic" in *95 Poems;* and of four visitors to a cathouse (21). Introducing these various portraits, the sonnet "so many selves(so many fiends and gods" (11) suggests the variety of selves within one man and warns the reader against reducing men, as poor portraits sometimes do, to simple categories. Of this many-faceted man, the poet notes that "his briefest breathing lives some planet's year, / his longest life's a heartbeat of some sun"—a kind of paraphrase of the Biblical statement that "one day is with the Lord as a thousand years, and a thousand years as one day" (ii Peter 3:8).

Cummings turns toward an overt use of Christian imagery in his later poems, and the allusion may be intentional, especially in the context of the final lines: "—how should a fool that calls him 'I' presume / to comprehend not numerable whom?" This "whom" may simply be the individual in all his variety, incomprehensible to those who elevate the ego to the status of capital "I." But, as in the "sun of whom" (*50 Poems*, 39), the "not numerable whom" may also be infinite God. Such a "whom," says the poet, is incomprehensible to the vanity that inflates self larger than transcendent Deity.

Cummings, hater of the New Deal and as staunch a Republican as his fellow New Hampshire voters mentioned in *Adventures in Value*,[7] turned positively caustic at the idea of trade-unionism and socialism. One of his most concise expressions of scorn for the "unanimal mankind" who would rather strike than work is the sonnet "when serpents bargain for the right to squirm" (22). Drawing his analogies from the natural world, where such collective pressure is inconceivable, Cummings suggests that only when nature begins to behave like strikers will he be less than incredulous at such behavior in man. Not only about social conditions, the poem is also about art: the notion that "every thrush may sing no new moon in / if all screech-owls have not okayed his voice" suggests the danger of carrying collective action into matters of artistic judgment. For all that Cummings was sympathetic to the plight of his individual fellows, he resisted mightily the increasing emphasis on man as a collective being and the corresponding decline of the majesty of the individual. Art, never a product of committees and democratic action, seemed to him to be in grave danger if society no longer permitted individuals to act alone.

Moving away from the previous portraits, "when serpents bargain" introduces a series of poems less personal than allegorical. One of these, "three wealthy sisters swore they'd never part:" (23), makes up in complexity what it lacks in length. The three sisters are "Soul" (who was "seduced by Life"), "Heart" (who married "Death"), and "Mind." The three, who also appear in " 'summer is over," embody an oblique allusion to the Christian "great commandment": emphasizing these three qualities, Jesus declared that one must "love the Lord thy God with all thy heart, and with all thy soul, and with all thy mind" (Matt. 22:37). In this poem, Soul (feeling, intuition) has been seduced by experience, action, the vitality of being—and is probably the better for it, since the union would produce something closer to the whole man. Heart, the merely romantic emotionalist, counterfeits real feeling; she marries, appropriately, the opposite brother, Death, implying the inevitable end of such sentimentality. The poem ends with "Poor Mind." Left a spinster, mind is sterile: the intellect, uncompanioned by its sister intuition and unwed to any sort of experience, is nothing but pitiable.

Two of the poems in this volume fomented a good deal of controversy: "one day a nigger" (24) and "a kike is the most dangerous" (46). In a letter the year *Xaipe* appeared, Cummings indicates his awareness of the potential difficulties. He reports that a friend urged him not to include these poems in the book "on the ground that the word 'nigger'(like the word 'kike')would hurt a lot of sensitive human beings & create innumerable enemies for the book. Of course I said tohellwith him;but the incident depressed me . . . ."[8] In a later letter to Friedman, Cummings called the first poem "an 8line expose of all dogoodery." Stars, he says, used to shine by day, until "a blackman . . . caught a star in his hand & told her 'i'll never let you go until you make me white.' " The problem, however, is that the blackman "could only see-&-resent his own blackness in terms of . . . nonblack("white")ness . . . ." As Friedman comments, "the point is, obviously, that Cummings wants the Negro to be himself, that for the Negro to want to become white is a loss

rather than an improvement. And for dogooders to want to res-
cue the Negro from his blackness by making him white like
themselves—that is, respectable and middle-class—is the ultimate in condescension."⁹ That annoyance at condescension is
the same impulse which, as he says in a later poem, "disposes
me to shoot / dogooding folk on sight" (*73 Poems,* 26). What is
remarkable about "one day a nigger" is not that, as late as 1950,
Cummings was still using the word "nigger"; it is that, as early
as 1950, he saw the need for preserving the distinctness of the
black culture. The word "nigger" is, in fact, the point of the
poem. Only a mere "nigger" mentality would envy the whiteness of the stars; blacks would have no business with such
counterfeiting.

Perhaps it is the inclusion of sympathetic portraits of blacks
elsewhere in Cummings' canon that prevented this poem from
causing much explosion. The same may be said, however, for
poems about Jews, as the marvelous portrait of Goldberger (*50
Poems,* 36) demonstrates. Interestingly enough, the poem on
Goldberger was wholly ignored by those who, attacking Cummings for his "kike" poem, delved into earlier volumes to trot out
damning evidence. In reaction against his receipt of the Academy of American Poets Award in 1950, *Congress Weekly*
(August 1951) presented a battery of views on the question of
Cummings' alleged anti-Semitism. The editors solicited opin-
ions pro and con from such figures as Ludwig Lewisohn ("Fundamentally he is nothing"), Stanton A. Coblentz ("socially . . .
vicious"), Leslie A. Fiedler ("an extraordinary sensibility" with a
"chaotic and imperfect heart"), and William Carlos Williams
("We give the artist freedom requiring only that he use it to say
Whatever He Chooses to Say").¹⁰ None, however, paid much attention to the poem itself; and none caught Cummings' use of
"kike" as a reference not to Jewish individuals but to a fabri-
cated stereotype made by the "yankee ingenuity" of bigots. Sev-

eral of Cummings' letters make clear his position. As he wrote to his biographer, "a jew is a human being;whereas 'a kike' is a machine—the product of that miscalled Americanization,alias standardization(id est dehumanization)which,from my viewpoint,makes out&out murder a relatively respectable undertaking."[11] Seen in this light, the poem takes its place among the scores of others that blast not the man made by individuality but the mankind made by contemporary mores.

One of the nice moments of balance in this volume comes in the pairing of "one day a nigger" with the poem that follows it, "pieces(in darker" (25). Each comprises two quatrains of short lines; each has to do with bringing the firmament down to earth. The black man in the first poem destroyed nature's brilliance and his own individuality by trying to reduce stars to his own level. The broken pieces of mirror lying in the street in the second poem, however, are each "whole with sky," each filled completely with the reflection of blue. In this dismal city environment—a "darker / than small is dirtiest" street—the mirror manages to bring the purifying clarity of sky right to the place where it is most needed. A cogent symbol, the mirror here suggests the purifying influence of the sky, which, untouched by the earth's dirt, is constantly there to redeem it. It also overturns the things "people say," the old wives' tale of bad luck and broken mirrors: for a mirror "whole with sky," broken or otherwise, suggests completeness and transcendence. The irony is in the conjunction of these two poems: what misguided human willfulness failed to accomplish in the first is done in the second by mere accident.

That these dirty streets can be redeemed is the message of "who sharpens every dull" (26), a joyous and expansive piece of artistry. Like poem 58 ("after screamgroa"), it is about the craftsman and his grindstone; like poem 62 ("in / Spring comes(no-"), it tells of the itinerant "mender / of things" who, in an earlier age, was a not uncommon figure in the city. Like the tinker, this man "sharpens every dull," and his bell calls out "maids mothers widows wives." The rhyme-word here is significant: one of Cummings' nine work-sheets for this poem lists some 125 possible near-rhymes for "i"—none of which appears in the finished product. Here, "wives" leads us to expect, in context, "knives." But what these people bring, instead, are "their very oldest lives," a word emphasized by virtue of its being the only perfect rhyme in the poem. No mere tinker, then, this "only man" repairs not mere things but existence itself. Significantly, the "dull" and "oldest" lives are not objects of scorn, as they had been in such earlier lines as "the godless are the dull" (*50 Poems*, 13) and such earlier images as that of the razor blades which have reached "the mystical moment of dullness" (*is 5*, "One," II). Resharpening—the renewal of the commonplace by the inspiration of this redeemer—is the result here, and whether one can pay him or not is beside the point. Like the poet, his work is with words: heightening the general to the individual, he "sharpens is to am," and elevating the prosaic to the poetic he "sharpens say to sing." As a moralist (perhaps, given the context of this volume, like Jesus) he "sharpens wrong" into "right," providing a finer moral perception and overturning evils. When "lives are keen," he departs. But, as the last stanza affirms, he has left his mark, for

> we can hear him still
> if now our sun is gone
> reminding with his bell
> to reappear a moon.

Sun, here, seems to stand for the harsh light of commonplace worldly or scientific attitudes: caught in such a narrowing sense of reality, says the poet, we will find this figure of redemption passing out of our hearing, and, presumably, of our lives.

Seeing not with sun but with moon—with the inner light of poetry and intuition—we will continue to hear him, and our sharpened lives will bear witness to his work. Throughout this parable, the echoing oppositions—of sun to moon, science to art, thinking to feeling, understanding to intuition, harshness to mellowness, fact to dream, dullness to sharpness—suggests that this tinker, like the earlier organ-grinder, is the poet himself, whose songs refresh the drab and revitalize the sordid. Probably no more appropriate self-portrait could be constructed for Cummings, who, seeing himself as something of an outcast living penuriously on the fringe of society, sang "Xaipe" to the world's gloom and sought again and again for the language of praise that would resurrect.

With poem 29 a sequence of winter poems begins. The first two are brief impressions, perhaps of scenes in Washington Square Park. The second ("snow means that," 30) observes that "life is a black . . . / tree" which, stripped of its leaves against the winter landscape, resembles an upended cannon spreading its charge into the sky. By a peculiar shift in viewpoint—as though he were in the sky looking back down on the park—the poet then describes the "Face" of the park, where the few people ("3ghosts") are like the "eyes" and features. Then "infinite jukethrob smoke & swallow to dis" (31) recalls the opposition of peaceful snow outside and barroom racket inside which Cummings had previously explored in "i was sitting in mcsorley's" (&, "Post Impressions," VIII). Like the earlier poem, this one explores the effect of disjointed syntax ("gorgedis reswal / lowing spewnonspew clutch") and dialect ("a fair / y . . . shrieks Yew May / n't Dew Thiz Tew Mee") to capture the denizens of this smoky din. With "blossoming are people" (32), the tone shifts to an oddly evocative lyric celebration of a snowstorm, where snow is the renovator and "i am you are i am we." The sequence ends with two Christmas poems. The first (33) appears to de-

scribe one of the quick sketches of elephants he was fond of giving Marion for Christmas, Valentine's, April Fools', and birthday reminders. The second (34), restored to more standard
form, tells of "a thrown-away It with something silvery bright
and mysterious, a wisp of glory prettily clinging," which reveals
itself to be "a thrown-away Xmas tree." Cummings, who years
before had written "little tree" (*XLI Poems*, "Chansons Innocentes," II), was fond of Christmas trees: a letter to his mother in
1920 records an early instance of his interest.[12]

   That a transcendent ethic does not necessarily restrict itself to
a lyric simplicity is proved by "quick i the death of thing" (36).
The "death of thing" which the narrator "glimpsed" is the demise of the objective world: seeing in a flash of truth the unreality of the physical universe, the narrator avoids the consequences of his realization (the swooping mountains, gaping
earth, and falling sky) only by his quickness. What allows him to
escape—what harbors him in his transcendent reality untouched by the collapse of this delusion—is "love." Those who
can not love will not conceive how he has seen such truth and
yet managed to escape unharmed. It is a moment of realization
like that at the end of Nabokov's *Invitation to a Beheading*,
where all that the senses report about the world with such authority is seen to be a sham.

   Another sham surfaces in the vitriolic "F is for foetus(a" (37),
a diatribe against Roosevelt ("F . . . D . . . R"). Here the poet
rages at that "great pink / superme / diocri / ty" in words emphasizing ("superme") the politician's ego. First published
shortly after the war, the poem suggests that Cummings, far
from sharing the general jubilation of the victorious, was sick-
ened by war-mongering. The threat of increasing government
control, a common enough worry in our age, loomed larger to
him than to most of his contemporaries: "it's / freedom from
freedom / the common man wants," he noted, ending his poem

with a Joycean version ("honey swoRkey mollypants") of the motto "Honi soit qui mal y pense"—"shame be to him who thinks evil of it."

Other responses to the war follow. One of the more interesting is "i'm" (40), a poem recording only one side of a dialogue (perhaps an overheard telephone conversation) between a returning G.I. and his wife or lover. Giving only such details as are necessary, the poet compels the reader to fill the ellipses in the soldier's talk. After the first three lines ("i'm / asking / you dear to"), the reader must add *forgive me;* after the fourth line ("what else could a"), something like *soldier do;* after the fifth ("no but it doesn't"), something like *make any difference to us.* The tale unfolds of the returning soldier trying to excuse himself for his indiscretions while abroad: "war," he tries to tell the woman who has stayed behind, "just isn't what / we imagine." The final line reveals the final excuse: "i am / dead." It is not clear whether the poet intends this to be, as in Hardy, the report of one literary deceased or, as in Eliot, the plaint of one spiritually insensible. The impact, however, is undiminished as the language rises in intensity, marking the frustration of one who cannot make himself understood.

Less specifically on war, but certainly inspired by current events, are two brief poems, "o to be in finland / now that russia's here" and "when your honest redskin toma." The former (43) echoes Browning's lines "O to be in England / Now that April's here," lines which have already been parodied in two poems in *is* 5. But "now that russia's here" in America—now that socialism has overtaken us, with communism not far behind—the poet longs for "finland." It is an ironic longing, since Russia is there, too, and in force. There, however, the influence is unequivocal and admitted; here it is disguised under the cloak of Roosevelt's policies. Less pointed, but more technically interesting, is "when your honest redskin toma" (45). The rhyme depends on pronouncing the names of the punctuation marks, which are set off from the words by intervening spaces. Hence "toma" rhymes with the *comma* after line two, "stalin" with semi-*colon*, and "spoil the rod" with the final *period*. The Indians, says the poet, were at least honest: they did not try to justify their wars with grand self-righteous schemes that made the world safe for democracy or saved it from Stalin. Inverting the old saw, the poet ends by having the "palmist"—a psalmist without the *s*, or a palm-reader, or one who spanks—tell us that to "spare the child" is to "spoil the rod." Beneath the humor lies a grim view of war: if you would keep your weapons from spoiling, you must exercise them in warfare, even at the cost of not "sparing" the victims.

In "whose are these(wraith a clinging with a wraith)" (41), Cummings borrows a landscape from the Gothic novelists— thunder, night, howling wind, beach, and "futuring snowily" whitecaps—as the background for his meditations. "This is a poem of persuasion," notes Friedman in a sound analysis;[13] and surely the poet and his lover are present. But the poem, in keeping with the thrust of this volume, goes beyond persuasion into transcendence. The last lines may be no more than an invitation to seize the day; but they also suggest something larger, as though these lovers, no longer absorbed by each other in a face-to-face relationship, are standing side by side and contemplating the "Now" of immeasurable imagination.

In "no time ago" (50), this imagination is specifically Christian. The narrator, "walking in the dark" of worldly confusion, "met christ / jesus." The enjambment isolates "jesus" so that, like Hopkins' "(my God) my God"[14] and like the "Jesus" in "Buffalo Bill 's" (*Tulips and Chimneys*, "Portraits," VIII), the word is both exclamation and name. The meeting was either "no time ago" (the opposite of *some time ago*, and hence either *never* or *right now*) or else "a life" ago, in boyhood, perhaps, or in some preexistence. In any case, the response was one of stunned passivity. The experience is likened, by this simple language, to that of seeing a celebrity pass in the street, although in context "passed" has overtones of "passed on" (died) and also "bypassed" (went on indifferent to the narrator). He was "as close as i'm to you / yes closer," says the narrator, addressing the reader directly. The voice is that of the poet, who, although his physical body may be miles away from the reader, is as close to him as the words are on the page we read. So, too, Jesus is "close" to the narrator through words, "closer," perhaps, in that the words of the Gospels may strike deeper than the words of this poem. In this close-up view the narrator perceives a telling characteristic of Jesus: he was "made of nothing / except loneliness." Made of no material substance ("nothing"), Jesus was able, according to the Gospels, to walk on water and appear or disappear as he needed. The word "loneliness," however, has all sorts of ramifications. Is the central characteristic that of individuality, or isolation, or uniqueness, or sorrow? Is it, as in the later "1(a" (*95 Poems,* 1), oneness, singleness, unity of vision? The poem, not unlike Cummings' own responses to Christianity, is thoughtfully ambiguous, a cryptic comment which nevertheless draws a bond of sympathy between the poet and the Master: Jesus, isolated from common understanding by his redemptive trade, resembles the poet who, in the likeness of organ-grinder, tinker, and street-vendor, is isolated by his. The two poems that brace this one give additional insights into Cummings' religious attitudes. In "this is a rubbish of human rind" (49), the poet speaks of conventional orthodoxy as "a deaf dumb church and blind / with an if in its soul / and a hole in its life." True to his generation, Cummings rejects organized religion without losing respect for Jesus' teachings. The Sonnet "who were so dark of heart they might not speak" (51) tells of salvation through "a little innocence." It is a bit sentimental, for the redemptive power of Christianity needs, in a skeptical age, a more tough-minded explanation of innocence. It nevertheless focuses on that characteristic of Jesus which in the octave heals the blind, dumb, and despairing, and in the sestet overcomes death itself.

The three poems that follow ring changes on the same theme. Like Jesus, who overcomes death, the artist in "to start,to hesitate;to stop" (52) proceeds slowly (note the progressively more final punctuation marks in the first two lines, from comma to semicolon to colon) toward his "masterpiece." He begins by "kneeling" not in prayer but "in doubt"; yet persistence conquers hesitation as, spelling THAED in the capital letters of the poem, he reverses the word "death" and produces life. The artist in "mighty guest of merely me" (53)—a poem which, because of the repeated "be thou gay," Friedman takes as the title poem for *Xaipe*—addresses his soul, the "guest" that inhabits the "merely me" of the body. In the time-honored tradition of poetry, Cummings produces here a poem on divine themes which embodies the language of the earthly love lyric: for this is really a *carpe diem* poem, addressed not to his lover but to his soul. The last poem of the group ("maybe god," 54), employing some of the same imagery as the earlier "Spring is like a perhaps hand" (&, "N," III), is another effort to come to terms with a definition of God. God brings us a "papery weightless diminutive / world / with a hole in / it"—a world which, whether it is to be interpreted as delicate and lovely or fragile and brittle, is nevertheless "diminutive" in its relative insignificance. Out of the hole, "demons with wings"—devils—would be "streaming," except that something has happened. Speculating on that something, the poet suggests that "maybe they couldn't agree," that evil, after all, is self-destructive because constantly at war with its own unity. The poem, fittingly, ends with an *o* isolated from the word "into." Visually, the *o* suggests the hole in the world;

metaphorically, it suggests both the wholeness of this world and the vast emptiness of the space "into" which it is floating. Read in this way, the poem is an apt conclusion to the sequence of religious poems preceding it: the last word, a preposition, has for object only the white space on the bottom of the page below the poem. The world created by such religious insights, then, is open-ended, a world of infinite possibilities. Read, however, as the poem beginning the upcoming sequence of Joy Farm poems, the "papery . . . / world" full of "demons with wings" is simply a wasps' nest. Such a reading complicates the poem in significant ways. A child bringing us, even "very carefully," a wasps' nest may well fill us with fright unless we know that the wasps are gone. If "god" here does what the child does, then our response must be similar, full of both dread and fascination, fear of the sting of the "demons" but awe at their architectural finesse. Like "no time ago," the poem offers little consolation to those who wish to pin down Cummings' religious convictions.

The sequence of Joy Farm poems takes as subjects a light rain (55), a country woman like a "grey / rock" in a field (56), a "Portrait" (as it was titled in its magazine publication) of a man sharpening a scythe on a foot-pedaled grindstone (58), a newborn colt (59), and a "friendly / himself of / a boulder," perhaps the husband of the grey-rock woman (60). The affection Cummings shows for these country people has a parallel in *Adventures in Value*, where the originals for these poems can perhaps be found. The most interesting is "(im)c-a-t(mo)" (57), which, although not positively identified with a country scene, may well be meant as a portrait of a barn cat. Dense and tangled, the poem has confused many who ought to have known better. These include William Carlos Williams, who in Book v of *Paterson* has an interviewer read him a few lines of the poem and ask, "Is this poetry?" Williams replies that "it may be, to him, a poem. But I would reject it. I can't understand it. He's a serious man. So I struggle very hard with it—and I get no meaning at all."[15] Cummings, patient with the puzzled, was willing to explain : "an *immobile* cat suddenly puts on an acrobatic act:&*fall-leaps*, becoming *drift-whirl-fully float-tumblish;*& then *wanders away,exactly as if nothing had ever happened."*[16] One of his most felicitous experiments, it nicely captures both the playful antics and the arch indifference so typical of cats, and the swiftness with which one becomes the other.

The last eleven poems in the volume consider spring, sunlight, singing, love, and other things about which one might exclaim "Xaipe!" The first of the series ("if(touched by love's own secret)we,like homing," 61) ends with an image not so much of overcoming as of outfacing time, the "colossal hoax of clocks and calendars." The interweaving of sounds—the creation of the word "clocks" out of the consonants and vowels already assembled in "colossal" and "hoax," and the development of these sounds into "calendars," which picks up the slant-rhyme of "stares"—testifies to the care with which Cummings learned his early lessons in assonance, consonance, and alliteration. Taking us back to the poems of *Tulips and Chimneys*, "in / Spring comes(no" (62) echoes both "in Just-" and "Spring is like a perhaps hand" in its imagery of "eager / fingers" and its metaphor of the "mender / of things" who, like the "little / lame balloonman," appears as a harbinger of spring. It is not as interesting as the earlier scissors-grinder poem ("who sharpens every dull," 26), to which it bears a more than tangential relationship: Cummings, tinkering with numbers, may well have intended that the second poem's number (62) reverse that of the first (26). These poems emphasize the redemptive qualities associated with the poet and the tinker, both of whom busy themselves "remaking" castoffs. Were it not for the saving grace of this seasonal repairman, "-wise we" should have thrown away not only our pots but perhaps even (in the words of the earlier poem) our "very oldest lives." That we stand perilously close to a kind of final exhaustion, and that spring renews us in more than metaphoric ways, is a theme which runs throughout this final sequence; Cummings, it would seem, is becoming increasingly conscious of his advancing age.

Perhaps that consciousness leads him to the next sonnet, "honour corruption villainy holiness" (63), which, in a more than usually sprung rhythm, describes Chaucer's Canterbury pilgrims on their way to honor their saint. Unlike the earlier satires, where "you and i" are not like "mostpeople," the narrator here observes in these pilgrims an egalitarian unity. Riding "side by side," "equally all alive," they each are in search of the same "sweet forgiveness." The sestet turns the argument slightly: all these characters "come up from the never of when" (Chaucer's imagination) into "the now of forever"—into a permanent place in literature, into an ongoing embodiment that allows them to come "riding alive" into Cummings' imagination without interference from the six hundred years between them. The final couplet carries the argument another step: these characters forever "come" because they are literary figures, while real people—"children . . . of dust"—must "go" into "nothing's own nothing." The paradox, playing against our usual conceptions of reality and fiction, suggests that poetry produces characters who are forever "alive," while human existence produces readers who turn to dust.

One of Cummings' best-known sonnets, "i thank You God for most this amazing" (65), is good enough that one wishes it were better. Revealing itself cleanly on a single reading, it has been dismissed, in Robert Grave's words, as "intrinsically corny."[17] A religious poem, it has neither the vibrant intellectuality of Hopkins, the cool ambiguity of Eliot, nor the resonance of Thomas. It depends, especially in the third stanza, on assertion rather than demonstration, and is finally a bit too facile. Nevertheless, it has some very good moments. The first line, for example, makes excellent use of the transposed adverb. We expect "most" to modify either "thank you" ("i thank you most, God") or "amazing" ("for this most amazing day"). Splitting the difference, Cummings places the word in a position where it does double duty. And the progression in the fourth line— "everything / which is natural which is infinite which is yes"— crescendoes toward abstraction, affirmation, and simplicity all at once. Perhaps for Cummings it is what "And death shall have no dominion" was for Thomas: a statement of faith that is too clear, too simplified, and hence too dishonest. In any case, it stands as a significant marker in the path of Cummings' development of transcendental and religious themes.

The lyric "when faces called flowers float out of the ground" (67) is almost entirely affirmative, pointing out negative qualities only in the third line of each stanza. As Alan Nadel has shown, it is an extraordinary piece of craftsmanship in rhyme and repetition.[18] It succeeds by sheer energy in becoming a poem of praise that is neither corny nor sentimental. The effectiveness of such lines as "—alive;we're alive,dear:it's(kiss me now)spring!" resides not only in the exclamatory vigor of its repeated words, its punctuation, and its paraphrasable content. It also inheres in the closely woven patterns of sound: "alive;we're" rhymes with "alive,dear"; "it's" and "kiss" are assonant; "me" echoes the vowel in "we're" and "dear"; "now" anticipates the beginnings of the three following lines; and "spring," picking up the "i" used earlier in the line, actually seems to spring out of the line while at the same time lending it the finality and containment of a closed syllable.

Recapitulating the seasonal theme, "now all the fingers of this tree(darling)have" (69) moves from summer through winter and out again into the promise of spring. A sober love poem, it notes that our "shining . . . now" will turn to "then," and "our

then shall be some darkness during which / . . . i have no you."
Like natural things, we must endure death and separation.
Then, like trees in winter, we will blossom again, for "also
then's until" (*then* is also *until*), and *until,* the last word of the
poem, is a word rich with implication of future promise.
Wegner notes that the poem was "inspired" by the elm in the
corner of Washington Square Park, which Cummings described
as "newyorkcity's Biggest,so far as am aware,Tree."[19] Many of
Cummings' impressions and brief descriptions probably owe
their impulse to that tree. This poem, however, goes so far
beyond attachment to place or specific detail that its inspiration
can only be attributed to the ferment of ideas long held. In
these terms it charts a progression in Cummings' work. Many
an early poem begins with an impression of place which is then
attached to a more abstract idea. Many later ones, on the other
hand, seem to begin with ideas and attach themselves, as necessary, to the details of place that provide the metaphor. As
though to prove himself still capable of straightforward impression, however, he follows this poem with "blue the triangular
why" (70), a description of a chalk drawing on a sidewalk which,
abstract in its design, suggests either a house or a kite. Like everything else in spring, this sidewalk, although filthy, is "blossoming glory" in this flowerlike and evanescent drawing.

In the first poem in this volume, the moon, rising just at sunset, was full. In the final poem ("luminous tendril of celestial
wish," 71), the volume has circled to the "new moon." The poet
apostrophizes this "luminous tendril" in the first nine lines before naming it. He then makes his request: just as the moon, by
a "miracle of . . . / sweet innocence," causes the "dull cowardice called the world" to vanish, so, prays the poet, "teach disappearing also me the keen / illimitable secret of begin." Like the
seasons, the moon too knows the secret of starting anew. As
though to summarize the pervasive theme of redemption in this

volume (notice the use of "keen," a central word in "who sharpens every dull"), the "disappearing" poet—"disappearing" from our experience as we close the book, and already in his fifty-sixth year—fittingly ends the volume with the word "begin."

Chapter 11

95 Poems

95 Poems (1958), Cummings' longest volume, brings together eight years' work. Earlier volumes had come more frequently, never more than six years apart. Here, as he exercises more patience, he expresses a quieter and more meditative outlook. Turning his attention largely to things held in high regard (Joy Farm, Washington Square Park in the rain, the less physical aspects of love), he does not shrink from those things—the cosmeticized mother, the apathetic reader, the bickering housewife—which deserve ridicule. But it is to Horace rather than Juvenal that the few satires here owe their allegiance: only "THANKSGIVING (1956)" recalls the rancor of earlier years. Noting the "consistently maturing transcendentalism" of this volume, Friedman observes that "Cummings' affirmations were never more strong."[1] And Winfield Townley Scott, reviewing *95 Poems* for the *Saturday Review*, observed that Cummings' work was "the latest important expression of the New England Transcendental tradition."[2] It is a volume full of praise for human goodness and wonder at nature's marvels.

As such, it is Cummings' most risky volume. Praise, as a glance at the best of modern literature attests, does not come easily to our age. The affirmations that were the stock of popular poetry as recently as the *Georgian Anthology* of 1915 came to seem, to a more burdened age, too facile, too superficial in their assurances, too cheaply attained. To a generation raised on cold wars and New Criticism, the standard of human dealings appeared to be suspicion and the touchstone of great art irony. Nor was 1958 the beginning of a general reversal: the very next year saw the publication of two volumes, Lowell's *Life Studies* and Snodgrass's *Heart's Needle*, which took as their subject not the universalized glory of natural and spiritual beauty but the personalized and "confessional" agony of disintegration. Honesty was still taken as the hallmark of the finest poetry; but, as it was generally held that the truth of the human condition was more nearly anguish than satisfaction, more nervous worry than buoyant hope, honesty was to be realized in the poet's assessment not of his confidences but his insecurities.

It was into this milieu, sensitized to the fraudulent and impatient with the glib, that the affirmations of 95 *Poems* came. Yet Cummings, after years of practice at distinguishing the merely sentimental from the genuinely affirmative, the "pansy heaven" from the "heaven of blackred roses" (*ViVa*, XLIII), had learned his balance well. Refusing to give over his skills at organization, his ear for nuance, and his fertile metaphoric imagination, he welded this book into a collection which helps demonstrate Robert Creeley's proposition that "FORM IS NEVER MORE THAN AN EXPRESSION OF CONTENT."[3] Here, it seems, is proof that a poet can refuse conformity to the "poetical" subject matter favored by his age and still attain a high standard of craftsmanship.

Craftsmanship inheres not only in individual poems but overall arrangements. "95 Poems," Cummings wrote to Francis Steegmuller, "is,of course,an obvious example of the seasonal metaphor—1,a   falling   leaf;41,snow;73,nature(wholeness   innocence eachness beauty the transcending of time&space)awakened."[4] The reader taking this general hint can observe, as in earlier volumes, some more extensive groupings. Poems 1–4 invoke autumn and early winter; poems 40–45 all deal with winter or snow; poems 63–66 take up spring; and poems 73–83 are all poems of the country. Knowing Cummings' habits—October through May in Greenwich Village, June through September at Joy Farm—the reader can see even more correspondences. In the autumn-winter sequences, poems 24–27 center on Washington Square Park and poems 28–34 are all, one way or another, portraits of individuals set against a city background. Later, sandwiched between the spring poems and the country poems, comes a short sequence (poems 69–71) dealing with the marvelous, the miraculous, and the mysterious. The direction of the volume—generally, though not rigorously—is once again from worldly to transcendent, from (as he says to Steegmuller) "dirty" to "clean."[5]

Another aspect of Cummings' craftsmanship is evident here as well: the painterly. In composing 95 *Poems* the poet, as Harold C. Schonberg noted in a 1959 article in the *New York Times* (Sunday) *Magazine*, "paid a great deal of attention to the visual effect of facing pages." Schonberg quotes Gerald Gross, an editor with Harcourt Brace, as saying, " 'The sequence was terribly important to him. . . . On one page a wrong poem was inserted. Cummings thought that the two pages clashed, and he wrote a new poem to take care of the situation.' "[6] This sense of visual design is evident within individual poems as well. The second poem in the book uses its shape—a crescent—to help the reader identify the poem's subject ("this how / patient creature") with the (unnamed) moon. A later poem (24) uses a nearly square second stanza with an isolated "e" at each corner to suggest a city park. And the well-known opening poem— "1(a"—is appropriately arranged in the shape of a figure 1.

Like the first pieces in 50 *Poems* and 1 x 1, this introductory poem is a brief description of autumn. Had Cummings been merely an imagist, he might have written simply "a leaf falls: /

loneliness." The brevity, the evocation of an experience visually apprehended, the intervening colon functioning as an equals sign, and the implied analogy between natural image and human feeling would qualify it for inclusion in any imagist anthology. But Cummings has done more. Focusing on oneness, the poet structures his letters to highlight the numerous appearances of the number *one*. The first line, "l(a," uses both the number and the indefinite article; the second line uses the French definite article "le"; line 5 ("11") has two ones; line 7 ("one") spells out the word; line 8 ("1") isolates the digit; and line 9 ("iness") suggests both Cummings' customary first person pronoun ("i") and a lower-case Roman numeral one, attached to a suffix making them into nouns of condition or quality. Even the number (1) which precedes the poem is significant. Visually, Cummings structures the poem so that two different aspects of its design—the overall shape and the inner movements among the lines—draw attention to the two sides of its equation, oneness and the leaf. The overall shape is that of a tall figure 1 resting on a flat base. And the patterns within the poem suggest a leaf drifting downward from a tree. The eye, like a leaf, moves slowly earthward in a gently rocking and somewhat repetitive motion: "l(a" shifts to "le"; "af" flips over into "fa"; the quick straight drop in the middle of the poem ("11," resembling an upended equals sign) is slowed by the extended line "one"; and the eye finally lands on the longest line of the poem, resembling a little heap of leaves already fallen.

Cummings' central perception here is that "loneliness" contains "oneness"—or rather "one-one-one-iness"—and that the single leaf falling is metaphor for both physical and spiritual isolation. Furthermore, by splitting open "loneliness" and inserting the brief sentence about the leaf, he has made the word for the human condition contain the natural image. The choice is important: a falling leaf does not *contain* loneliness any more than, in such poems as "Hello is what a mirror says" (*1 x 1*, xxx), the world of objects contains any meanings of itself. It is the state of mind—the loneliness—that contains and hence determines the outward and objective state. Not content to remain within the usually negative emotional value of loneliness, he instead calls these into question by equating loneliness with oneness. Out of context, as it is usually read, "1(a" speaks of sadness. But seen along with Cummings' other work—the joyous brightness of his autumnal paintings, for example, or the delight, mentioned in the next poem, of autumn's "not . . . / imaginable mysteries"—the focus shifts to the beauty of isolation and quietness. Cummings, more hermit than socialite, no doubt saw both feelings in the approach of winter: the stillness of autumn must have delighted him, but the impending return from the summer landscape to the city came to disturb him more and more. Hence the aptness of his leaf image, which can call up both the serene rightness of a sense of completion and the foreboding of doom. To read the poem in only one of these ways is to oversimplify a remarkably subtle statement.

Subtle, too, is the device Cummings adopts in this volume to avoid direct satire: he writes poems in praise of people or things which are themselves agents for satirizing others. The device at its simplest underlies "crazy jay blue)" (5), a poem saluting a "vivid voltaire" of a bird, full of a "scorn of easily" and a "hatred of timid." Earlier, Cummings himself would have scorned and hated. Here, standing back, he writes a poem which praises while it attacks. A similar device appears in "dominic has" (8), portraying the "icecoalwood" man whose truck has left and right rear mudflaps labelled respectively "ZOOM" and "DOOM." These two words illumine the central distinction in the poem: that "we & worlds," busy zooming along, "are / less alive / than dolls & / dream." The "doll" which Dominic has rescued and carries on the grill of his truck was once "doomed" to the ash-barrel. Out of that death, says the narrator, comes a greater life. It is a life where love is expressed by "mrs dominic" in restoring the doll and by Dominic himself in the "most tremendous hug" he gives the narrator. The poem is less satire against "most-people" than praise for a man who lives peacefully at right angles to social conformity.

In "maggie and milly and molly and may" (10), the poet becomes a painter of group portraits. Like Sargent's *Daughters of Edward D. Boit* (the comparison is apt, for all that Cummings despised Sargent) the poem has a superficial decorum that appears almost bland. The portrait of Boit's four daughters seems conventional enough at first blush. Only with deeper probing does the viewer uncover the remarkable distinctions among character that Sargent delineates: the intelligence, the petulance, the denseness, and the easygoing vacuity that characterize the daughters in turn. Cummings manages a similar depth, the clue to which is in the statement that "it's always ourselves we find in the sea." These girls, in other words, are to be identified by what they find. Maggie, the "sweetly" troubled one, finds a singing shell. Milly, "languid" and friendly, takes pity on a "stranded" starfish. Molly, both "chased" and, as Bethany Dumas notes, chaste, is an active imaginer of horrors, and appropriately locates her objective correlative in a crab. May is the dreamer, who in her "smooth round stone" comes upon a symbol resisting simple categorization. Not unlike Cummings, she envisions a situation where normal values are reversed: the "world" is "small," while "alone" is "large." Like "l(a," this poem suggests the two sides of loneliness; "alone" is a quality that looms large in may's experience, yet, being large, it is hardly a confining and stifling place.

If, like so many of Cummings' poems, this one is also about poetry, then these four playmates may stand for four different sorts of writing. Going down to the shore of the unconscious, not unlike the people in Frost's "Neither Out Far nor In Deep," they return with different sorts of images. Poetry, to some, is simply a sweet singing that covers up troubles. To others it is a means of social justice, a way to call attention to the plight of the stranded. To many it is an exercise in surreal fantasizing. To still others it is a search for the transcendental. Losing egotism ("a you or a me"), we are able to find "ourselves," our real identity, in this sea of the unconscious and, for that matter, in poetry. Cummings is again insisting that meaning does not reside within the poem: we will find in the words, as in the sea, whatever meanings we bring.

The sonnet that follows (11) begins with two fine lines: "in time's a noble mercy of proportion / with generosities beyond believing." Thereafter the demands of the form weigh heavily; and by the sestet the poem has degenerated into a pale echo of popular song and Ecclesiastes. Several poems later, however, Cummings proves himself equal to the demands of carefully balanced form in a poem ("So shy shy shy(and with a," 13) which John Berryman, reviewing the volume, found most effective.[7] A portrait of a "shy," "wrong," "gay," "young" girl, the poem describes the paradoxically ennobling effect these qualities have on her admirers. Metrically precise—it is syllabic verse, with only two minor variants from the pattern in lines 3 and 15—it is clear enough in meaning and regular enough in form to invite a musical setting.

Similarly songlike is "in time of daffodils(who know" (16). The message is vintage Cummings: flowers teach us how to behave. As though to highlight the kind of person who ignores their advice, "for prodigal read generous" (17) describes the atrophied sense of wonder Cummings found so prevalent in the readers around him. The word "prodigal" sends us back to the Bible, where we encounter the story of a father's forgiveness of his wastrel son. The poem seems a comment on the average reader's inability to read such a story correctly: eviscerating the tale, the reader reduces the prodigal youth to a merely generous middle-aged son, the "sheer wonder" and "ecstasy" of his father to "mere surprise" and "contentment," and the poetic qualities of the narrative to "prose." Then, turning the page and closing his eyes, he drifts mindlessly and soullessly. The message to readers of 95 Poems should be clear: those who find something less than "sheer wonder" in this volume will find themselves described in this poem.

That content should be exactly embodied by form is the message of poem 19, "un(bee)mo." Like "l(a," it too can be spelled out as an imagist poem: "bee in the only rose / unmoving, are you asleep?" But the bee, after all, is *in* the rose, as the tmesis here makes clear. Again, it is not the image that contains the question, but the question that surrounds—almost ingests—the image. Several other impressions follow: "joys faces friends" (21) is the poet's response to an old cellar-hole engulfed by the woods; and "albutnot quitemost" (23) describes his reaction to a hillside graveyard, with tombstones "still u / ntumbled but slant / ing drun / kenly." Each of these, however, goes beyond mere impression. The poet in the former focuses on the imagined inhabitants of the old house, and rises, in the penultimate stanza, to a series of images reminiscent of the "Time Passes" section of Virginia Woolf's *To the Lighthouse*. In the latter the tombstones remind the narrator of "noone i ever & / someone . . . i never . . . heard . . . of." Turning from the dead to the living ("o my / darling") and from the tombs to what is evidently (although he does not name it) the sky, the poet ends in a rhapsody that fuses the immensity of the sky with the depth of the grave and the vastness of eternity, involving them all as metaphors for the extent of his love. How far Cummings has come in his comprehension of things transcendent can be charted by comparing this poem with "it is funny,you will be dead some day" (&,

"Sonnets—Actualities," II), where the language refuses to come to terms with the deeper meanings of the issue.

Sightlessness, central to poems 25 and 26, is a virtue in "jack's white horse(up" (27). That horse is "high in / the night / at the end / of doubleyou / 4th." Like the signs in "-G O N splashes-sink" (&, "Sonnets—Actualities," XVIII) and "when i am in Boston" (*XLI Poems,* "Sonnets," XIII), this horse is an illuminated sign atop a building at the end of West 4th Street. The sign makes the narrator think of Lady Godiva, famous for her nudity. And that "(for no reason at / all)" reminds the narrator that the "cheerfulest goddamned / sonofabitch / i ever met" was "a blindman." His cheerfulness is perhaps the product of his disability: to be blind to the world, and to the visual allure of sensuality represented in Lady Godiva, is to be in the "cheerfulest" state. "And if thy right eye offend thee," said Jesus, also talking about sensuality, "pluck it out" (Matt. 5:29).

The eleven poems that follow are, one way or another, portraits. Depicted here are Joe Gould (28), a woman who has everything ("It," "what," and "which") except the "who" of personality (29), a "Flop" who experiences nothingness (30), a drunken pencil-seller (31), the "platinum floozey" who is "toothfully leering" at herself in a mirror (32), a "babyfaced" drunk (33), the participants in a barroom brawl (34), some "or . . . / dinary / a / meri / can b / usiness . . . / me / n" (36), three soldiers (37), and a collapsed drunk (38). These are the *dramatis personae* from the early sections of most of Cummings' books. In one way or another they all share the plight of the "Flop" in 30: "what got him was nothing," the emptiness of not knowing or feeling anything, the apathy and lassitude that Cummings saw in so much of humanity. In this void it is difficult to determine identities and to assess the purposes of human action.

This difficulty is expressed (or, rather, rendered inexpressible) in "ADHUC SUB JUDICE LIS" (34), a poem about four

or perhaps five brawlers who act and react for inscrutible reasons. Like "from the cognoscenti" (*ViVa*, xxiv), the poem is intentionally obscure. The fact that we cannot (as any judge must)
sort out the causes of this scuffle and assign recognizable mo-
tives to the actors is nicely summarized by the title. "Gramma-
tici certant et adhuc sub judice lis est," wrote Horace in *Ars
poetica*, a phrase which translates, "Grammarians dispute, and
the case is still before the courts." Why people behave as they
do, why the world is composed of the humanity here portrayed,
is a mystery neither grammarians nor courts will fathom. Neither will they learn why the world sends off three soldiers
(named "handsome," "clever," and "he") to fight its wars (37).
Like the soldier in "come,gaze with me" (*is 5*, "Two," viii),
"handsome" and "clever" are perfectly adapted to the demands
of society. They become the "cleanest keenest bravest / killers"
imaginable, and return to their homes after the war to perpetu-
ate their warlike attitudes in future generations. But "he," the
real individual ("himself was him"), questioned the purpose of
war and was killed by it. The final poem (38), when reassembled
out of its fractured but perfectly ordered words, reads "stirs this
once man collapsed in sunlight ('ah, go on, you don't fool me') to
itself whispering." The irony is that, in attempting to dismiss
the images that haunt his drunkenness, the man addresses himself: even the drunk, while realizing that we don't fool ourselves, nevertheless knows that it is our own foolish selves
that frighten us.

These portraits, appropriately, provide an overture for
"THANKSGIVING (1956)" (39), the only biting satire in the
book. The poem, about the invasion of Hungary by Russia and
the passive isolationism of the United States during that conflict, spawned some controversy when Cummings selected it for
reading as the Festival Poem at the Boston Arts Festival in
1957.[8] Norman Friedman thought the poem "merely disagree-

able" in its coarseness.[9] The problem, however, may run deeper. An anomaly among Cummings' poems, it argues *for* military intervention. Cummings told Charles Norman that, on hearing of the Hungarian uprising, "I was so frantic and sick, I felt I would die if I couldn't do something in this situation. Then the poem came."[10] Perhaps it came too slickly; perhaps it came too much as therapy, as a mere purging of undigested emotion; perhaps it has not fully come to terms with the contradictory impulses to avoid war (an opinion Cummings has aired from the very first in his poetry) and to go to fight for freedom. Rather than coming to terms with the situation, the poet merely lashes out: more interested in shocking readers than seeking answers, he can only counsel that we "bury the statue of liberty / (because it begins to smell)."

Having exorcised his rage, however, he turns immediately to a subject which, while different in tone, naturally follows Thanksgiving: winter. "THANKSGIVING" was full of bitter irony; winter, ironically, is no dark night of the soul but a time of beauty and peace. The first of the winter poems, "silence" (40), is the best. A three-part poem in the imagist tradition, it speaks of silence as "a / looking / bird," the bird as "the / turn / ing;edge of / life," and the combination of these things as "inquiry before snow." The surprising word, here, is "life"; typically, Cummings replaces the more specific word (we expect "the season" or "the day" instead) with the more abstract. In this way he defines not only the particular silence, the sense of expectancy and prophecy (the "inquiry") before a snow, but suggests a more universal state of meaning and feeling as well. The next poems describe snowfalls (41–42), the responses of people toward the snow (43–44), and images of winter and sunlight (45). Poem 46, a Valentine's Day poem, advances into February.

The five poems from 47 to 51 form a tight sequence linked by references to twilight and the moon. The first speaks of moonrise as the coming of the "onlying / world" in the "bloodlight" of a colorful sunset. And the last ("f / eeble a blu," 51) pictures the moon on the wane, a "poor shadoweaten / was / of is" which, like the fragmented letters of this poem, is "a blu / r of cr / umbli / ng." Cummings, fond of crescent moon images, used them not only in poems. Some of his paintings picture the moon as a precise fine arc, "thinner than a watchspring" (*ViVa*, XIV); in some, however, it is a blur, a crumbling hunk of paint distinctly "shadoweaten."

The progress out of the city and into nature, like spring with its periods of warmth and frost, is not uniform, and these poems are followed by portraits of three city women. The "once beau / tiful la / dy" (52) who sits sewing is followed by the "old almos / tlady" (53) feeding perhaps the same six English sparrows that appeared earlier in "dim" (24). The last of these (54), the most critical, is best. Here, the "noN . . . / She" is the product of "ardensteil-henarub-izabeth," a wonderful word combining Elizabeth Arden's beauty treatments with hens, henna, rubs, and perhaps a curiously New York spelling of *style*. The product of such treatments, "allgotupfittokill," has a "p-e-r-f-e-c-t-l-y-d-e-a-d" voice that frightens even the park's boldest pigeons. In a final image that suddenly renders real her killing ways, she obliviously showers "cigaretteash" over her screaming offspring.

A different look at the relationship between youth and age appears in "old age sticks" (57). The aged, standing for tradition, conservatism, the establishment, erect signs that warn youth to "Keep / Off"; they cry "No / Tres) . . . (pas) / . . . (sing," and they scold "Forbid / den Stop / Must / n't Don't." Youth laughs and rebels—and "goes / right on / gr / owing old." Cummings, well past his own rebellious youth when this poem appeared in 1950, knew the danger of ignoring history. Having seen how readily youthful radicalism hardened into reactionary middle age, he nevertheless must have wondered at the pace with which some of the cronies of his youth were "growing old." In a similarly autobiographical vein, "a total stranger one black day" (58) records an interior combat with a "fiend" who "knocked living the hell out of me." The stranger turns out to be "myself"; once the identity is recognized, "fiend and i" become "immortal friends" and become each other. The poem may well suggest, as Friedman notes, the recognition on Cummings' part that his world consists not only of the transcendental but of the "descendental" as well.[11] But it is also true that the stranger, battling with the narrator, freed him from the necessity of living in the "hell" of the unworld. The combat has not been easy, and "forgiveness" was "hard"; but the struggle for a transcendent vision, with the aid of the "fiend" to purge him of the worldly, has been successful.

The transcendent vision itself is the subject of poem 60, which begins "dive for dreams / or a slogan may topple you." Without an ideal, says the poet, man is prey to clichés and catch-phrases; without vision he is subject to the conformity of the commonplace. The explanation is a cryptic image: "trees are their roots / and wind is wind." A tree is only as strong as its roots, and will topple in the wind unless well rooted. So we, too, unless we "dive" deep, may be toppled by the winds of slogan. The second stanza tells us to abide not by reason but by feeling ("trust in your heart") if unreasonable things happen ("if the seas catch fire"). The third suddenly descends into a tone dangerously close to that of the "slogan" he decries: the phrase "honor the past / but welcome the future," sound advice, nevertheless sounds less like Cummings than Polonius. But irony and wit begin to jell with the word "wedding." The fourth stanza betrays the narrator's "never mind a world" stance: the poem, after all, is simply a variant on the familiar *carpe diem.* Ignore the world, it counsels, and do what you are made to do. In this context, the earlier advice to go for the ideal and trust the heart is designed to seduce. That the narrator urges a passionate abandon to one's fate is evident in such images as "wind is wind," "the seas catch fire," and "live by love." But the irony may be deeper still. We who take this to be simply a poem addressed to a lady may find, instead, that the *carpe diem* theme is only a metaphor for the seizing of a transcendental vision, and that Cummings is laughing at us for being "toppled" by such slogans as *carpe diem* into a less elevated interpretation of this poem. Such a reading suggests one of the ways Cummings' poetry has developed. Where earlier poems corralled all sorts of images to serve the end of persuading his lady, the later poems make the *carpe diem* theme itself serve higher ends.

With "precisely as unbig a why as i'm" (63), the volume at last arrives at spring. Awakening, mercy, sunlight, and April are woven together in a correspondence which makes this poem a fitting beginning for a sequence whose poems speak of "one violet" (64), the "first robin" (65), and April, "the / greatest / of / living magicians" (66). These are a prologue for the exploration of oneness and individuality in "this little huge" (67). Cummings had earlier refined his thoughts on oneness in such poems as "one's not half two" (*1 x 1*, XVI) and "if everything happens that can't be done" (*1 x 1*, LIV). And he had delved into Yeatsian notions of masks in suggesting that "so many selves(so many fiends and gods / . . . is a man" (*Xaipe*, 11). Here he rejects the idea of a personality made of "many selves" in favor of the unified and integrated being. Reconstructed, the poem reads "this little huge-eyed person (nearly bursting with the inexpressible numberlessness of her selves) can't understand my only me." A highly structured arrangement of visual rhythms, the poem is constructed of alternating one- and three-line stanzas. The first and fourth of the long stanzas are built so that at each corner is a hyphen: a structure recalling "dim," whose second stanza is boxed by four isolated *e*'s at the corners. The second and third three-line stanzas here also build patterns: the second with its two-letter lines, the third by a triangular pattern designed around two corner hyphens in the first line and a parenthesis in the center of the last line. The central line in each stanza balances three things: two three-letter syllables around a parenthesis ("son(nea"), two hyphens around a word fragment ("-expressib-"), two three-letter syllables around a central word ("ess of her"), or two letters around a word ("d of o"). The pattern here nicely expresses the point: while this lady is a bundle of contradictions ("little huge") who is "nearly bursting," the "only me" of the poet is capable of producing poems as poised and well-balanced as the spheres, where separate things are drawn together into a unified and stable synthesis.

Anticipating the long sequence of Joy Farm poems beginning with 73 is a brief three-poem sequence (69–71) which has as its common feature the mysterious, the miraculous, and the marvelous. The best of these is 70 ("whatever's merely wilful"), a poem about artistic creation and beauty. That which is "wilful" rather than "miraculous"—those poems or paintings created with great academic skill but devoid of the *élan vital* of genius—must "wither fail and cease." Beauty, however, knows no better than "to grow." The goal of those who have made beauty is (when *is to* is inserted at the comma in line 9) to "outglory glory"—to raise glory to new heights. And if beauty should touch "a blunder / (called life)," then life itself becomes "her [beauty's] wonder" and both life and beauty are renewed in an everlasting union. For all its elliptical syntax, the poem is one of great loveliness and grace. Balancing its patterns carefully, it demonstrates the kind of "miraculous" quality that poetry must have to raise it above the "merely wilful" and abstractly intellectual statements of aesthetics.

With poem 73 ("let's,from some loud unworld's most rightful

wrong") the eleven-poem Joy Farm sequence begins. Several of these, focusing on rural birdlife, recall Cummings' comment to Pound that he had learned much from "a very few birds(who have honoured me with their friendship)."[12] Poem 74 ("sentinel robins two") invokes the protection of a pair of robins to guard poet and lover from "hate and fear." The lucid gives way to the cryptic in the second stanza: the "which of slim of blue / of here" is, it seems, the robin's egg, which, hatching, will "who / straight up into the where"—take on its own individuality (exchange "which" for "who") and fly up into the limitless air. All this happens because "so safe we are." Cummings, who delighted in watching the animal life around the farm from his porch, may have been responding to a nest so close to the house that he could watch the eggs. Even in such proximity, however, birds are "safe" and eggs can hatch. The birds, in return, are the poet's sentinels, guarding his creative energies so that they, too, can hatch and take flight. It is a fine symbiosis, in which each couple protects the other. In another bird poem, "(hills chime with thrush)" (75), Cummings describes the "chinoiserie" of a pair of humming-birds, a bird for which, as Charles Norman reports, he had a special affection[13] and about which he later composed a shaped poem (*73 Poems*, 55) emphasizing the long slender bill.

The two poems that follow, uncommonly lucid in the exposition of their ideas, are frankly religious in character and need to be seen as a set. The first, "these from my mother's great-grandmother's rosebush white" (76), blends together images of heaven, roses, and mothers: like the "heaven of blackred roses" in his tribute to his mother (*ViVa*, XLIII), these white roses are "improbable" in their beauty and perfection, creations of "omnipotent He." The roses are metaphors for poems: " 'and who' i asked my love 'could begin / to imagine quite such eagerly innocent whoms / of merciful sweetness except Himself?' " Her answer is that such roses (or poems) can only be imagined by someone " 'who holds Himself as the little white rose of a child' "—by someone who apprehends God Himself with the innocence and devotion of a child holding a white rose, or by someone, like Jesus "Himself," who holds himself to be the perfect child of God.

These ideas prepare the way for one of Cummings' best-known poems, "i am a little church(no great cathedral)" (77). Read as the Festival Poem for the Boston Arts Festival in 1957, it was the result of an extended effort that produced the eighty pages of drafts now in the Houghton Library. An early version begins simply as an impression, an apostrophe to a little church "with your bells within / you and your dead behind you sitting in a green field."[14] The lines are meant to transcribe a visual image: a nearby note refers to a picture of Saint-Germain-de-Charonne which Cummings found in a book of photographs entitled *Paris imprévu*.[15] Succeeding pages show that, while the last stanza was the first completed, the other five were slower in coming. In finished form the poem is built on many oppositions: "splendor and squalor," "rapture and anguish," and so forth. That these were not haphazard selections is indicated by a list of possible words on a typescript draft, a list including *hurry, bustle, hubbub, chaos, din, discord, tumult, confusion, turmoil, thunder, tension, sham, storming, terror, strife, warfare, conflict, hustle, rancor, malice,* and many more.

Starting as it does from a photograph, the poem might have become another of his visually oriented poems, depending for its meaning on the shapes of words on the page. In fact, however, Cummings departs somewhat from his own visual tradition and shows himself responsive to the demands of poetry meant to be read aloud. In the tradition of the poetry of praise from the Psalms forward, it develops a simple idea, the metaphor of the individual as "little church" rather than "cathedral," through repetition of phrasing and restatement of idea. In the tradition of oral poetry, it fixes upon certain recognizable syntactical patterns, establishes them early, and adheres to their form while varying their content. On several occasions a form introduced in one line is repeated later: the phrase "my life is the life of" is followed in the next line by "my prayers are the prayers of," and in the first stanza, "i do not worry if" is followed by "i am not sorry when," a pattern repeated in the fourth stanza. A conventional grammatical structure typically introduces both subject and verb within the first five words of each independent clause. Many of the lines are end-stopped, and most of these are in apposition with one another. Cummings' use of the coordinating conjunction *and* fits both the Biblical tradition and the necessities of oral presentation: demanding no shift of grammatical form, the conjunction simply appends a second clause to an already established sentence structure. Sometimes the word joins opposites. Sometimes it links, as in "sun and rain" or "the reaper and the sower," expected collocations of ideas. And sometimes it permits the introduction of words in series ("finding and losing and laughing and crying," "birth and glory and death and resurrection") which all serve the same grammatical function. The hearer, then, is not called upon to parse and reconstruct, as he is in so many of Cummings' poems. He can receive with a minimum of effort the poet's message.

The danger of such easy reception, however, is that it can favor clichés. For surely the easiest message to send is the one which has already been received countless times. Cummings runs that risk; and some readers complain that this poem is, in Friedman's words, "mawkish and sentimental."[16] The charge is not entirely unjust: references to sun and rain making April, to reapers and sowers, and to the peace of nature are certainly not

new. Nor, in context, are they entirely accurate. The trouble
comes from the impression of a poet speaking more out of wishful thinking than experience and conviction. Coming in the context of a body of work about cathouses, burlesques, derelicts in
city parks, and much of the paraphernalia of modern society,
the poem stretches us a bit far in asking us to credit the poet's
assertion that "my life is the life of the reaper and the sower."
Metaphorically we may agree: writing poetry and painting pictures resembles planting and gathering. That the poem expresses a desire for these things—for a humble country life, for
a disassociation from the "frantic / world" which, in its "rapture
and anguish," is both terribly appealing and terribly enervat-
ing—we can believe. Literally, however, we are forced to
demur: the problem is one of overstatement. Such hyperbole
leads us to question the significance of his final lines: are they
pronouncing a wholesale religious commitment, or do they
make up in fervor what they lack in conviction? Perhaps too
clearly, they mark out a particular state of faith—too clearly,
because for Cummings experience was never this simple. One
feels, for all his assertion and in spite of the beauty of the lines,
that "the deathless truth of His presence" is an idea with which
the poet has not quite come to terms, a presence not adequately
realized. Nevertheless it points a direction—and the direction,
for a poet growing out of the mundane and into the transcendent, is a most significant one.

In some ways, "how generous is that himself, the sun" (84) is
a better version of the religious ethos Cummings attempted to
express in "i am a little church." The difference is that it takes
the sun as subject, letting the reader make the simple but essential metaphoric connection between sun as source and God
as Source. Not especially meant for reading aloud, some passages are knotty: "till of more much than dark most nowhere no
/ particle is not a universe" means, on distentangling, "until

every particle of darkest nowhere is an entire universe by itself." The ending, eschewing the capital letters which sat uneas-
ily in "i am a little church," makes a similar point: "we are himself's own self;his very him" suggests our identity as images of
the sun and of God, and implies that our effect on our world is
like the sun's effect on its universe. And lest the reader show
concern that Cummings, by this time, is only repeating old
themes in new dress, poem 87 (beginning "now(more near ourselves than we) / is a bird singing in a tree") includes an astute
self-definition of its own style: "who never sings the same thing
twice / and still that singing's always his." Like Cummings' poetry, birds' songs are never exactly the same, yet similar enough
that the creator can be identified.

The last eight poems in the volume turn their attention to
love. Here Cummings returns to his earlier habit of ending volumes with sonnets, in which form all but three of these are
written. Moving away from the specifics of time and place that
characterized the Joy Farm poems, these subsist on the abstract: their subjects are such things as "your complete fearless
and pure love" (88), "your fear" (89), "The whole truth" (91),
and "spring!" (93). In some cases that abstraction leads him into
difficulties: "i carry your heart with me(i carry it in" (92) is a bit
repetitious, an over-extended piece that loses economy in need-
less proliferation. And "being to timelessness as it's to time"
(94), suffering an old complaint, begins bravely enough—indeed, with a provocative line that turns on the definition of
"it's"—and then lapses into a series of affirmations that come to
sound, especially in the final "all's well," a shade too hollow.
The points it expresses are, once again, laudable and remarkably true: but the slickness of their expression ignores the difficulties attendant upon realizing their truth.

Two of these last poems, however, escape the blight of mere
abstraction by sheer lyricism. In "rosetree,rosetree" (90),

Cummings composes a carefully wrought song in praise, perhaps, of the same white rosebush celebrated in 76. In nine six-
line stanzas of syllabic verse (counted 4-6-6-5-5) he works an
intricate system of rhyme, near-rhyme, and reversed rhyme:
the first two lines of each verse, for example, end with such inverted rhymes as "rosetree / see:whose," "wish no / roguish,"
and "least the / three,must." As Friedman's extensive analysis
indicates, this poem required some 175 worksheets; the result,
as he says, is a "ceremonial ode for the earth's birthday" in
which the rosetree is seen as the symbol of all things that tran-
scend mind (stanza 3), fact (stanza 4), time (stanza 5), and despair (stanza 6).[17]

The volume's final poem knits lyric affirmation to abstract language: "if up's the word;and a world grows greener" (95) is indeed, as Berryman thought, a "most effective" poem.[18] The ecstatic rhythm, composed largely of anapests, captures the verve
of a celebratory dance. Lines like "—let's touch the sky;with a
to and a fro / (and a here there where)and away we go" depend
less for their effect on meaning than on rhythm and sound; they
are cousin to such nonsense refrains as "With a hey, and a ho,
and a hey nonino" from the Shakespeare poem which Cummings read as part of his second Harvard nonlecture. Woven
into this lyric texture are some of the most quotable of Cummings' lines: "in even the laziest creature among us / a wisdom no
knowledge can kill is astir" is typical in its dependence on careful distinctions ("wisdom" versus "knowledge"); and his archetypal vocabulary is threaded smoothly into the lines "it's brains
without hearts have set saint against sinner; / put gain over
gladness and joy under care." Like the final lines in *50 Poems*
("whole truthful infinite immediate us") and *1 x 1* ("we're wonderful one times one"), the final lines here celebrate not individuality but communion: "—let's touch the sky:with a you and
a me / and an every(who's any who's some)one who's we." The

earlier poems, more cognitive in their appeal, also had more to say about the evils of the world they were resisting. Here, in keeping with the reduced emphasis on satire in 95 *Poems*, the poet speaks almost entirely in the affirmative: the second stanza, for example, which could talk in denigrating terms about the "laziest creature among us," instead singles out one of that creature's good qualities ("wisdom") for praise. Perhaps, as he progressed, Cummings came to feel less dependent on the demands of the prosaic and more comfortable in the presence of the simple lyric. Perhaps it was in lyricism that he most clearly approached "the wisdom no knowledge can kill."

Chapter 12

73 Poems

Cummings' last volume was published the year after his death in New Hampshire on September 2, 1962. Like earlier volumes, 73 *Poems* intermixes new work with poems previously published in periodicals. Unlike earlier volumes, the contents were not arranged by Cummings but by his bibliographer, George Firmage. "In early December 1962," Firmage recalls, "Marion Cummings handed me a folder containing typescripts for 28 hitherto unpublished poems and asked me to make fair copies of these as well as any other poems I knew of that had been published but had not, as yet, been collected in one of Estlin's books. . . . I made no attempt to imitate Estlin's previously published volumes in arranging the . . . poems; I merely tried, as best I could, to find a pleasing reading order."[1] The final text included forty-six previously published poems and twenty-seven of the unpublished ones.

While nothing of Cummings' intentions can be deduced from the sequence, the volume does mark a certain progress beyond 95 *Poems*. Although it levels its share of satiric darts—at "mrs somethingwitz / nay somethingelsestein" (18), at the "fearlessandbosomy . . . / gal" of eighty (20), and even at Aphrodite, Hephaestus, and Ares (27)—these pieces tend to be soft at the tip, written less in biting anger than bemused aversion. The world, with its "Mostpeople" who scream for "international /

measures that render hell rational" (30), is still a "sub / human superstate" (31) descending on "the path to nothingness" (62). But that world, for Cummings, is no longer too much with us; he looks with increasing serenity at a better one. "Only at the close of his life," as Lane notes in his commentary on the penultimate poem in the volume, "did Cummings approach the lofty tone of late Goethe or Yeats, facing . . . death with a dignified but idiomatic simplicity, a distanced but intensely personal vision, and a serene but passionate conviction in transcendence."[2]

As conviction increased, so did limpidity. Syntax here is less demanding, vocabulary less challenging, and words are less often fragmented than in earlier volumes. There is a growing proportion of extremely short poems, poems with no more than thirty words and sometimes no more than ten.[3] It is a simplicity born not of senility but of wisdom, a capacity for concise statement coupled with lyric evocation. Fittingly, a number of these poems recall earlier ones: Cummings in these years was of a mind, it seems, to reexamine his earlier successes. In many ways it is a poetry of triumph, marking the victory of the feeling he always preached over the thinking he struggled to refine.

The volume opens with "O the sun comes up-up-up in the opening." A boistrous celebration about animals awaking to the sunrise, it features birds, dog, cat, cow ("who-horn"), colt ("prance"), chicks ("fluffies"), and a "ree ray rye roh / rowster" who crows in the dawn with a loud "rawrOO." Unlike Ted Hughes, whose *Lupercal* had appeared three years before *73 Poems*, Cummings sees in animals not deadly violence but lively joy, an exuberance that blends the noisy onomatopoeia of his contemporary Wallace Stevens with the precise observation of his friend Marianne Moore. The poem also indicates something of the distance he had come from an earlier dawn poem, "O It's Nice To Get Up In,the slipshod mucous kiss" (&, "Sonnets—

Realities," I) which celebrated morning as a time for the "chuckles of supreme sex." Following what is already his own well-established genre of animal pieces, Cummings includes in this volume poems about kingbird (2), songbird (11), thrushes (48), a hummingbirds' nest (55), a chickadee (56), a "drea(chipmunk)ming" (58), a purple finch (64), and something which may be a cricket (49). He also describes "2 little whos" (60), who, like the pair of porcupines in "porky & porkie" (*New Poems*, 21) and the pair of birds in "sentinel robins two" (*95 Poems*, 74), are probably small forest animals. These last, like most of his animals, stand in instructive juxtaposition to the "grown / -up i&you- / ful world of known," which includes the poet and his love. Nature, hardly red in tooth and claw, is sympathetic to Cummings' fauna: over them is not Dylan Thomas' hawk crying "dilly dilly . . . Come and be killed"[4] but a "wonderful tree" radiant with autumn foliage and "aflame with dreams."

If nature is friendly to animals, man is not always so, as "Me up at does" (12) suggests. Here the poet, finding a "poisoned mouse," brings together contradictory impulses into a single image. Mice, to the owner of a country residence like Joy Farm, gnaw their way into great nuisance unless poisoned. But mice—to a poet who delighted in "the eyes of mice" as a symbol for a reality beyond literature (preface to *is* 5) and who found himself sharing his meals with a mouse (&, "Sonnets—Actualities," xx), comparing a mouse with love (*is* 5, "4," III), and writing an elegy for a dead mouse (*No Thanks*, 14)—represented something friendly and affectionate. Cummings, both owner and poet, feels both sides of the issue: this mouse, asking "What / have i done that / You wouldn't have," opens in that accusing question a number of points for speculation. Pursuing his own mousey ways, living the only way he knows, he has been poisoned. Is this, perhaps, an image for the poet grimly rewarded by the "numb . . . unworld" (19) of inhumanity for doing what he must do? Concise and simple, the poem refuses even the imagist equation of a tangible perception with an intangible state of thought or feeling; it provides simply a brief impression, leaving the reader the task of seeing significance.

"Me up at does," brief in its twenty-six words, is by no means among the shortest of Cummings' poems here. The thirteen words of poem 3 represent a style that Cummings brings to its fullest in this volume. Here, without the fragmentation common in his shorter poems, he deploys traditional devices: metrical lines, off-rhyme, repetition (of "truth" and "path"), and a syntactical ambiguity that lets us read the final lines both with a pause after "where" and, alternatively, with a pause after "is" ("all paths lead where truth is, here"). Read in the first way, paths are seen to be a danger, leading us astray to "where"— somewhere else—and away from "here," the present moment. Read in the second way, paths are merely a redundancy, since we are already where truth is. Ultimately, both readings are correct. Paths, after all, are worn by the feet of conforming generations which, as in Hopkins' "God's Grandeur," "have trod, have trod, have trod."[5] Truth, for Cummings as for Hopkins, is not found in acquiescence; it is indigenous, a kingdom within, and its seeker need go no farther than "here" to find it. Several other poems capture the same brevity and penetration: "now is a ship" (9) talks of waking from sleep into dream, and poem 34 varies Paul's observation that "unto the pure all things are pure" (Titus 1:15) into a neatly turned epigram.

"SONG" (4), one of only two titled poems in the volume, recalls Cummings' penchant for titles in his earliest volumes. It also recalls, in its comment that "worlds are made / of hello and goodbye," the world which, in "into the strenuous briefness" (*Tulips and Chimneys*, "Post Impressions," iii), is made "of roses & hello: / (of solongs and,ashes)." Lyric not only by title and stanza structure, "SONG" also depends on studiously balanced repetition to suggest a tuneful refrain. The line "big little and all" alternates between lines 6 and 4 in the first four stanzas, settling down to line 8 in the final stanza. Each stanza builds on a simple contrast between what "we" have and what "they"— the inhabitants of "worlds"—claim to possess. The major opposition is between "love" and "worlds." Developing this dialectic, each stanza also contains its own pair of opposed contraries. In the first, "we've the may / . . . to sing" (the month, as well as the permission), while "worlds" have only "the must to say." Where they have "the when to do"—the timebound pressure to keep busy—we have, in stanza 2, "the now to grow." Where love in stanza 3 gives us "the gift to live," they are provided only with "the trick to seem." And where good, by cyclical inevitability, turns into bad for them in stanza 4, we find "our summer in fall / and in winter our spring"—the recollection of past beauty ("summer") and the promise of renewal ("spring") even when seasons would tell us otherwise.

Several pieces here evidence Cummings' flair for building poems from colloquial statements strung out down the page. When the strategy works, as it does in "it's / so damn sweet when Anybody—" (7) the statement is a plain one expressed with simple force, withholding its conclusion until the final word. When the strategy is less successful, as in "because it's" (10), the statement repeats well-worn ideas and even repeats itself. In this case, Cummings falls victim to his occasional weakness for starting off well and finishing poorly. Here the beginning—"because it's / Spring / thingS / dare to do people"—has a wit about it that by the end has evaporated.

Often the strung-out poems are molded into shape by a precise stanza structure. Such is the case in "e / cco the uglies / t" (16), a poem about the drabness of the wintry New York skyline under an "eggyellow smear" of sunset. Balancing word fragments, Cummings builds an artful pattern here: one-letter lines in stanza one are echoed by similar lines in stanza 5; the one-two-three progression of stanza 2 ("s / ub / sub") is reversed in stanza 4 ("hou / se / s"); and the whole poem, because of increasingly long lines in stanzas 1, 3, and 5, has the shape of a right triangle—a shape echoed in the stanzas 2 and 4. Less crafted, the following poem ("n / Umb a," 17) groups its word fragments into four-line stanzas to describe another city scene: a sidewalk graced with "6 / twirls of do / gsh / it" and three hideous voices. Recalling the "sawdust voices" high in the tenements in "(one!) / the wisti-twisti barber" (&, "N," VI), the poem may also spin a coterie joke for Cummings' friends. The line "s 3 m," exhibiting the kind of balance he loved, may also be a diminutive of *S. 4. N.*, a periodical from the twenties in which "POEM, OR BEAUTY HURTS MR. VINAL" first appeared. Similar in stanza structure is "nite)" (23), an intriguing poem which, while it may simply be about intercourse ("2 ph / antoms clutch / ed in / a writhewho room . . . / e / xploding"), is more probably about a midnight catfight interrupted by the charge of a mongrel ("moangrowl"). As the racket peaks to a scream, the animals vanish into the stillness of the poem's last word, "aRe(n't." Perhaps it is a metaphor for the poet, who in three lines of the last stanza ("e / AM / e") signs his initials and lists his occupation.

The volume includes a number of other brief poems skillfully patterned in their stanzas. Poem 24 ("insu nli gh t") counts letters carefully to suggest the regular motion of a newspaper blowing over and over in the wind. Poem 42, which on recombination simply says "nothing can surpass the mystery of stillness," regularly returns to the one-letter line. Poem 58 ("& sun &") alternates one- and four-line stanzas, matches the line lengths of stanza 2 with stanza 6 and of 4 with 8, and suggests visually a chipmunk standing upright on the flat base of a boulder. And "one" (61), a poem about a snowflake on a gravestone whose first word is also its last, pivots upon its central line ("ght") and mirrors the pattern of its first seven lines in the perfect reflection of the last seven. One of the most interesting of the short poems is "t,h;r:u;s,h;e:s" (48), a collection of one- and three-line stanzas which, if reduced to a nearly standard English, might read "thrushes are silent now; in silvery not-quiteness is a dream of the moon." Read so, the poem is an exercise in imagism, evoking twilight at Joy Farm. In fact, however, it is more correctly read as an exploration of the margin at which reality becomes illusion. By extracting "-it-" out of "notqu / -it- / eness," the poet uses the word perhaps to suggest the magical presence or state which, silencing the thrushes, has not quite arrived to the waiting world. In this state of half-light dreams *a the of moon*, a particular and defined object which is a piece of the moon. The tmesis of "dre(is)ams" compels the word to suggest both illusion (the moon "dreams") and reality (the moon "is"), while simultaneously welding the described outer scene to the felt inner world (the moon "am") as moon and poet merge. "Through syntax and typography," says Wegner in his ingenious reading of this poem, "splintered vision is made whole."[6]

With "nobody could / in superhuman flights" (18), Cummings limbers up his satiric arm. Like the portait of the mother who, wholly absorbed in herself, sprinkles cigarette ashes over her child ("ardensteil-henarub-izabeth," *95 Poems*, 54), "this dame" is more involved in politics than motherhood. Out campaigning, she is overheard to say that "politics,as everyone knows,is / wut ektyouelly metus" (what actually matters). The poet, assessing the woman's humanity by her treatment of others, can hardly agree: the child who limps along beside her "might less frenziedly have cried / eev mahmah hadn chuzd nogged id entwhys" (if mama hadn't just knocked it endways). Politics, after all, is the tool whereby individuals convert their autonomy into mass action, where the "I" becomes the "we"; and Cummings has wasted no opportunity to make his feelings for the herd state clear in such earlier poems as "when serpents bargain for the right to squirm" (*Xaipe*, 22). More cryptic, but no less scathing, is "everybody happy?" (19). The poem, as Lane observes, depends on our knowledge of the political philosophy of Jeremy Bentham, who found fame in asserting that the goal of political action is the greatest happiness for the greatest number—a notion which Carlyle branded "pig philosophy."[7] Cummings, who knew about these things, was not misled in alluding to the three little pigs in line two ("WE-WE-WE"), which also suggests agreement (*oui-oui-oui*) and asserts the collective "we" over the individual "I." Pigs may lurk behind "chappy" as well, which seems an oblique reference to the "grintgrunt wugglewiggle" who "champychumpchomps" his food in the first poem in this volume. If you can't lick 'em (or dent 'em), join 'em, urges the sarcasm in the lines "if you can't dentham / comma bentham." After all, "science" reigns supreme and knows only "1 law for the lions & / oxen." Poetry, however, knows where such a sense of law gets us: "One Law for the Lion & Ox," declared Blake in *The Marriage of Heaven and Hell*, "is oppression."[8] Drifting to insentience, the world sinks into an apathy where it sells its soul for a dream of political happiness. Asking "how numb can an unworld get?" the narrator answers his own question with "number," the great word of majority rule and of mathematical science.

Several of the satires return to the regular form of Cummings' earlier work. The somewhat unusual rhythm of "if seventy were young" (26) results from a simple figure: each stanza comprises three feminine pentameter phrases which have been broken into trimeter and dimeter lines, and which are followed by a single trimeter line with a masculine rhyme. The strategy of composition is no less orderly. The first three stanzas, in the manner of "as freedom is a breakfastfood" (*50 Poems*, 25), set up impossible conditions: "if broken hearts were whole," "if sorrowful were gay," and so forth. These are followed by lines whose general meaning is *come what may:* "dingdong:dong-ding" in the first stanza, "fare ill:fare well" and "cry nay:cry yea" in the next two. Each stanza ends with the extraordinary paradox that would exist if the conditions were true. If, says the poet, all things were pleasant, amenable, easy, and without challenge, then "to say would be to sing," "a frown would be a smile," and "november would be may." Were that the case, "you and i'd be quite / . . . another i and you"—individuality would be lost in the general blandness of "such perfection." Fear of that loss "disposes me to shoot / dogooding folk on sight"—to shoot those who hawk schemes for perfecting humanity. The message, from one who so often speaks of escaping the world to a transcendent state where such paradoxes are welcome, may seem contradictory. Cummings' point, however, is that the attempt to salvage mortality (rather than to rise above it into immortality) is the most dangerous counterfeit of real transcendence, a sham perpetuated by "dogooding folk" who, rather than seeking to grasp the nature of transcendence, busy themselves in the mundane affairs of others.

Nearly as serious, and far funnier, is "in heavenly realms of hellas dwelt" (27). Here Cummings retells the classical tale of Aphrodite ("someone wholly beautiful"), her husband Hephaestus ("cunning ugly lame"), and her lover Ares ("handsome strong and born to dare"). Vigor of language proves Cummings' credentials both as forger of words and narrator of tales. Blowing up the rhetoric and undercutting the formality, Cummings recalls here the tone of "come,gaze with me upon this dome" (*is* 5, "Two," VIII): the mock-heroics of long sentences and archaic diction are larded with conversational turns of phrase ("as you'll shortly comprehend," "flee one another like the pest"). Like the "trumpets clap and syphilis" of "come,gaze with me," the end strikes a wry note that reduces the famous classic to moral homily: "my tragic tale concludes herewith: / soldier,beware of mrs smith." Even in such a light moment Cummings, like "Cunning" the "marvelous artificer," remembers his craft: after thirtynine lines of off-rhyme (and, in one instance, perfect feminine rhyme), the final couplet clicks into perfect masculine rhyme. Cummings, whose name Edmund Wilson once rendered "hee hee cunnings," may have seen himself in this poem.

Dealing another hand of rhymed and rhythmic verse, Cummings produces two city poems that focus on reactions to the unconventional: " 'right here the other night something" (28), and "one winter afternoon" (30). The first recounts a tale told to the poet by "charlie," who describes a street-corner encounter with "a tall strong young / finelooking fellow,dressed / well but not over" who asked him for "three cents please." Charlie, having no change, gave him "one whole buck"—at which the panhandler fell to his knees in gratitude. The narrator asks " 'then . . . what happened?' " Charlie's response is a whispered " 'i ran.' " Like "i met a man under the moon" (ViVa, XLVI), this poem is a portrait of an incomprehensible. So contradictory are Charlie's impressions—a well-dressed man begging, a beggar asking for only three cents (which, by the sixties, was a pointlessly small amount), a beggar who so effusively shows his gratitude—that he cannot construct from them a portrait of anything recognizable. He cannot, in other words, reduce this character to a label: neither "bum," "con man," nor "religious fanatic" will work here. Having no way to come to terms with the experience, he flees.

That there are other ways of dealing with expressions of acute individuality is demonstrated by "one winter afternoon" (30), in which the narrator himself meets "a bespangled clown / standing on eighth street" who hands him a daisy. Nobody else, we are told, has observed the clown, because he represents "whatever . . . / mostpeople fear most: / a mystery for which i've / no word except alive." Ending with the famous couplet—"i thank heaven somebody's crazy / enough to give me a daisy"—the poet comes to terms with this magical figure by seeing in him the antithesis of the "international / measures that render hell rational," of the intellection that rationalizes the world's horrors instead of mitigating them. Whether or not the clown is meant to be real or imagined is unimportant. What matters is the way one deals with the "miraculous whole" of such a being, an individuality possessed of "not merely a mind and a heart / but unquestionably a soul." It is a problem Cummings has raised from the earliest poems. His response here, in keeping with the joyous tone of his later work, is to thank heaven.

With "your homecoming will be my homecoming—" (40) Cummings shows himself still master of the sonnet in the Renaissance tradition. A simple conceit for lover and beloved, this poem is elaborated in graceful and lucid language. The sonnet dwells largely on the beloved's absence, the conceit being that on leaving she takes with her "my selves" and leaves behind only "an almost someone always who's noone." It ends, fittingly, with reconciliation: "joy's perfect wholeness we're." There is nothing paraphrasable here that has not been said for years in popular songs; but liberties of syntax, elliptical expressions ("my very life who's your"), typical vocabulary ("noone," "selfish i," "joy's perfect wholeness"), and characteristic turns of phrase ("the forever of his loneliness") all brand the style with Cummings' own mark. Telling much the same message as "your homecoming," the syllabic stanzas and careful rhymes of "without the mercy of" (47) speak of the "namelessness" of the poet's condition without "the mercy" of the lover's presence. That unspeakable condition vanishes at the "thrill of your beauty," and "my whereful selves they put on here again"; the selves put on the quality of *hereness,* take up their abode in the present once again. The last stanza, tangled in artful arabesques, may be paraphrased to say that all this happens "as [at the time when] all these small thankful birds are wholly singing to one livingest star."

Depending more on specific image than abstract idea, "a round face near the top of the stairs" (41) describes the sleeping house with a grandfather clock bonging at mignight, a mantle-piece clock chiming at one, a moon in the sky, and "i and my love . . . alone." A wholly different view of clocks emerges in the sonnet beginning "what time is it?it is by every star / a different time" (45). Here "clocks have enough to do / without confusing timelessness with time." Pondering metaphysics and rising above the "falsely true" notions of "subhuman" time, the poet asserts that he and his love are "hosts of eternity;not guests of seem," and are, by escaping into "timelessness," undying. The poem begs comparison with an earlier one beginning in the same words; but "what time is it i wonder never mind" (*ViVa*, XIV), an aubade dealing with "lust," chose not to rise into time-lessness but to seize the moment. The change in emphasis from time and lust to timelessness and love is characteristic of Cummings' later work. Where time is irrelevant, the moment need not be seized; the emphasis on timelessness, in fact, accounts for the virtual disappearance of the *carpe diem* theme in these last volumes.

Characteristic, too, are the elegies in this volume. Unlike earlier portraits, the three commemorative poems here do not identify their subjects. The first (14) speaks simply of "a great / man" gone: references to mountains, sky, sun, and stars point to the Joy Farm landscape and suggest that the man may have been one of the rural Yankees Cummings so admired. The sense of loss ("what absolute nothing") at the end of "but" (51) registers the depth of grief the narrator feels at the loss of the "miracle" of friendship. The last ("of all things under our," 53) is

less an elegy than a poem of consolation for "eliena,my dear."
Eliena Eastman, with whom Cummings had some correspondence,[9] was the wife of Max Eastman, former editor of the Marxist organ *Masses* (1911–17) and friend and supporter of Cummings for years—although Eastman himself, who outlived Cummings, is not the subject. None of these elegies makes any effort to come to terms with death: eschewing the layering of perception of Milton's "Lycidas," the monumental praise of Yeats's "In Memory of Major Robert Gregory," and the religious assertions of Thomas's "Do not go gentle into that good night," Cummings here sticks simply to his feelings. What he felt was grief, absence, and nothingness: and that is what he reported.

As though to battle his way out of that gloom, Cummings writes "now does our world descend" (62), a poem describing the corrupt state of the world and his desire to flee it. Cummings' model is probably Sir Walter Ralegh's "The Lie," a poem of some thirteen stanzas which begins:

> Go, soul, the body's guest,
> Upon a thankless errand;
> Fear not to touch the best;
> The truth shall be thy warrant.
> Go, since I needs must die,
> And give the world the lie.

Cummings' poem begins:

> now does our world descend
> the path to nothingness
> (cruel now cancels kind;
> friends turn to enemies)
> therefore lament,my dream
> and don a doer's doom.

Similar in form (each is composed in a stanza of six trimeter lines rhyming *ababcc*), these poems follow parallel courses. Ralegh speaks to his "soul"; Cummings speaks in turn to "my dream," "my life," "poor dishonoured mind," "my heart," and "my soul." Ralegh inveighs against courts, churches, statesmen, artists, and a host of others; Cummings complains less about the evildoers than the evils themselves, which lead to the condition where "create is now contrive" and "wrong's the only right." Ralegh ends in unmitigated virulence: "Spare not to give the lie," he urges his soul, because "No stab the soul can kill" and the truth will be victorious. Cummings, however, knows another way out: where dream, life, mind, and heart must "lament," "lie down," "hide," and "despair," the final line commands his soul to "arise . . . and sing." In accord with the prevailing tenor of these last poems, the poet rises above the mire of the world; even in the face of all its evil the soul must sing. What illusion, human vigor, rationality, and courage could not accomplish in the first four stanzas is to be done, and done singingly, in the fifth by soul. As for Ralegh, so for Cummings soul is victor.

The two last poems in the volume are, in very different ways, among the finest in the canon. The three pentameter lines of "wild(at our first)beasts uttered human words" (72) compress into twenty-four words a compendious history of the world. Ascending from "beasts" to "birds" and on into "stars," the images move progressively upward and away from earth. In the beginning, says the poet, we were children uttering strangely word-like sounds. In maturity our presence made "stones sing like birds"—made the inanimate universe take on the qualities of animation, joyousness, and freedom. Cummings, again, implies that the things of the world—stones, in this case—have no expressive qualities of their own. Hence they have no meanings until given them by the user of language who, like the banished duke in *As You Like It,* finds "sermons in stones." The first two lines, then, account for human life; but the poem has a third line, moving on to considerations of immortality. Where life for the early Cummings was a matter of birth, maturity, and decay, for the late Cummings it consists in birth, maturity, and transcendence. The "starhushed silence" is our third state, an ascendent condition in which, words and songs quited, the silence of a deeper communion prevails. This is the silence that appears at the end of "all which isn't singing is mere talking" (32): there, "the very song . . . / of singing is silence," for as singing is superior to talking, so silence is the very essence of the power of song.

The word "silence" shows up rather frequently in Cummings' earliest and latest work. In fact, as a quick check of the concordance shows, more than half of his uses of the word occur in his first two and his last two volumes.[10] In the first volumes, however, it was not infrequently the silence of death that the poet invoked. In *Tulips and Chimneys* cannons lay "fists of huger silence" on soldiers ("La Guerre," I), lovers flee from "death, / silence, and the keenly musical light / of sudden nothing" ("Sonnets—Actualities," III), and the sea "through her blind miles / of crumbling silence seriously smiles" ("Sonnets—Unrealities," VI). In *&* the word suggests the deathly spectacle of lust. The girl with "long hard eyes" keeps "silence on her dress" with "long hard hands" ("Sonnets—Realities," XVIII), the girl whose "hair was like a gas / evil to feel" smelled of "silence" ("Sonnets—Realities," VI), and the consummation of lust is ominously seen as a "nude / and final silence" ("Sonnets—Actualities," IV). By the end of his career, however, Cummings saw in silence an image for the transcendent and the metaphysical. Seeing it also as the finest eloquence, he associated it with poetry and song. In *95 Poems* the moon is "the onlying / world) / whose / silence are cries / poems children dreams" (47), the countryside is "a cloverish silence of thrushsong" (73), and with the coming of love "all . . . words of words / turn to a silence who's the voice of voice" (88). In 73 *Poems*, as the clown gave the poet a daisy, "the silence of him / sang like a bird" (30). It is, then, to this metaphysical and metapoetical stillness that the last poems turn, a "starhushed silence" in which the merely human ear is quieted and man can respond to the things of soul.

As silence is the keenest quality of sound, so a vision of love is the sharpest focus of sight. And just as no human ear will be adequate to the first, so mere worldly seeing will not encompass the second. That is the message of the last poem, "all worlds have halfsight, seeing either with" (73). For Cummings, "worlds" are limited and loveless places inhabited by most-people and utterly without grace. Worlds are places made not by fact but by consent, not by matter, society, or time but simply by belief. Seen for what it is, the world can be rendered harmless: "this world(as timorous itsters all / to call their cowardice quite agree) / shall never discover our touch and feel," says the poet in *Xaipe* (66). And although "down come blundering / proud hugenesses of hate / sometimes called world," birds continue singing (73 *Poems*, 11). It is these worlds, then, which have only "halfsight." They see one of two ways: with "life's eye(which is if things seem spirits)," or, "(if spirits in the guise of things appear)," with death's. If a kind of airy pantheism prevails, they see in things the presence of spirits; if a stolid materialism, the unspiritualized molecular stuff. Insofar as they limit vision in either way—and "any world," by definition, "must always half perceive"—they cannot grasp wholeness. The only one who can perceive the whole is he "whose vision can create the whole": for wholeness, not a quality of the objective world per se, is the result of one's view of that world. And the only one who can see in that way is "love," the entity that "strolls the axis of the universe," the being who lives easily at the very heart of existence. The trademark of the world is denial, the negation of the promise of love. But "your lover . . . / timelessly celebrates the merciful wonder" of love. The pronoun "your" may be read as the general and colloquial term contrasting the lover, for example, with "your pedant" or "your soldier." But "your" may also be read as a specific identifying term, especially if this poem is meant to be addressed to "my lady" from "your lover." In the latter reading, lover is poet, and the wholeness of love's vision becomes that of poetry's vision. Uniting opposite modes of vision and rising above them, the lover is paradoxically "foolishwise" and "proudhumble"; seeing with more than world's sight, he is "free into the beauty of the truth," and sees a universe far beyond that of either life or death.

This sort of poem demands a reading in context. Isolated from the slowly developing themes that progress through Cummings' earlier poetry, it appears somewhat plain. But in that context there are very few words used here that do not come to this poem charged with significance. The idea of halves versus wholes, the distinction between the seeming and the real, the words "steep," "beauty," "truth," "timelessly," and "merciful," derive their impact from use in numerous prior poems; each draws sustenance and originality from the accretion of definition built up throughout Cummings' entire career. Most notable is the word "love." If Cummings has one subject, that is it. It begins in *Tulips and Chimneys* as an echo of popularly romantic notions, and it grows in early volumes to a sometimes amorphous phenomenon seasoned by a not entirely unselfish lust. By these last poems, however, it has come to be a purified and radiant idea, unentangled with flesh and worlds, the agent of the highest transcendence. It is not far, as poem after poem has hinted, from the Christian conception of love as God. It is this sense of God that Cummings' poems of praise have celebrated, this sense that his satires have sought to protect. It is this sense that Cummings, whose entire body of work is finally an image of himself, would have us see as the source of his own being.

Appendix

This Appendix refers the reader to explications and useful comments on individual poems. Intended to be selective rather than comprehensive, it cites those portions of articles and books which help the reader to an understanding of particular poems and which contribute significantly to the literature on the poem.

Poems are listed in order of appearance in their original volumes, and are cited by section (when applicable), number, first line, and title (when applicable). Citations to books and articles are in chronological order of appearance.

Frequently mentioned books:

Dumas, Bethany K. *E. E. Cummings: A Remembrance of Miracles.* New York: Barnes & Noble, 1974.

Friedman, Norman. *E. E. Cummings: The Art of His Poetry.* Baltimore: Johns Hopkins University Press, 1960. (Cited as Friedman, *Art.*)

—— *E. E. Cummings: The Growth of a Writer.* Carbondale: Southern Illinois University Press, 1964. (Cited as Friedman, *Growth.*)

Lane, Gary. *I Am: A Study of E. E. Cummings' Poems.* Lawrence / Manhattan / Wichita: The Regents Press of Kansas, 1976.

Marks, Barry A. *E. E. Cummings.* New York: Twayne, 1964.

Wegner, Robert E. *The Poetry and Prose of E. E. Cummings.* New York: Harcourt, Brace & World, 1965.

Collections of essays:

Baum, S. V. ΕΣΤΙ: *e e c: E. E. Cummings and the Critics.* East Lansing: Michigan State University Press, 1962.

Friedman, Norman. *E. E. Cummings: A Collection of Critical Essays.* Englewood Cliffs, N.J.: Prentice-Hall, 1972. (Cited as Friedman, *Essays.*)

Readers desiring more complete bibliographies are referred to Baum and to Friedman, *Art.*

Tulips and Chimneys (1923)

Epithalamion ("**Thou aged unreluctant earth who dost**"). Marks, pp. 67–68.

Of Nicolette ("**dreaming in marble all the castle lay**"). Richard S. Kennedy, "E. E. Cummings at Harvard: Verse, Friends, Rebellion," *Harvard Library Bulletin* (July 1977), 25:258–59.

Songs, III ("**Thy fingers make early flowers of**"). Friedman, *Art*, pp. 72–73; Marks, pp. 68–69.

Songs, IV ("**All in green went my love riding**"). Barry Sanders, *The Explicator* (November 1966), vol. 25, item 23; Will C. Jumper, *The Explicator* (September 1967), vol. 26, item 6; Cora Robey, *The Explicator* (September 1968), vol. 27, item 2; William V. Davis, "Cummings' 'All in green went my love riding,' " *Concerning Poetry* (1970), 3:65–67; Irene R. Fairley, "Syntactic Deviation and Cohesion," *Language and Style* (1973), 6:221–23; Philip J. West, "Medieval Style and the Concerns of Modern Criticism," *College English* (March 1973), 34:784–90; Lane, pp. 59–63.

Songs, VI ("**when god lets my body be**"). Doris Dundas, *The Explicator* (May 1971), vol. 29, item 79; Irene R. Fairley, "Syntactic Deviation and Cohesion," *Language and Style* (1973), 6:223–27; Lane, pp. 56–59.

Puella Mea ("**Harun Omar and Master Hafiz**"). Sheridan Baker, "Cummings and Catullus," *Modern Language Notes* (March 1959), 74:233 (footnote 4).

Chansons Innocentes, I ("**in Just-**"). Marvin Felheim, *The Explicator* (November 1955), vol. 14, item 11; Marks, pp. 46–47; C. Steven Turner, *The Explicator* (October 1965), vol. 24, item 18; Lane, pp. 26–29.

Chansons Innocentes, III ("**Tumbling-hair**"). Irene R. Fairley, "Syntactic Deviation and Cohesion," *Language and Style* (1973), 6:218–19; Richard S. Kennedy, Introduction to *Tulips & Chimneys*, George J. Firmage, ed. (New York: Liveright, 1976), p. xii.

Amores, I ("**consider O**"). Friedman, *Art*, pp. 161-64.

La Guerre, I ("**the bigness of cannon**"). William R. Osborne, *The Explicator* (November 1965), vol. 24, item 28.

La Guerre, II ("**O sweet spontaneous**"). Marks, pp. 69-71.

Impressions, V ("**stinging**"). Laura Riding and Robert Graves, "Modernist Poetry and the Plain Reader's Rights," in Baum, pp. 34-43.

Portraits, VIII ("**Buffalo Bill 's**"). Cleanth Brooks and Robert Penn Warren, *Understanding Poetry* (New York: Henry Holt, 1938), pp. 296-98; Louis J. Budd, *The Explicator* (June 1953), vol. 11, item 55; David Ray, "The Irony of E. E. Cummings," *College English* (January 1962), 23:282-90; Wegner, pp. 93-97; Earl J. Dias, "e. e. cummings and Buffalo Bill," *The CEA Critic* (December 1966), 24:6-7; Rushworth M. Kidder, " 'Buffalo Bill 's'—an Early E. E. Cummings Manuscript," *Harvard Library Bulletin* (October 1976), 24:373-80.

Portraits, X ("**somebody knew Lincoln somebody Xerxes**"). Wegner, pp. 87-89.

Sonnets—Realities, I ("**the Cambridge ladies who live in furnished souls**"). R. P. Blackmur, "Notes on E. E. Cummings' Language," in Baum, pp. 60-61; Lane, pp. 74-77.

Sonnets—Unrealities, V ("**a wind has blown the rain away and blown**"). John Clendenning, "Cummings, Comedy, and Criticism," *Colorado Quarterly* (Summer 1963), 12:50-53.

Sonnets—Actualities, I ("**a thing most new complete fragile intense**"). Julia P. Stanley, "An Analysis of E. E. Cummings' 'Actualities: I,' " *College Composition and Communication* (October 1966), 17:130-34.

Sonnets—Actualities, V ("**notice the convulsed orange inch of moon**"). Lane, pp. 20-22.

ℒ (1925)

Post Impressions, I ("**windows go orange in the slowly**"). John Clendenning, "Cummings, Comedy, and Criticism," *Colorado Quarterly* (Summer 1963), 12:48.

Post Impressions, V ("**Paris;this April sunset completely utters**"). R. P. Blackmur, "Notes on E. E. Cummings' Language," in Baum, pp. 64-65.

Post Impressions, XII ("**suppose**"). Lane, pp. 63-67.

Post Impressions, xiv ("**inthe,exquisite**"). Edith Sitwell, *Aspects of Modern Poetry* (London: Duckworth, 1934), pp. 252–56.

Portraits, i ("**being**"). Wegner, pp. 91–92.

Portraits, iii ("**ta**"). S. V. Baum, "E. E. Cummings: The Technique of Immediacy," in Friedman, *Essays*, pp. 115–17; G. R. Wilson, *The Explicator* (November 1972), vol. 31, item 17.

Portraits, v ("**raise the shade**"). Marks, pp. 78–80; William Heyen, "In Consideration of Cummings," *Southern Humanities Review* (Spring 1973), 7:138–39.

Portraits, x ("**here is little Effie's head**"). Wegner, pp. 92–93; Lane, pp. 85–89.

N, i ("**i will be**"). Theodore Spencer, "Technique as Joy," in Baum, pp. 119–20; Marks, pp. 76–77; Richard Gid Powers, *The Explicator* (February 1970), vol. 28, item 54.

N, vi ("**(one!)**"). Louis C. Rus, *The Explicator* (March 1957), vol. 15, item 40; George C. Brauer, *The Explicator* (December 1957), vol. 16, item 14.

N, vii ("**who knows if the moon's**"). Friedman, *Growth*, p. 46.

Sonnets—Realities, i ("**O It's Nice To Get Up In,the slipshod mucous kiss**"). Richard S. Kennedy, Introduction to *Tulips & Chimneys*, George J. Firmage, ed. (New York: Liveright, 1976), p. xiii.

Sonnets—Realities, xvii ("**whereas by dark really released,the modern**"). Marks, p. 72.

Sonnets—Realities, xxii ("**life boosts herself rapidly at me**"). Fred E. H. Schroeder, "Obscenity and Its Function in the Poetry of E. E. Cummings," *Sewanee Review* (Summer 1965), 73:474.

XLI Poems (1925)

Song, i ("**the / sky / was**"). John Arthos, "The Poetry of E. E. Cummings," *American Literature* (January 1943), 14:383–85.

Chansons Innocentes, ii ("**little tree**"). Marks, pp. 53–54.

Portraits, iii ("**Picasso**"). Richard S. Kennedy, Introduction to *Tulips & Chimneys*, George J. Firmage, ed. (New York: Liveright, 1976), pp. xiii–xiv.

Portraits, iv ("**the skinny voice**"). Marks, pp. 54–56.

Sonnets, xi ("**who's most afraid of death? thou / art of him**"). R. P. Blackmur, "Notes on E. E. Cummings' Language," in Baum, pp. 63–64.

is 5 (1926)

One, I, ii ("**she puts down the handmirror. 'Look at' arranging**")
["MAME"]. Friedman, *Art*, pp. 75–76.

One, II ("**take it from me kiddo**") ["POEM, OR BEAUTY HURTS
MR. VINAL"]. Emmett Dunn, "The Coming of Cummings,"
S.4.N. (March–April 1923), 25: [11]–[13]; Matthew Josephson,
"More Letters: Cummings." *S.4.N.* (May–August 1923), 25–29:
[94]–[95].

One, III ("**curtains part)**"). E. E. Cummings, *i: Six Nonlectures*
(Cambridge, Mass.: Harvard University Press, 1953), p. 25;
Marks, p. 71; Wegner, pp. 18–19.

One, V ("**yonder deadfromtheneckup graduate of a**"). Margaret
Schlauch, *The Gift of Tongues* (New York: Viking, 1942), p. 251.

One, IX ("**death is more than**"). Friedman, *Art*, pp. 82–83.

One, X ("**nobody loses all the time**"). William V. Davis, "Cummings'
'nobody loses all the time,' " *American Notes and Queries* (April
1971), 9:119–20.

One, XIX ("**she being brand**"). Marks, pp. 74–75.

One, XXVII ("**stop look &**") ["MEMORABILIA"]. Clyde S. Kilby,
The Explicator (November 1953), vol. 12, item 15; Ben W. Grif-
fith, Jr., *The Explicator* (May 1954), vol. 12, item 47; Cynthia
Barton, *The Explicator* (December 1963), vol. 22, item 26; H.
Seth Finn, *The Explicator* (January 1971), vol. 29, item 42; Lane,
pp. 81–85.

One, XXX ("**(ponder,darling,these busted statues**"). G. R. Wilson,
Jr., "Cummings' '(ponder,darling,these busted statues,' " *South
Atlantic Bulletin* (November 1972), 37:66–69.

Two, III (" **'next to of course god america i**"). William V. Davis,
"Cummings' ' "next to of course god america i,' " *Concerning Poetry* (1970), 3:14–15.

Two, X ("**my sweet old etcetera**"). Fred E. H. Schroeder, "Obscenity and Its Function in the Poetry of E. E. Cummings," *Sewanee Review* (Summer 1965), 73:472–73.

Three, II ("**Among / these / red pieces of**"). Laura Riding and Rob-
ert Graves, *A Survey of Modernist Poetry* (New York: Doubleday,
Doran, 1928), pp. 84–88; Edith Sitwell, *Aspects of Modern Poetry*
(London: Duckworth, 1934), pp. 256–57; John Peale Bishop, "The
Poems and Prose of E. E. Cummings," in Baum, p. 102; Marks,
pp. 33–38.

Four, VII ("since feeling is first"). Friedman, *Art*, p. 57; Wegner, pp. 85–86; William Heyen, "In Consideration of Cummings," *Southern Humanities Review* (Spring 1973), 7:133–34.

Four, X ("you are like the snow only"). Edith Sitwell, *Aspects of Modern Poetry* (London: Duckworth, 1934), pp. 259–62.

Five, I ("after all white horses are in bed"). Edith Sitwell, *Aspects of Modern Poetry* (London: Duckworth, 1934), pp. 262–64.

Five, V ("if i have made,my lady,intricate"). Lane, pp. 22–26.

ViVa (1931)

I (",mean-"). Marks, pp. 49–53.

V ("myself,walking in Dragon st"). Wegner, pp. 101–5.

VI ("but mr can you maybe listen there 's"). Wegner, pp. 106–8.

VII ("Space being(don't forget to remember)Curved"). Richard B. Vowles, *The Explicator* (October 1950), vol. 9, item 3.

XIII ("remarked Robinson Jefferson"). Donald R. Read, "The Lay of the Duckbilled Platitude," *Satire Newsletter* (Fall 1965), 3:30–33.

XXV ("murderfully in midmost o.c.an"). Wegner, pp. 13–14.

XXX ("i sing of Olaf glad and big"). Dumas, pp. 84–85.

XLIII ("if there are any heavens my mother will(all by herself)have"). Wegner, p. 35.

LXIII ("be unto love as rain is unto colour;create"). Friedman, *Growth*, pp. 77–79.

LXV ("but being not amazing:without love"). Marks, pp. 139–41.

LXVI ("nothing is more exactly terrible than"). Marks, pp. 138–39.

LXX ("here is the ocean,this is moonlight:say"). Friedman, *Art*, p. 94.

No Thanks (1935)

1 ("mOOn Over tOwns mOOn"). Friedman, *Art*, pp. 41–42.

3 ("that which we who're alive in spite of mirrors"). Edith A. Everson, *The Explicator* (March 1974), vol. 32, item 55.

4 ("a)glazed mind layed in a"). Marks, pp. 98–99.

7 ("sonnet entitled how to run the world)"). Friedman, *Art*, pp. 85–86; Michael L. Lasser, *The Explicator* (January 1966), vol. 23, item 44; Lane, pp. 48–51.

9 ("**o pr**"). Sheridan Baker, "Cummings and Catullus," *Modern Language Notes* (March 1959), 74:231–34.

13 ("**r-p-o-p-h-e-s-s-a-g-r**"). Sam Hynes, *The Explicator* (November 1951), vol. 10, item 9; Friedman, *Art,* pp. 123–24; Wegner, pp. 41–42; Dumas, pp. 70–71.

15 ("**one nonsufficiently inunderstood**"). Friedman, *Art,* pp. 76–77.

16 ("**may i feel said he**"). Fred E. H. Schroeder, "Obscenity and Its Function in the Poetry of E. E. Cummings," *Sewanee Review* (Summer 1965), 73:476–77.

20 ("**go(perpe)go**"). Friedman, *Art,* pp. 117–18; Nat Henry, *The Explicator* (April 1962), vol. 20, item 63.

26 ("**what does little Ernest croon**"). Friedman, *Art,* pp. 52–53.

27 ("**little joe gould has lost his teeth and doesn't know where**"). J. D. Shuchter, "E. E. Cummings and Joe Gould's 'Oral History,' " *American Notes & Queries* (June 1966), 4:148–49.

42 ("**out of a supermetamathical subpreincestures**"). Marks, pp. 81–82.

43 ("**theys sO alive**"). Mick Gidley, *Poetry Review* (Autumn 1968), 49:186–89.

46 ("**swi(/ across!gold's**"). Friedman, *Growth,* pp. 83–84; Marks, pp. 103–7.

48 ("**floatfloaflolf**"). Richard Crowder, *The Explicator* (April 1958), vol. 16, item 41.

50 ("**much i cannot)**"). Marks, pp. 86–89.

59 ("**b / eLl / s?**"). John W. Crowley, "Visual-Aural Poetry: The Typography of E. E. Cummings," *Concerning Poetry* (1972), 5:51–54.

60 ("**sh estifl**"). Nat Henry, *The Explicator* (May 1963), vol. 21, item 72; Marks, pp. 82–84; Patrick B. Mullen, "E. E. Cummings and Popular Culture," *Journal of Popular Culture* (Winter 1971), 5:508–9.

61 ("**love's function is to fabricate unknownness**"). Gerald Levin, *The Explicator* (December 1958), vol. 17, item 18; Lane, pp. 102–5.

70 ("**brIght**"). Wegner, pp. 154–57; Robert M. McIlvaine, *The Explicator* (September 1971), vol. 30, item 6.

71 ("**morsel miraculous and meaningless**"). Friedman, *Art,* pp. 25–26.

New Poems (1938)

1 ("**un**"). Dumas, pp. 79–81.

2 ("**kind**)"). Paul O. Williams, *The Explicator* (September 1964), vol. 23, item 4.

4 ("**(of Ever-Ever Land i speak**"). Marks, pp. 57–58.

5 ("**lucky means finding**"). Edward A. Levenston, *The Explicator* (January 1976), vol. 34, item 36.

9 ("**so little he is**"). Lloyd Frankenberg, "Cummings Times One," in Baum, pp. 157–58; Rushworth M. Kidder, " 'Twin Obsessions': The Poetry and Paintings of E. E. Cummings," *The Georgia Review* (Summer 1978), 32:342–68.

10 ("**nor woman**"). Nat Henry, *The Explicator* (September 1963), vol. 22, item 2.

12 ("**The Mind's(**"). Nat Henry, *The Explicator* (February 1962), vol. 20, item 49; W. Yeaton Wagener, *The Explicator* (October 1962), vol. 21, item 18.

14 ("**hanged**"). Marks, pp. 61–62.

22 ("**you shall above all things be glad and young**"). Friedman, *Growth*, pp. 91–92.

50 Poems (1940)

1 ("**!blac**"). S. V. Baum, "E. E. Cummings: The Technique of Immediacy," in Friendman, *Essays*, pp. 118–20; Wegner, pp. 143–47.

6 ("**flotsam and jetsam**"). Lane, pp. 11–13.

8 ("**the Noster was a ship of swank**"). Luther S. Luedtke, *The Explicator* (March 1968), vol. 26, item 59.

11 ("**red-rag and pink-flag**"). Friedman, *Art*, p. 81.

13 ("**proud of his scientific attitude**"). Lane, pp. 77–81.

14 ("**the way to hump a cow is not**"). Friedman, *Art*, p. 79; Fred E. H. Schroeder, "Obscenity and Its Function in the Poetry of E. E. Cummings," *Sewanee Review* (Summer 1965), 73:473.

22 ("**nouns to nouns**"). John Clendenning, "Cummings, Comedy, and Criticism," *Colorado Quarterly* (Summer 1963), 12:49–50.

29 ("**anyone lived in a pretty how town**"). Herbert C. Barrows, Jr., and William R. Steinhoff, *The Explicator* (October 1950), vol. 9, item 1; Arthur Carr, *The Explicator* (November 1952), vol. 11,

item 6; Robert C. Walsh, *The Explicator* (May 1964), vol. 22, item 72; Marks, pp. 38–45; Wegner, pp. 49–52; Charles L. Squier, *The Explicator* (December 1966), vol. 25, item 37; S. John Macksoud, "Anyone's How Town: Interpretation as Rhetorical Discipline," *Speech Monographs* (March 1968), 35:72–76; David R. Clark, "Cummings' 'anyone' and 'noone,' " *Arizona Quarterly* (Spring 1969), 25:37–43; Jan Aarts, "A Note on the Interpretation of 'he danced his did,' " *Journal of Linguistics* (April 1971), 7:71–73; Lane, pp. 97–102.

34 ("**my father moved through dooms of love**"). Robert E. Maurer, "Latter-Day Notes on E. E. Cummings' Language," in Friedman, *Essays*, pp. 91–92; Peter H. Mott, "E. E. Cummings: Two Texts on the God in Man," *Dissertation Abstracts International* (1973), 33:2386A (Columbia); Orm Överland, "E. E. Cummings' 'my father moved through dooms of love': A Measure of Achievement," *English Studies* (April 1973), 54:141–47; Lane, pp. 41–48.

36 ("**i say no world**"). Tomaz Lozar, "E. E. Cummings: The Poem as Improvisation," *Acta Neophilologica* (1971), 4:66–68.

37 ("**these children singing in stone a**"). Edwin M. Moseley, *The Explicator* (October 1950), vol. 9, item 2; Nat Henry, *The Explicator* (June 1955), vol. 13, item 51.

42 ("**love is more thicker than forget**"). Friedman, *Growth*, pp. 132–33.

43 ("**hate blows a bubble of despair into**"). Friedman, *Growth*, pp. 128–29.

48 ("**mortals**"). George Haines IV, ": : 2 : 1 : The World and E. E. Cummings," in Friedman, *Essays*, pp. 24–26.

1 x 1 (1944)

I ("**nonsun blob a**"). Marks, pp. 26–33; Richard Gunter, "Sentence and Poem," *Style* (Winter 1971), 5:26–36.

III ("**it's over a(see just**"). Friedman, *Growth*, pp. 135–36; Wegner, pp. 158–62.

VIII ("**applaws**"). Joseph Axelrod, "Cummings and Phonetics," *Poetry* (November 1944), 55:88–94; Karl Shapiro, "Prosody as the Meaning," in Baum, pp. 134–35.

XIII ("**plato told**"). Friedman, *Art*, pp. 114–15.

XIV ("**pity this busy monster,manunkind**"). John Britton, *The Expli-*

cator (October 1959), vol. 18, item 5; James W. Gargano, *The Explicator* (November 1961), vol. 20, item 21.

XVI ("**one's not half two. It's two are halves of one:**"). Friedman, *Art*, pp. 64–65; Friedman, *Growth*, p. 136; Lane, pp. 94–97.

XIX ("**when you are silent,shining host by guest**"). G. J. Weinberger, "E. E. Cummings's Benevolent God: A Reading of 'when you are silent,shining host by guest,' " *Papers on Language and Literature* (Winter 1974), 10:70–75.

XX ("**what if a much of a which of a wind**"). Stephen E. Whicher, *The Explicator* (November 1953), vol. 12, item 14; Frederick H. Candelaria, "Cummings and Campion," *Notes and Queries* (April 1959), 6:134–36; Friedman, *Art*, pp. 38–39; John Ciardi, "What If a Much of a Which of a Wind," *Saturday Review* (October 24, 1964), 47:18, 72; Marks, pp. 59–60; Robert E. Maurer, "Latter-Day Notes on E. E. Cummings' Languge," in Friedman, *Essays*, pp. 97–98; Laurel Maureen O'Neal, *The Explicator* (September 1973), vol. 32, item 6.

XXVII ("**old mr ly**"). Theodore Spencer, "Technique as Joy," in Baum, p. 121.

XXXI ("**a-**"). Friedman, *Art*, pp. 104–5; Wegner, pp. 150–54.

XXXV ("**except in your**"). William V. Davis, "E. E. Cummings's 'except in your,' " *English Language Notes* (June 1974), 11:294–96.

XXXVI ("**true lovers in each happening of their hearts**"). Friedman, *Art*, pp. 102–3; Wegner, pp. 111–13.

XXXVIII ("**yes is a pleasant country**"). Lane, pp. 32–34.

XXXIX ("**all ignorance toboggans into know**"). Friedman, *Growth*, pp. 137–38.

XLIV ("**these(whom;pretends**"). Friedman, *Art*, pp. 119–20.

LII ("**life is more true than reason will deceive**"). Friedman, *Art*, p. 71.

LIII ("**o by the by**"). Lane, pp. 36–38.

LIV ("**if everything happens that can't be done**"). Jack Steinberg, *The Explicator* (December 1949), vol. 8, item 17; Friedman, *Art*, pp. 73–75.

Xaipe (1950)

6 ("**dying is fine)but Death**"). Wegner, pp. 55–57; Lane, pp. 67–70.

11 ("**so many selves(so many fiends and gods**"). Lane, pp. 51–53.

16 ("**if the**"). Wegner, pp. 9–10.

22 ("**when serpents bargain for the right to squirm**"). Dumas, pp. 97–98.

23 ("**three wealthy sisters swore they'd never part**"). Friedman, *Art*, p. 19.

24 ("**one day a nigger**"). Friedman, *Growth*, pp. 153–54.

26 ("**who sharpens every dull**"). Friedman, *Growth*, pp. 161–62.

37 ("**F is for foetus(a**"). Wegner, p. 131.

41 ("**whose are these(wraith a clinging with a wraith**"). Friedman, *Art*, pp. 69–70.

46 ("**a kike is the most dangerous**"). Alex Jackinson, "[The Question Posed]," in Baum, p. 176; Friedman, *Growth*, pp. 154–55.

50 ("**no time ago**"). Friedman, *Art*, pp. 83–84.

56 ("**a like a**"). Irene R. Fairley, "Syntax as Style: An Analysis of Three Cummings Poems," in Charles E. Gribble, ed., *Studies Presented to Professor Roman Jakobson by His Students*, pp. 107–10 (Cambridge, Mass.: Slavica Publishers, 1968); Fairley, "Syntactic Deviation and Cohesion," *Language and Style* (1973), 6:217–18.

62 ("**in**"). Wegner, pp. 110–11.

67 ("**when faces called flowers float out of the ground**"). Alan M. Nadel, *The Explicator* (February 1974), vol. 32, item 47.

68 ("**love our so right**"). Friedman, *Growth*, pp. 159–60.

69 ("**now all the fingers of this tree(darling)have**"). Friedman, *Art*, pp. 164–67; Wegner, p. 163.

95 Poems (1958)

1 ("**1(a**"). James E. White, *The Explicator* (September 1962), vol. 21, item 4; Friedman, *Art*, pp. 171–72; Marks, pp. 21–26; Dumas, pp. 72–73.

10 ("**maggie and milly and molly and may**"). Dumas, pp. 104–5.

13 ("**So shy shy shy(and with a**"). Allan A. Metcalf, "Dante and E. E. Cummings," *Comparative Literature Studies* (September 1970), 7:381–83.

16 ("**in time of daffodils(who know**"). Friedman, *Art*, pp. 180–82.

25 ("**that melancholy**"). John Logan, "The Organ-Grinder and the Cockatoo: An Introduction to E. E. Cummings," *The Critic* (October–November 1961), 39–43.

39 ("a monstering horror swallows") ["THANKSGIVING (1956)"].
Friedman, *Growth*, 163–64.

43 ("who(is?are)who"). Marks, pp. 48–49.

48 ("someone i am wandering a town(if its"). Friedman, *Art*, p. 175.

49 ("noone and a star stand,am to am"). Friedman, *Art*, pp.
175–76.

63 ("precisely as unbig a why as i'm"). Friedman, *Growth*, pp.
169–70.

73 ("let's,from some loud unworld's most rightful wrong"). Mary S.
Mattfield, *The Explicator* (December 1967), vol. 26, item 32.

76 ("these from my mother's greatgrandmother's rosebush white").
Friedman, *Art*, pp. 173–74.

77 ("i am a little church(no great cathedral)"). Friedman, *Growth*,
pp. 166–67.

84 ("how generous is that himself the sun"). Friedman, *art*, 174–75.

90 ("rosetree,rosetree"). Friedman, *Art*, pp. 128–58.

94 ("being to timelessness as it's to time"). Norman Friedman, Introduction to Friedman, *Essays*, pp. 8–10.

73 Poems (1963)

4 ("but we've the may") ["SONG"]. Lane, pp. 105–7.

7 ("it's"). David R. Clark, *The Explicator* (February 1964), vol. 22,
item 48.

12 ("Me up at does"). Irene R. Fairley. "Syntactic Deviation and
Cohesion," *Language and Style* (1973), 6:219–20; Fairley, *E. E.
Cummings and Ungrammar* (Searington, N.Y.: Watermill Pub-
lishers, 1975), pp. 89–92.

19 ("everybody happy?"). Lane, pp. 89–91.

27 ("in heavenly realms of hellas dwelt"). Laurence Perrine, "In
Heavenly Realms of Hellas," *Notes on Contemporary Literature*
(January 1971), 1:2–4.

48 ("t,h;r:u;s,h;e:s"). Wegner, pp. 42–46.

72 ("wild(at our first)beasts uttered human words"). Lane, pp. 70–72.

73 ("all worlds have halfsight,seeing either with"). Jane Donahue,
"Cummings' Last Poem: An Explication," *Literatur in Wissenschaft
und Unterricht* (Band 3, Heft 1, 1970), 3:106–8; Lane, pp. 108–10.

Notes

1. INTRODUCTION

1. *i: Six Nonlectures* (Cambridge: Harvard University Press, 1953), p. 4.

2. *The Best Times* (New York: New American Library, 1966), pp. 83, 84.

3. Interview with William O'Brien, New York City, June 14, 1973.

4. "Ivan Narb: Abstract Sculptor of the Cosmic," in George J. Firmage, ed., *E. E. Cummings: A Miscellany Revised*, p. 188. (New York: October House, 1965). Hereafter cited as *Miscellany.*

5. See Charles Norman, *E. E. Cummings: The Magic-Maker* (rev. ed. Indianapolis and New York: Bobbs-Merrill, 1972), ch. 11 (hereafter cited as *Magic-Maker*); Robert Tucker, "E. E. Cummings as an Artist: *The Dial* Drawings," *The Massachusetts Review* (Spring 1975), 16:329–53; Dagmar Reutlinger, "E. E. Cummings and *The Dial* Collection," *ibid.*, 353–56; Rushworth M. Kidder, "E. E. Cummings, Painter," *Harvard Library Bulletin* (April 1975), 23:117–38; Kidder, " 'Author of Pictures': A Study of Cummings' Line Drawings in *The Dial*," *Contemporary Literature* (Fall 1976), 17:470–504; Frank Gettings, *E. E. Cummings: The Poet as Artist* (December 2, 1976–February 6, 1977; exhibition catalogue, Hirshhorn Museum, Washington, D.C., 1976); Rushworth M. Kidder, " 'Twin Obsessions': The Poetry and Painting of E. E. Cummings," *The Georgia Review* (Summer 1978), 32:342–68; Kidder, "Cummings and Cubism: The Influence of the Visual Arts on Cummings' Early Poetry," *Journal of Modern Literature* (April 1978).

6. bMS Am 1892.8 (24); bMS Am 1823.7 (25), sheet 192; bMS Am 1823.7 (25), sheet 109. These call numbers refer to material in the Cummings collection in the Houghton Library, Harvard University, Cambridge, Massachusetts.

7. See bMS Am 1892.8 (1), folders 246 and ff.

8. "Minnie (1)," in *Adventures in Value* (New York: Harcourt Brace Jovanovich, 1962), 4:7.

9. Edmund Wilson, *The Twenties* (New York: Farrar, Straus, and Giroux, 1975), p. 206.

10. *The Best Times,*, p. 87.

11. "Notes on E. E. Cummings' Language," *Hound and Horn* (January–March 1931), 4:163–92; later collected in *The Double Agent* (1935) and *Language as Gesture* (1952); reprinted in S. V. Baum, ed., EΣTI: *e e c: E. E. Cummings and the Critics*, pp. 50–67. (East Lansing: Michigan State University Press, 1962). Hereafter cited as EΣTI.

12. Blackmur, in Baum, EΣTI, p. 50.

13. *Ibid.,* p. 67.

14. *Ibid.,* p. 66. In a review of *50 Poems* published in *The Southern Review* (Summer 1941), 7:187–213, Blackmur considerably modified his earlier strictures. His review is reprinted in Norman Friedman, ed., *E. E. Cummings: A Collection of Critical Essays,* pp. 75–78. (Englewood Cliffs, N.J.: Prentice-Hall, 1972).

15. *i: Six Nonlectures,* p. 7.

16. That this view has great currency is suggested by the words of a student who, seeing me check out a book on Cummings from the Harvard library, mentioned her admiration for his poetry. We fell into conversation; on learning that I intended to write a book about Cummings' poetry, she was scandalized. A poet like Cummings, she asserted, would be ruined by "analysis," which was bound to dispel all the wonderful feeling in the poems. Somewhat taken aback, I asked her whether she understood all of Cummings' poems. She replied with some disdain that of course she didn't—mere understanding being hardly an essential for the sort of interpretation she favored.

17. T. S. Eliot, "East Coker,"*Four Quartets* (New York: Harcourt, Brace, 1943), pp. 16–17.

18. Jerzy Pelc, in "Some Methodological Problems in Literary History," observes, "A literary work is a linguistic entity and as such is subject to a semiotic analysis that should take into account three types of relations: syntactic, semantic, and pragmatic. The first holds between the various elements of a text; the second, between a text, or its elements, and its (their) extra-textual referents; the third, between a text, on the one hand, and its producer and readers, on the other." Such analysis requires "triple competencies: linguistic, philosophical, and psychological" (*New Literary History* [Autumn 1975], 7:91). Perhaps the problem with much of the Cummings criticism lies in its emphasis on the third of these "types of relations," to the neglect of the other two.

19. "Ivan Narb," *Miscellany,* p. 188.

20. bMS Am 1823.7 (23), sheet 257.

21. "Wallace Stevens and E. E. Cummings," *The New Republic* (March 19, 1924), 37:102; reprinted in Baum, EΣTI, p. 25.

22. Letter to Richard Church, "9th December 1935," in Constantine FitzGibbon, ed., *Selected Letters of Dylan Thomas,* p. 161. (New York: New Directions, 1967).

2. TULIPS AND CHIMNEYS

1. *Eight Harvard Poets* (New York: Lawrence J. Gomme, 1917). Cummings contributed four sonnets and four poems in free verse. For details of publication, see Norman, *Magic-Maker*, ch. 4, "The Making of a Book."

2. Letter to his father, Edward Cummings (EC), April 17, 1923; quoted in Kidder, "E. E. Cummings, Painter," p. 117.

3. Letter to EC, December 3, 1923, in *ibid.*

4. Letter to EC, January 9, 1923, Houghton Library collection.

5. Letter to EC, April 11, 1924, Houghton Library collection.

6. bMS Am 1823.7 (27), sheet 20.

7. See Norman Friedman, *E. E. Cummings: The Growth of a Writer* (Carbondale: Southern Illinois University Press, 1964), p. 38. Hereafter cited as Friedman, *Growth*.

8. Norman Friedman, *E. E. Cummings: The Art of His Poetry* (Baltimore: Johns Hopkins University Press, 1960), p. 72. Hereafter cited as Friedman, *Art*.

9. Doris Dundas, *The Explicator* (May 1971), vol. 29, item 79.

10. Letter to EC, January 5, 1921, Houghton Library collection.

11. *Selected Letters of E. E. Cummings*, F. W. Dupee and George Stade, eds. (New York: Harcourt, Brace, and World, 1969), p. 70. Hereafter cited as *Letters*.

12. Interview, June 14, 1973, New York City.

13. See Rushworth M. Kidder, " 'Buffalo Bill 's'—an Early E. E. Cummings Manuscript," *Harvard Library Bulletin* (October 1976), 24:373–80.

14. *Letters*, p. 68.

15. *Ibid.*, p. 71.

16. "The Poet of Brattle Street," *A History of American Poetry, 1900–1940* (New York: Harcourt, Brace, 1947). Reprinted in Baum, EΣTI, p. 128.

17. Friedman, *Growth*, p. 42.

18. José Ortega y Gasset, *The Dehumanization of Art*, Helen Weyl, trans. (Princeton, N.J.: Princeton University Press, 1968), p. 48.

3. XLI POEMS AND &

1. In a selection of his poetry published in London (*One Over Twenty*, 1936), Cummings did list the poems from *XLI Poems* before those from &.

2. Letter to his mother, Rebecca Haswell Cummings (RHC), Houghton Library collection.

3. *Ibid.*

4. *Ibid.*, March 20, 1925.

5. "Gaston Lachaise," *Miscellany*, pp. 19–20.

6. "Jean Cocteau as a Graphic Artist," *Miscellany*, p. 100.

7. bMS Am 1892.7 (67).

8. "Modern Art," *The Dial* (January 1924), 76:102.

9. For drawings of Thayer, see Tucker, "E. E. Cummings as an Artist," and Reutlinger, "E. E. Cummings and *The Dial* Collection."

10. Friedman, *Growth*, p. 45.

11. *The Best Times*, p. 82.

12. Letter to RHC, March 20, 1925, Houghton Library collection.

13. Letter to RHC, Houghton Library collection.

14. *Ibid.*

15. *Ibid.*

16. This painting is reproduced in Kidder, " 'Twin Obsessions.' "

17. bMS Am 1892.5 (766), sheet 41.

18. Letter to RHC, April 15, 1918, Houghton Library collection.

19. See Joseph Mitchell, *McSorley's Wonderful Saloon* (New York: Duell, Sloan, and Pearce, 1943).

20. For a particularly good explication of this poem, see Louis C. Rus, *The Explicator* (March 1957), vol. 15, item 40.

21. bMS Am 1823.7 (25), sheet 119.

22. Horace Gregory and Marya Zaturenska, "The Poet of Brattle Street," in Baum, EΣTI, pp. 125–26.

4. IS 5

1. Letter to RHC, February 1926, Houghton Library collection.

2. "Gaston Lachaise," p. 19.

3. Friedman, *Growth*, p. 47.

4. "The typical case history of the American modern artist of this period [the twenties] reveals a general evolution from fervent radicalism to conservatism, from experimentation with the brashest new forms to their assimilation for more conventional purposes or to their final abandonment. . . . By 1929 the doctrine of art-for-art's-sake had already begun to lose its hold on American art." Milton W. Brown, *American Painting from the Armory Show to the Depression* (Princeton; N.J.: Princeton University Press, 1955), p. 196.

5. "Cummings: One Man Alone," *Yale Review* (Spring 1973), 62:337.

6. Quoted in Norman, *Magic-Maker*, p. 24.

7. *i: Six Nonlectures*, pp. 29–30.

8. bMS Am 1892.8 (1), sheet 3093.

9. Gregory and Zaturenska, in discussing this poem, refer the reader to John Wilmot's "Et Caetera," in Baum, EΣTI, p. 129.

10. For Cummings' interest in George Herriman's *Krazy Kat* cartoons, see his "A Foreword to Krazy," *Krazy Kat* (New York: Henry Holt, 1946), reprinted in *Miscellany*, pp. 323–28.

11. See above, pp. 44–46.

12. bMS Am 1823.5 (150)

5. VIVA

1. Letters to RHC, October 4 and October 10, 1926, Houghton Library collection.

2. "ViVa: e. e. cummings," *Contempo* (April 1, 1932), 1:1.

3. "The Last of Lyric Poets," *The New Republic* (January 27, 1932), 69:299.

4. Letter to RHC, March 2, 1922, Houghton Library collection.

5. "The Adult, the Artist, and the Circus," *Miscellany*, p. 111.

6. For an account of Crosby's career, see Malcolm Cowley, *Exile's Return* (New York: W. W. Norton, 1934), pp. 242–88.

7. *Letters*, p. 70.

8. Richard S. Kennedy, "E. E. Cummings at Harvard: Verse, Friends, Rebellion," *Harvard Library Bulletin* (July 1977), 25:262.

9. Bethany K. Dumas, *E. E. Cummings: A Remembrance of Miracles* (New York: Barnes and Noble, 1974), p. 35.

6. NO THANKS

1. *Starting Out in the Thirties* (Boston: Little, Brown, 1965), p. 4.

2. *Ibid.*, p. 12.

3. *On Native Grounds: An Interpretation of Modern American Prose Literature* (New York: Doubleday, 1956), p. 153.

4. *Starting Out in the Thirties*, p. 12.

5. *The Twenties: American Writing in the Postwar Decade* (New York: Viking, 1955), p. 25.

6. Quoted in Norman, *Magic-Maker*, p. 284. For a detailed discussion of this pattern, see Richard Kennedy's introduction to the typescript edition of *No Thanks* (New York: Liveright, 1978).

7. Hoffman, *The Twenties*, p. 210.

8. April 22, 1931, p. 32.

9. *Growth*, p. 85.

10. *Letters*, pp. 270–71.

11. *The Explicator* (April 1962), vol. 20, item 63.

12. Joseph Mitchell, *Joe Gould's Secret* (New York: Viking, 1965).

13. Barry Marks, *E. E. Cummings* (New York: Twayne, 1964), p. 81.

14. See Kidder, " 'Author of Pictures,' " for reproductions of some representative drawings in this genre.

15. Friedman, *Growth*, pp. 86–87.

16. Quoted in Kidder, "E. E. Cummings, Painter," p. 130.

17. bMS Am 1823.5 (185).

18. *The Explicator* (September 1971), vol. 30, item 6.

7. NEW POEMS

1. Material quoted in these paragraphs is from Norman, *Magic-Maker*, pp. 286–90.

2. *i: Six Nonlectures*, p. 8.

3. Quoted in Marks, *E. E. Cummings*, p. 57.

4. Norman, *Magic-Maker*, p. 146.

5. Nat Henry, *The Explicator* (September 1963), vol. 22, item 2.

8. 50 POEMS

1. *Letters*, p. 147.

2. *Ibid.*, pp. 148–49.

3. *Ibid.*, p. 151.

4. Quoted in Robert E. Wegner, *The Poetry and Prose of E. E. Cummings* (New York: Harcourt, Brace and World, 1965), p. 144. Hereafter cited as *Poetry and Prose*.

5. *I Am: A Study of E. E. Cummings' Poems* (Lawrence/Manhattan/Wichita: The Regents Press of Kansas, 1976), p. 12.

6. *Letters*, p. 253–54.

7. Friedman, *Art*, p. 81.

8. *Ibid.*, p. 79.

9. "Gaston Lachaise," p. 19.

10. "Spring," *The Poems of Gerard Manley Hopkins*, W. H. Gardner and N. H. MacKenzie, eds. (4th ed.; London: Oxford University Press, 1967), p. 67.

11. "Cummings, Comedy, and Criticism," *Colorado Quarterly* (Summer 1963), 12:49.

12. *Adventures in Value*, 3:1.

13. *The Complete Works of Ralph Waldo Emerson* (Boston: Houghton Mifflin, 1903), 1:106.

14. "I see the boys of summer," *The Collected Poems of Dylan Thomas* (New York: New Directions, 1953), p. 2.

15. *i: Six Nonlectures*, pp. 8–9. For a brief biography of Cummings' father, see Richard S. Kennedy, "Edward Cummings, the Father of the Poet," *Bulletin of the New York Public Library* (1966), 70:437–449.

16. Lane, *I Am*, p. 45.

17. *Congress Weekly* (August 20, 1951), 18:11–13, reprinted in Baum, EΣTI, pp. 173–82.

18. *Letters*, pp. 258–59.

9. 1 X 1

1. Friedman, *Growth*, p. 139.

2. bMS Am 1892.5 (765), sheet 56.

3. *Letters*, p. 253.

4. Eleanor M. Sickels, "The Unworld of E. E. Cummings," *American Literature* (May 1954), 26:235.

5. *Letters*, p. 247.

6. R. P. Blackmur, "Notes on E. E. Cummings' Language," in Baum, EΣTI, p. 55.

7. *Letters*, p. 205.

8. Wegner, *Poetry and Prose*, p. 8.

10. XAIPE

1. *Letters*, p. 193.

2. Unpublished letter to Howard Nelson, October 10, 1949, at the Humanities Research Center, University of Texas, Austin.

3. See Friedman, *Growth*, p. 152.

4. *Letters*, p. 195.

5. For Cummings' interest in organ-grinders, see Kennedy, "E. E. Cummings at Harvard," p. 274.

6. Lane, *I Am*, p. 70.

7. "Minnie (1)," *Adventures in Value*, 4:7.

8. *Letters*, p. 210.

9. Friedman, *Growth*, pp. 153–54.

10. Reprinted in Baum, EΣTI, pp. 173–82.

11. Norman, *Magic-Maker*, p. 319.

12. *Letters*, pp. 67–68.

13. Friedman, *Art*, pp. 69–70.

14. "Carrion Comfort," *Poems of Gerard Manley Hopkins*, p. 100.

15. *Paterson* (New York: New Directions, 1963), p. 224.

16. *Letters*, p. 268.

17. Review of *i: Six Nonlectures*, *The New Statesman and Nation*, June 12, 1954, p. 761. Reprinted in Norman Friedman, ed., *E. E. Cummings: A Collection of Critical Essays* (Englewood Cliffs, N.J.: Prentice-Hall, 1972), p. 174.

18. *The Explicator* (February 1974), vol. 32, item 47.

19. Wegner, *Poetry and Prose*, p. 163.

11. 95 POEMS

1. Friedman, *Growth*, p. 162.

2. *The Saturday Review* (January 3, 1959), 42:13.

3. Quoted in "Projective Verse," *Selected Writings of Charles Olson*, Robert Creeley, ed. (New York: New Directions, 1966), p. 16.

4. *Letters*, p. 261.

5. *Ibid.*

6. "At 65, Our Rebel Poet Still Rebels" (October 11, 1959), pp. 37, 66.

7. Berryman, "The Revolving Bookstand," *The American Scholar* (Summer 1959), 28:388–90.

8. For an account of the controversy, see Norman, *Magic-Maker*, pp. 328–38.

9. Friedman, *Growth*, p.163.

10. Norman, *Magic-Maker*, p. 333.

11. Friedman, *Art*, p. 178.

12. *Letters*, p. 205.

13. Norman, *Magic-Maker*, p. 12.

14. bMS Am 1823.5 (136).

15. Louis Cheronnet, *Paris imprévu*, with photographs by Marc Foucault (Paris: Editions "Tel," 1946), p. 128. Cheronnet, in discussing l'Église Saint-Germain-de-Charonne, quotes an earlier writer's comment: ". . . Charonne n'a que son église, édifice modeste qui date de quelques siècles. À l'intérieur comme au dehors, rien de remarquable" ["Charonne has only its church, a modest building some centuries old. Nothing remarkable either outside or inside"] (p. 138).

16. Friedman, *Growth*, p. 166.

17. Friedman, *Art*, p. 131.

18. Berryman, "The Revolving Bookstand," p. 388.

12. 73 POEMS

1. Letter to the author, March 28, 1977. The twenty-seven unpublished poems were 5, 10, 12, 13, 14, 17, 18, 27, 28, 35, 36, 38, 39, 42, 43, 46, 49, 50, 51, 52, 53, 55, 56, 62, 64, 67, and 72.

2. Lane, *I Am*, p. 71.

3. Nearly one-third of the poems in *73 Poems* have fewer than thirty words, compared with less than one-quarter in *95 Poems*.

4. "Over Sir John's hill," *Collected Poems of Dylan Thomas*, p. 188.

5. "God's Grandeur," *Poems of Gerard Manley Hopkins*, p. 66.

6. Wegner, *Poetry and Prose*, pp. 43–46.

7. Lane, *I Am*, pp. 89–91.

8. Quoted in Lane, *I Am*, pp. 89–91.

9. *Letters*, p. 191.

10. Katharine McBride and Rushworth M. Kidder, "A Concordance to Cummings' Complete Poems: 1913–1962" (unpublished computer printout, Wichita State University, 1975).

Index of First Lines

Significant explicatory passages are indexed in light face italic.

Subject Index

Academy of American Poets Award, 182

"A Chorus Girl," see "when thou hast taken thy last applause, and when," 32

Adventures in Value, 142, 165, 180, 191

Alcestis, 111

&, 44–46; individual poems in, 46–59; "A," 44, 46–52 ("Post Impressions," 46–48, "Portraits," 48–52); "N," 44, 52–55; "D," 44, 55–59 ("Sonnets—Realities," 55–56, "Sonnets—Actualities," 55, 56–59); dedication to Elaine Orr, 44–46; mentioned, 36

Antirational attitudes, 2, 3, 6

Anti-Semitism, alleged, 151, 181

Armory Show, 84

"Arthur Wilson," see "as usual i did not find him in cafés, the more dissolute," 39–40

Ash Can painters, 43, 54, 62, 91

Babbitt, Irving, 90

Barr, Alfred, 93

Barton, Anne, 83, 96

Barton, Diana, 83

Bentham, Jeremy, 226

Berryman, John, 203, 217

Bible: Corinthians, 172; Ecclesiastes, 203; Galatians, 144; Genesis, 149, 157, 164; Isaiah, 30; Jeremiah, 30; John, 161, 164; Matthew, 115, 205; Peter, 179; Proverbs, 110; Psalms, 99; Revelation, 23; Song of Solomon, 25–26; Titus, 222; see also Biblical imagery and allusions; Christianity; Jesus

Biblical imagery and allusions, 14, 41, 66, 94, 96, 102, 103, 107, 120, 123, 130, 136–37, 177; overt use of, in later poems, 180; parable of prodigal son, 203–4; parable of good Samaritan, 67; see also Bible; Christianity; Jesus

Bigelow, Josephine, 88

Blackmur, R. P., 6, 170

Blake, William, *The Marriage of Heaven and Hell*, 226

Boston Arts Festival, 206, 213

Broom, 28

Browning, Elizabeth Barrett, 34

Browning, Robert, 187

Buchanan, James, 89

Carlyle, Thomas, 226

Cambridge, Mass., 24, 32, 33, 36, 65

Censorship, 17, 36, 71, 73

Cézanne, Paul, 37–38

Charonnet, Louis, *Paris imprévu*, 213